THE SOLENT

CRUISING COMPANION

A yachtsman's pilot and cruising guide to ports and harbours
from Keyhaven to Chichester

Derek Aslett

John Wiley & Sons, Ltd

Photographs by Derek Aslett

Additional photography:
Page 3, 180 (top) ©Rolex/Daniel Forster; Page 4 ©Dick Durham/Yachting Monthly; Page 13 (top left), 17 (bottom), 62, 104
(top right), 110 (top) ©Isle of Wight Tourism (www.islandbreaks.co.uk); Cover picture, page 9 (middle), 15, 22, 28, 30 (bottom),
31 (middle), 45, 48, 49 (bottom), 64, 78, 82 (bottom), 83, 91, 103, 112, 114 (bottom), 139 ©Sealand Aerial Photography Ltd;
Page 7 (bottom right) ©Steve Guinn; Page 12 (bottom), 58, 75, 173, 174, 175, 176-7, 178 (bottom left), 179 (bottom), 182, 183,
184 (top), 185 187 ©onEdition; Page 17 ©Richard Temple; Page 46, 172 (top) ©Tony Dixon; Page 63 ©Kim Lyal/Classic Boat
Museum; Page 76, 90 ©Walking Distance; Page 11, 85 ©Premier Marinas; Page 128 (bottom right), 145, 155 (top right), 175
(bottom left), 177 (bottom left), 181, 184 (bottom), 186 ©Vanessa Bird; Page 157, 160 (bottom) ©Isle of Wight County Record
Office; Page 158 ©Fishbourne Roman Palace/Sussex Archaeological Society; Page 160 (top) ©Southampton City Council;
Page 161 (top), 167 ©English Heritage; Page 161 (bottom), 162-3 ©Portsmouth Museums and Records Service;
Page 164 ©Lord Montagu of Beaulieu; Page 165 ©Portsmouth Historic Dockyard;Page 168-169 ©Monty;
Page 170 ©Beken of Cowes; Page 178-9 ©Rick Tomlinson; Page 180 (bottom) ©P1/Crash

For Wiley Nautical
Executive Editor: David Palmer
Project Editor: Lynette James
Assistant Editor: Drew Kennerley

For Nautical Data
Cartography: Jamie Russell
Art Direction: Vanessa Bird and Jamie Russell
Cruising Companion series editors: Vanessa Bird and Lucinda Roch

ISBN-13: 978-0470988282

IMPORTANT NOTICE

This Companion is intended as an aid to navigation only. The information contained within should not solely
be relied on for navigational use, rather it should be used in conjunction with official hydrographic data.
Whilst every care has been taken in compiling the information contained in this Companion, the publishers,
author, editors and their agents accept no responsibility for any errors or omissions, or for any accidents
or mishaps which may arise from its use.

Neither the publisher nor the author can accept responsibility for errors, omissions or alterations in this book.
They will be grateful for any information from readers to assist in the update and accuracy of the publication.

Readers are advised at all times to refer to official charts, publications and notices.
The charts contained in this book are sketch plans and are not to be used for navigation.
Some details are omitted for the sake of clarity and the scales have been chosen
to allow best coverage in relation to page size.

Correctional supplements are available at www.wileynautical.com and on request from the publishers.

ACKNOWLEDGEMENTS
Derek Aslett would like to thank the Solent harbourmasters, marina staff and yacht club secretaries for their help while researching
this companion. Special thanks also go to Tony Dixon for the material he supplied on Uffa Fox, and John Bingeman for his
historical expertise on the Solent, as well as to Tony Bedingfield, William Daniels, Bill Dixon, Christine Graves, Mike Samuelson,
Celia Ward and the Chichester Harbour Federation for providing information and photography on the Solent racing fleets. Lastly,
thanks to Souter Harris for all his crewing and advice and to Derek's wife Ann for her constant help and encouragement.

Printed by Markono Print Media, Singapore

Contents

Preface

Having sailed in the Solent for some 35 years, I have never tired of this large expanse of protected water. Its diversity enables you to experience a broad range of cruising, from the modern-day facilities, bars and restaurants of ports such as Cowes and Portsmouth, to the rustic tranquillity of Newtown River, a favourite destination of mine.

And yet, if you want to compromise between these two extremes, the small harbours of Yarmouth, Beaulieu and Bembridge, with their pretty villages and traditional pubs, provide a perfect answer. At the eastern tip of the Solent is my home port of Chichester, where you could spend at least a week cruising its peaceful waters – although at weekends you will be sharing it with racing dinghies, RIBs, dayboats and other craft of every description.

Racing is an integral part of life in the Solent, an insight into which is included in this book to help you identify some of the more traditional fleets you are likely to encounter on passage. After enjoying many years of racing our former Contessa 32, albeit rather unsuccessfully, I know how appreciative racers are if cruising yachtsmen keep clear.

In this Cruising Companion, I have aimed to provide a complete yet straightforward pilot to the western and eastern approaches to the Solent, as well as to the ports themselves. Although you should be aware of the various well-charted spits, sandbanks and occasional rocks, the Solent is on the whole a relatively safe cruising ground (weather permitting), the biggest hazards probably being the commercial ships coming to and from Southampton and Portsmouth. Since the first edition of this book, you will find that there have been considerable changes to many of the Solent harbours, in particular Portsmouth, Cowes, Bembridge and Yarmouth, which mainly consist of additional berths and facilities for visitors.

Besides the navigational matters I have tried to provide a detailed account of each port, highlighting the facilites on hand and pinpointing the nearest shops, restaurants and places to visit. With centuries of history, predominantly spent protecting Britain's shores from military invasion, the Solent has no shortage of historic sites, both on the mainland and the Isle of Wight. In addition, the areas of outstanding natural beauty should not be overlooked, particularly the New Forest, which fringes Lymington, Beaulieu and Hythe.

I hope that this Cruising Companion will help you make the most of your visit to the Solent, both on the water and ashore.

Derek Aslett – November 2007

ABOUT THE AUTHOR

Derek Aslett, a photographer and designer, together with his wife Ann, has extensively cruised the whole of the Channel on board their Laurent Giles-designed 38-footer *Anne*. Built in 1985, the Giles 38 is a medium-displacement, long-keeled cruising yacht based on a 1950s classic design. With the boat berthed in Chichester Harbour, the Solent has become Derek and Ann's backyard. Here, they have spent much of their time over the past 35 years either cruising the harbours or racing around the cans in their former Contessa 32.

Introduction

The Solent is one of the most popular coastal areas in Britain, offering a variety of cruising grounds from the lively, bustling marinas of Cowes and Portsmouth to the quiet backwaters of Wootton Creek and Newtown River. As it is a centre of yachting excellence, you are never too far away from a chandlery or boatyard should you need any repairs carried out.

Stretching roughly 25 to 30 miles from Hurst Point in the west towards Chichester Harbour in the east, the Solent is an estuarine labyrinth of 12 harbours and estuaries. Its protected inshore waters have enabled significant ports to flourish over the years, and it is not surprising that the Solent has played a vital role in British history since the Roman times. Today, as a favourite recreational spot for locals and visitors alike, this stretch of water plays host to numerous key events, including the Southampton International Boat Show in September and Cowes Week in August. However, its sheltered location hasn't just been utilised by mankind; over three-quarters of the Solent's shores are protected areas providing a haven for an abundance of plant and animal marine life.

Right on the Solent's doorstep is the New Forest where ancient heaths and woodlands have remained relatively unspoilt since William the Conqueror created it as a hunting area in 1079. Renowned for its wild ponies, the Forest is an attractive place to walk, cycle or horse-ride, especially if you stop off at one of the many traditional pubs along the way.

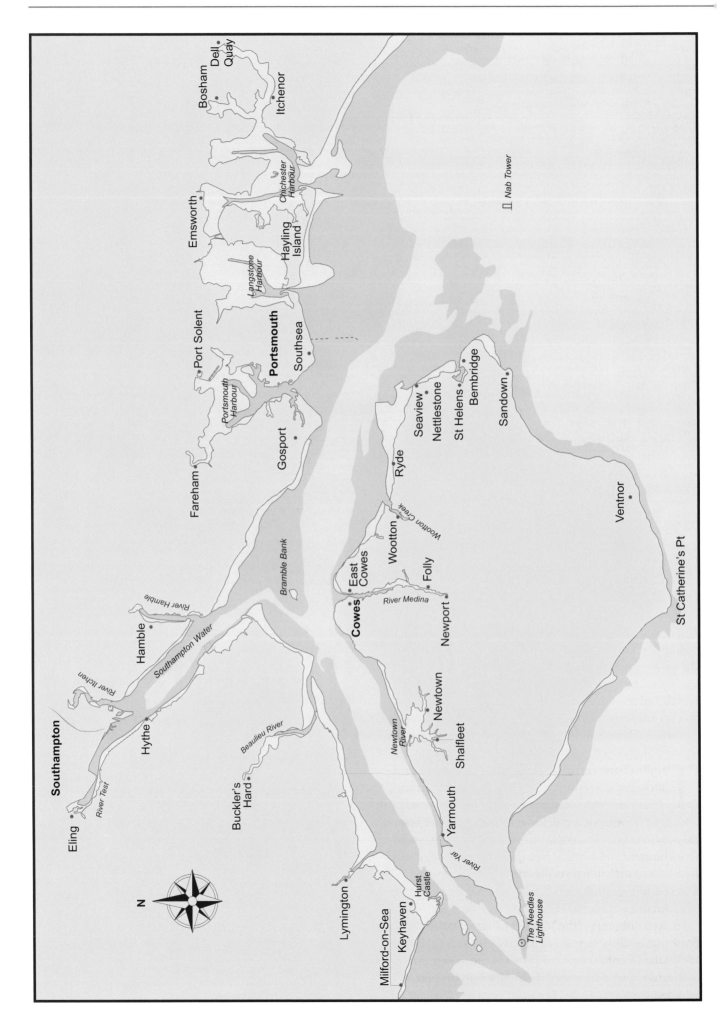

CRUISING STRATEGIES – APPROACHING THE SOLENT

As the Solent is among the busiest waters in Britain, you need to enter it with the due care and respect that it deserves. If approaching the Western Solent, you can't fail to spot the distinctive Needles Rocks at the western end of the Isle of Wight along with the adjacent chalk cliffs of High Down. By night the lighthouse at the end of the Needles flashes Oc (2) WRG 20s 24m 17-13M. A couple of good deterrents from getting too close to this area are the Goose Rock, situated about 50m west-north-west of the lighthouse, and the wreck of the Greek ship *Varvassi* which, laden with wine and oranges, sank about 150m west-south-west of the rock. West of the Needles Rock are the fairway buoys signifying the deep water entrance to the Needles Channel. To the north-west of the channel are the Dolphin Bank and Shingles Bank, the latter being one of the most prominent features in the Solent. Watch out for this bank as parts of it dry at Low Water and seas break on it even if there's not much swell. The channel is clearly marked and lit by the standard buoyage so if you stick to that you can't go wrong, although beware of the strength of the tide, particularly on the ebb when the stream sets in a west-southwesterly direction across the Shingles at a rate of about three to four knots.

To the south-east of the Needles Channel is the Pot Bank where the minimum depths are around 15m. Pay particular attention in bad weather to the Bridge, a reef that runs about ¾M west of the lighthouse, the end of which is marked by a WCM lt buoy. Also bear in mind that dangerous seas can form in the Needles Channel in southerly to westerly gales, particularly when the tide is on the ebb. In these circumstances you would be better off approaching the eastern Solent via the Nab Tower or, alternatively, sheltering in Poole Harbour.

Again in strong winds, or if coming from St Alban's Head or Poole, it may be preferable to use the North Channel, which is situated just north of the Shingles Bank. The North and Needles Channels merge south of Hurst Point, where you should to be aware of the Trap, a shoaling spit about 150m south-east of Hurst Castle.

If you want to approach the eastern Solent from France the passage is straightforward, although the commercial

Marking the two extremes of the Solent: the Nab Tower lies to the east, with the Needles lighthouse to the west

Give commercial shipping a wide berth

shipping tends to be pretty heavy. Head for the Nab Tower, which is approximately 4.5M east of Foreland. You will see that the main channel into the Solent is well marked and easy to follow.

Coming east along the low-lying coast from one of the Sussex ports you will eventually reach Selsey Bill, off which there are extensive rocks and shoals. These can be passed either via the Looe Channel, so long as conditions are favourable, or to seaward of the Owers SCM lt buoy. In good visibility, moderate conditions and during daylight hours, the Looe Channel, which runs in an east/west direction about 1M south of Mixon Beacon, is a preferable shortcut. However, make sure you have the tides with you (a west-going stream begins about an hour and a half

Portsmouth has its own dedicated Small Boat Channel

before High Water Portsmouth, with Springs running at around 2.5 knots). Also, keep an eye out for the lobster pots in this area. At night, or when conditions are bad, it is best to keep south of the Owers SCM lt buoy, which is about 6.5M south-east of Selsey Bill.

Due to the heavy shipping that you are likely to encounter when approaching the Solent, particularly towards the eastern end, a radar reflector is essential, and it is always useful to have an active radar responder or radar installed as well. Once in the Solent there are plenty of harbours and marinas to choose from, most of which offer all the necessary facilities including maintenance and repairs. A useful service for breakdowns at sea is Sea Start.Based in the Hamble, it can be contacted on Tel: 0800 88 55 00.

As far as crew changes go, it is probably easier to arrange these in the larger ports of Southampton or Portsmouth where there are direct trains to several major cities within the UK. Southampton also has a local airport with flights throughout Britain and the rest of Europe. However, several of the other Solent harbours have local railway stations and some of those mentioned on the Isle of Wight are linked to the mainland by ferry.

SOLENT TIDES

The Solent is renowned for its unusual tidal system which is reputedly one of the most complex in the world. The customary 6.5 hour flood and ebb is certainly inconsistent in this stretch of water, and the frequently-mentioned 'Double High Water' is due not, as is commonly believed, to the Solent's dual entrance but to the strange tidal rhythm in the English Channel as well as to the shape of the Solent itself. Both Colin Tubbs, author of *The Ecology, Conservation and History of the Solent*, and the Associated British Ports (ABP) use an effective analogy to explain the tidal flow in the English Channel.

They compare the Channel to a rectangular-shaped tank in which the water levels can be made to seesaw around a central axis. If you tilt the tank in one direction the water will automatically flow to the lower end, creating the effects of High and Low Water at either end. Although this has been very much simplified, the Channel works in a similar way, which is why Low Water at Land's End occurs when it is High Water in the Dover Strait (and vice versa). This happens twice a day and is known as an 'oscillation'. Outside influences created by the sun and the moon in relation to the earth produce the 'tilting' effect, evolving from the Atlantic pulse which takes a certain amount of time to circulate the UK, hence causing the High Water and Low Water to vary from port to port. Most sailors know that there is a fortnightly cycle between the highest Springs and lowest Neaps, with each stage in the cycle taking place at more or less the same time each day in a particular area. In the case of the Solent, the highest Springs and lowest Neaps occur around midday and midnight, while the highest Neaps and lowest Springs are in the early morning and early evening. As Colin Tubbs goes on to explain, however, in reality the Channel is not rectangular in shape, but is more 'funnel-shaped',

The ebb tide can be very strong past Hurst, particularly at Springs

Southampton Water experiences a 'young flood stand' about two hours after Low Water

'with the Cherbourg peninsula further reducing the cross-sectional axis. Thus the volume of water forced into the eastern Channel on the flood after half-tide, when the flow past the node is strongest, induces a secondary tidal oscillation resulting in a double High Water or long tidal stand.' A further 30 smaller tidal oscillations, which derive from the fact that the Solent has two entrances,

Even the smallest creeks are used for moorings

also play a part in the tidal pattern, culminating in the long flood tide, 'young flood stand' in Southampton Water and the short ebb.

The 'young flood stand' takes place about two hours after Low Water and is particularly prominent during Springs. It basically refers to a slackening in the tidal stream for about a two-hour period before a final surge to High Water, persisting for roughly three hours. The short ebb is a consequence of the flood and Double High Water. The flood in the western Solent flows for about six hours and is followed by the Double High Water, the whole process lasting for about nine hours. Therefore, as a complete tidal cycle is about 12.5 hours, it means the ebb tide can only run for between three and a half to four hours, which explains why the ebb is so strong, especially at Spring tides through Hurst Narrows and at the entrances to Chichester, Langstone and Portsmouth harbours.

As the western branch of the Solent is closer to the axis of the English Channel, the tidal range is far less than it is at the eastern end. The maximum tidal range in the east is around 4.5m whereas in the west it is about 2.8m. As the ABP points out in its Tide Tables, 'the times of High Water and Low Water in the two places differ by only an hour or so however, and the rising tide in the eastern end has to rise further in about the same time as the western end. It therefore overtakes it in height about an hour or so before High Water, though in both places the tide is still rising. This difference in level causes the Solent tidal stream to turn to the westward between one and two hours before High Water, and to continue in that direction near the following Low Water, when it again turns to the eastward.'

Weather and atmospheric pressure also has a bearing on the height of tides, with high pressure slightly decreasing tidal heights and low pressure increasing them. For information on weather sources, see p196.

Chartlets

All the chartlets in this book have been simplified and should not be used for navigation. The green shading indicates that the area dries at the Lowest Astronomical Tide (LAT), the dark blue signifies that there is up to five metres at LAT and the pale blue shading illustrates that there is over five metres of water at LAT. Soundings are represented in metres and tenths of metres, showing the depth of water above chart datum with the underlined soundings referring to drying heights above chart datum.

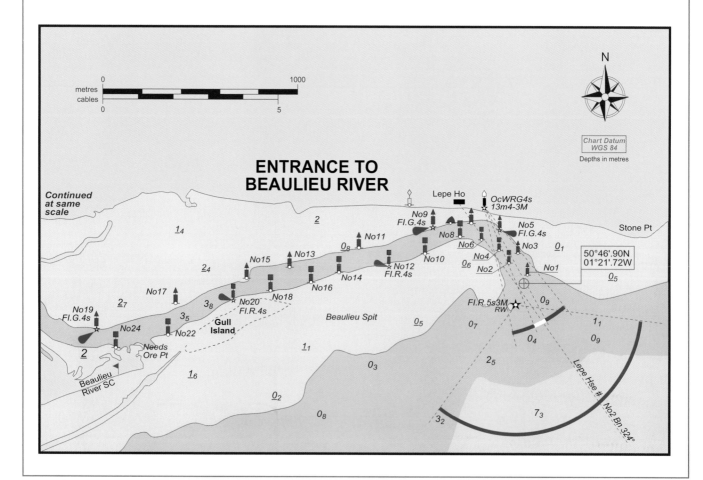

BEARINGS AND COURSES

All bearings and courses are true and so magnetic variation should be applied as shown on a current Admiralty Chart. Variation in the Solent is approximately 2½° west (2007), decreasing by about eight minutes annually.

WAYPOINTS

It is advisable to check the waypoints in this book, especially if using them with a GPS, and at regular intervals plot your own position manually on the chart in case your GPS should fail at any time. Our waypoints are referenced to the WGS 84 datum so positions must be adjusted before plotting on charts referred to the old OSGB 1936 datum. Waypoints of the harbour and marina entrances have usually been included under the port headings, firstly to make it easier for you to pinpoint the area on the chart and secondly to be used as a final waypoint in your passage plan.

DISTANCES

All distances relating to the sea are in nautical miles, written as 'M', (2,025 yards/1,852metres), cables (0.1M/ approximately 185m) and metres (1.094 yards).

MARINA CHARGES

Every effort has been made to include the most up-to-date information on marina charges for boats of varying lengths, although all harbours are likely to raise their

Yarmouth, a safe and convenient harbour

Swanwick on the River Hamble is a well-equipped Solent marina

You are always in sight of prominent landmarks

The Royal Solent YC, Yarmouth, and Seaview YC, Seaview, both of which have spectacular views over each end of the Solent

fees each year to keep in line with inflation. The charges mentioned in the book are inclusive of VAT and generally refer to the peak season rates.

YACHT CLUBS

The Solent is an international centre for yachting and this is reflected by the number of yacht clubs that have been set up here, many of which are among Britain's oldest and finest maritime establishments. Most of the clubs welcome visiting yachtsmen, especially if from an affiliated club, although one or two do not extend their hospitality to visitors, most notably the Royal Yacht Squadron in Cowes. If you are thinking of visiting a yacht club, it is best to check with the steward or secretary as to whether you are actually welcome there before using their facilities.

SOLENT COASTGUARD

For routine traffic and other information, the Solent Coastguard should be contacted on VHF Ch 67. Don't forget to always listen out before making a transmission and use the correct radio procedures. Note that Ch 16 should now be used for distress and urgency calls only. The Solent Coastguard broadcasts a weather forecast on Ch 86 and Ch 23 once an initial announcement has been made on Ch 16. For more information on broadcast times and other weather sources, see p196. All search and rescue operations (SAR) in the Solent area are coordinated by the Maritime Rescue Coordination Centre (MRCC) at Lee-on-Solent, whose MMSI is 002320011. The centre is manned round-the-clock by at least three coastguard officers who keep a watch on VHF Ch 16 and Ch 67.

Racers appreciate the right of way regardless of cruising rules!

The Isle of Wight Steam Railway will take you on a journey back in time

One of the Wightlink ferries running between Lymington and Yarmouth

TRANSPORT

Under each port you are able to find detailed travel information giving you the relevant telephone numbers of public or private transport within that particular area.

Rail: There are direct rail links from Portsmouth and Southampton to London Waterloo, with the journey taking just over an hour. For National Railway enquiries Tel: 08457 484950.

Car: The M3 and A3 are fast roads to London, which is only an hour or so away by car, while the M27 joins all the major towns along the South Coast of England. Car hire companies have been listed under the relevant ports or, alternatively, you can contact the nearest tourist office, which is again listed under each harbour.

Bus: There are a number of bus and coach operators connecting the cities, towns and villages throughout the Solent area and Hampshire, which are all listed under each individual port.

Air: Two local airports with connecting flights throughout the UK and Europe are Bournemouth (Tel: 01202 364000), not far west of Lymington, and Southampton (Tel: 0870 040 0009). The South Coast is also in close proximity to the two major British airports, Heathrow (Tel: 0870 000 0123) and Gatwick (Tel: 0870 000 2468).

Ferries: Wightlink runs ferry services between Portsmouth and Fishbourne on the Isle of Wight as well as between Lymington and Yarmouth and Portsmouth and Ryde (Tel: 0870 582 7744). Red Funnel offers routes between Southampton and East Cowes (Tel: 0870 444 8898). For information on ferries to northern France and the Channel Islands, call P&O on Tel: 08716 646464 and Brittany Ferries on Tel: 0870 536 0360.

DISTANCE TABLE

Approximate distances in nautical miles are by the most direct route, while avoiding dangers and allowing for Traffic Separation Schemes.

		1	2	3	4	5	6	7	8	9	10	11	12	13	14	15	16	17	18	19	20
1	Exmouth	1																			
2	Lyme Regis	21	2																		
3	Portland Bill	36	22	3																	
4	Weymouth	46	32	8	4																
5	Swanage	58	44	22	22	5															
6	Poole entrance	65	51	28	26	6	6														
7	Needles Lt Ho	73	58	35	34	14	14	7													
8	Lymington	79	64	42	40	20	24	6	8												
9	Yarmouth	77	63	40	39	18	22	4	2	9											
10	Beaulieu	84	69	46	45	25	29	11	7	7	10										
11	Cowes	86	71	49	46	28	27	14	10	9	2	11									
12	Southampton	93	78	55	54	34	34	20	16	16	9	9	12								
13	River Hamble	90	75	53	51	32	34	18	12	13	6	6	5	13							
14	Portsmouth	96	81	58	57	37	35	23	19	19	12	10	18	13	14						
15	Langstone Hbr	98	84	61	59	39	39	25	21	21	14	12	21	18	5	15					
16	Chichester Bar	101	86	63	62	42	42	28	23	24	17	15	23	18	8	5	16				
17	Bembridge	97	81	59	58	38	39	24	18	19	13	10	18	15	5	6	8	17			
18	Nab Tower	102	86	64	63	43	44	29	23	24	18	15	24	19	10	7	6	6	18		
19	St Catherine's	82	68	45	44	25	25	12	19	21	27	15	36	29	20	20	19	17	15	19	
20	Littlehampton	117	102	79	79	60	61	46	44	45	38	36	45	42	31	28	25	28	22	35	20

SYMBOLS AND ABBREVIATIONS

The following abbreviations and symbols may be encountered in this book; others may be found that are self-explanatory

✈	Airport	⊖	Fishing harbour/quay	☎	Public telephone
⚓	Anchoring	⊠	Fish farm	⇌	Railway station
⚓	Anchoring prohibited	FV(s)	Fishing vessel(s)	✕	Restaurant
Ⓑ	Bank	▮	Fuel berth	SWM	Safe water mark
☒	Boat hoist	Ⓛ	Harbourmaster	◄	Shore power
☒	Boatyard	Ⓗ	Heliport	⚲	Showers
Ca	Cable(s)	⇵	Holding tank pump-out	◢	Slipway
Ⓟ	Car park	⊞	Hospital	SCM	South cardinal mark
♫	Chandlery	ℹ	Information bureau	SHM	Starboard-hand mark
⊞	Chemist	IDM	Isolated danger mark	☒	Supermarket
⊹	Church	⊡	Launderette	SS	Traffic signals
H24	Continuous	Ldg	Leading	Ⓥ Ⓥ	Visitors' berth/buoy
○	Crane	✦	Lifeboat	WPT⊕	Waypoint
⊖	Customs office	Ⓐ	Marina	WCM	West cardinal mark
⚓	Direction of buoyage	NCM	North cardinal mark	⛵	Yacht berthing facilities
ECM	East cardinal mark	PHM	Port-hand mark		
☒	Ferry terminal	PA	Position approx.		
◄	Fishing boats	✉	Post office		

LIGHTS AND FREQUENCIES

FR	Fixed red light
FG	Fixed green light
Fl	Flashing light, period of darkness longer than light. A number indicates a group of flashes, eg: Fl (2). Most lights are white unless a colour follows the number of flashes, eg: Fl (2) G. The timing of the sequence, including light and darkness, is shown by the number of seconds, eg: Fl (2) G 10s. The range of the more powerful lights is given in nautical miles (M), eg: Fl (2) G 10s 20M
L Fl	Long flash, of not less than two seconds
Oc	Occulting light, period of light longer than darkness
Iso	Isophase light, equal periods of light and darkness
Q	Quick flashing light, up to 50/60 flashes per minute
VQ	Very quick flashing, up to 120 flashes per minute
Mo	Light flashing a (dot/dash) Morse single letter sequences, eg: Mo (S)
Dir	A light, usually sectored, RWG or RG, usually giving a safe approach within the W sector. Either fixed or displaying some kind of flashing characteristic

Chapter one
Western Solent

With considerably less commercial traffic and several tranquil harbours, the western Solent is popular with yachtsmen. The backdrop of the New Forest, which stretches along the shoaling shores of the mainland, and the unspoilt coastline of the Isle of Wight make it a particularly attractive cruising ground.

Apart from the Needles Channel (see p7), the western Solent has few serious hazards to watch out for, provided you keep to reasonable soundings. Along the Isle of Wight's shores, Black Rock, Hamstead Ledge, Salt Mead Ledges and Gurnard Ledge are all clearly marked with

buoys. In strong winds and tides heavy overfalls can occur at these particular spots but if you stay to the correct side of the buoyage you will be fine.

On the mainland coast, between Hurst Point and Lymington, the chart shows that you should not cut inshore where the shallow water off Pennington extends some three quarters of a mile from the land. East of Lymington's entrance, the Pylewell Lake shallows also protrude approximately a mile offshore while, to the west of the entrance to the Beaulieu River, the Beaulieu spit can easily catch out anyone making for the harbour. Patches of

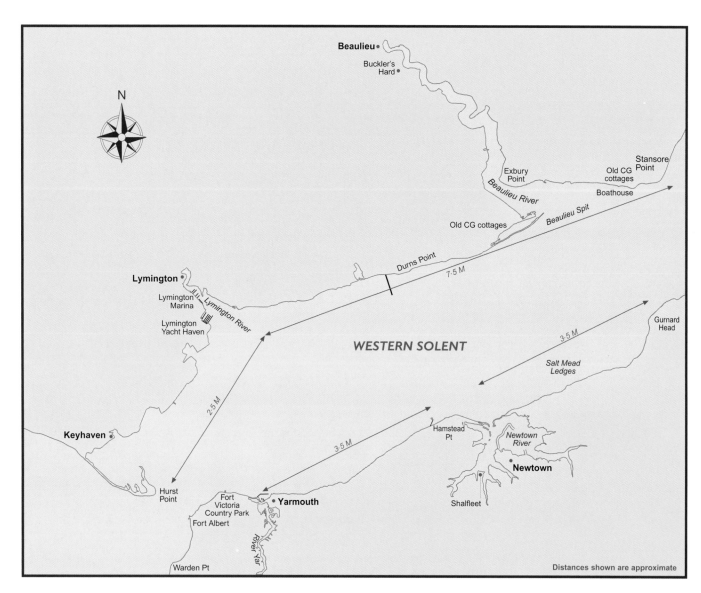

this sandbar dry to around 0.3m about 100m south of the spit, so it is important that you do not cut the corner.

In favourable conditions there are several pleasant anchorages along the north coast of the Isle of Wight. Keeping clear and to the north of the moorings, you can anchor in Yarmouth Roads to the west of the harbour entrance. Another option is just inside the western edge of the Newtown River approach channel, in the lee of Hamstead Ledge. Totland Bay and Alum Bay, off the Needles Channel, are very popular anchorages, too, although with their isolated rocks you need to use a large-scale chart and careful pilotage when navigating in this area. It is not a good idea to anchor in the rocky and shallow Colwell Bay, situated between Warden Point and Fort Albert.

On the mainland side of the Solent, inside Hurst Point, there is a useful anchorage if waiting for the tides (see p20). Note that due to obstructions, anchoring is prohibited west of Solent Bank between Hamstead Ledge on the island to about 550m west of Durns Point on the mainland.

It is worth remembering that even short hops between Solent harbours need to be planned using a tidal atlas, especially on Spring tides.

This north cardinal buoy lies off Sconce Point on the Isle of Wight

The Hamstead Ledge buoy lies just to the west of Newtown River

The South-West Shingles Buoy (FL R 2.5s) marks the Shingles Bank

Black Rock off Yarmouth is clearly marked with a starboard-hand buoy

Hurst Castle, built in 1544, and Fort Victoria (right), constructed in the 1850s, have both played a significant role in the Solent's history

Guardians of the Western Solent

Looking out over the entrance to the Western Solent is Hurst Castle. Situated at the seaward end of a shingle spit that extends about two miles from Milford-on-Sea, near Keyhaven, it was one of a string of coastal fortresses constructed upon the orders of King Henry VIII to protect England from invasion by the European Catholic powers (see p162). The castle, which was completed in 1544, lies only three-quarters of a mile from the Isle of Wight, making it an ideal spot to defend the western approaches to the Solent and the naval cities of Southampton and Portsmouth.

Hurst Castle continued to play a significant military role in the 17th century – it was here in 1648 that King Charles I was imprisoned before being taken back to London for his trial and execution in 1649 following defeat by the Parliamentarians in the second English Civil War (1648-9).

Since then, it has also been refortified several times to keep pace with technological advances. In the 1860s, as a result of the findings of the 1859 Royal Commission, instigated by Britain's Prime Minister, Lord Palmerston, in response to a volatile relationship with France (see p166), it received two new wing batteries, giving it the overall appearance that we see today. Hurst was garrisoned during both world wars and in the Second World War was equipped with coastal gun batteries and searchlights. Remaining part of the Coastal Artillery defences until 1956, it is today owned by English Heritage and is open to the public (see p21 for details).

Opposite Hurst Castle, on the shores of the Isle of Wight, sits Fort Albert, with Fort Victoria about half a mile further to the east. The fear of invasion by the French in 1852 (see p93 and p162-3) led to their construction in the mid-1850s as part of a string of fortifications. With its design allegedly conceived by Prince Albert himself, Fort Albert's foundations were dug into the sea and a drawbridge was put in place to connect it to the shore. A miniature railway was used to transport ammunition to its cannon emplacements. Today, the fort is privately owned and has been converted into luxury flats. As there is no public access to even the cliffs above it, Fort Albert is best viewed from the sea or Hurst Castle. Fort Victoria, on the other hand, is still open to the public (see p26). Forming part of the Fort Victoria Country Park, the remains of this fort now enclose a marine aquarium, a seabed archaeology exhibition, a planetarium and a model railway.

The Needles Battery also played a significant part in the Western Solent's defence. Sometimes referred to as the Old Battery (completed in 1863) to distinguish it from the nearby New Battery (completed in 1895), it guards the island's westernmost tip and provides the closest view of the Needles from land. It was again built as a result of the 1859 Royal Commission report, and both batteries played a significant role in the two world wars, with the New Battery being used in the mid-1950s to 1960s to test the Black Knight and Black Arrow space rocket engines. The National Trust acquired the site in 1975 and, after an extensive restoration of the Old Battery, opened it to the public in 1982. For details, Tel: 01983 741020.

The Needles Battery stands on the western tip of the Isle of Wight

Keyhaven

Keyhaven harbour entrance: 50°42'.85N 01°33'.22W

Keyhaven is situated at the western tip of the Solent and forms part of a nature reserve extending over 2,000 acres of saltings and mudflats. Tucked away behind the historic Hurst Castle (see p17), it is really only accessible to small craft that can take the ground, although there is a small, moderately deep-water anchorage just inside the entrance.

NAVIGATION

Charts: Admiralty Charts: SC5600, 2021, 2035; Imray: C15, 2200; Stanfords: 11, chartpack 24, chartpack 25, L9, L10

Tides: Double High Waters occur at or near Springs, with predictions referring to the first High Water. Off Springs, there is a stand for about 2 hours, in which case predictions relate to the middle of the stand.

HW Springs at Hurst Point are 1 hour 15 minutes before and HW Neaps 5 minutes before HW Portsmouth.
LW Springs are 30 minutes and LW Neaps 25 minutes

before LW Portsmouth. MHWS: 2.7m; MHWN: 2.3m; MLWN: 1.4m; MLWS: 0.7m.

Approaches: The entrance to Keyhaven lies about half a mile north-west of Hurst Point. From a distance it can be quite difficult to locate the mouth of the channel, approximately half a mile north of Hurst Tower Light (Fl [4] WR 15s 23m 13/11M Iso WRG 4s 19m 21-17M). The entrance is flanked by a low shingle bank to the south and mudflats beyond. On approach from the east you will not encounter any real dangers, although look out for the regular Lymington to Yarmouth ferries. From the west, be aware of both the Shingles Bank, over which seas can break, and the Trap, just inside Hurst Point, which should be given a wide berth.

It is not advisable to enter Keyhaven in strong easterly winds, especially as the bar is constantly shifting, and for yachts with a 1.5m draught accessibility is limited to two hours either side of High Water. If you keep to the transits, however, shallower draught yachts can find sufficient water at most states of the tide.

The low-lying entrance to Keyhaven can be hard to identify, but lies about half a mile west of Hurst Point. Note the anchorage tucked in behind North Point

Pilotage: The waypoint 50°42′.73N 01°32′.58W brings you to within half a mile of the entrance. From here two leading red and white-striped beacons, positioned on the mudflats just inside the entrance, bear 283°. It is quite hard to spot them until you are fairly close in and you may well find that you pick up the port and starboard-hand entrance buoys more easily. At times, there are strong tides across the entrance, particularly on the ebb, which makes the approach rather difficult.

Keep to a bearing of 283° between the port and starboard-hand buoys until you clear the pink port-hand buoy, then turn to port to bring the green starboard-hand buoys close to. The depth just inside the North Point entrance is only 0.3m LAT. Once in the channel, the deepest water is close to the line of moorings on your port-hand side. Yachts that draw over 1.75m (5ft 7in) are advised to enter no further than the No 20 mooring. Keep rigorously to the channel and do not attempt to cross any open water or make the mistake of following the shallow-draught ferry, as you may end up running aground.

Shortly afterwards, the fairway turns to the north-west, but the moorings still need to be followed closely until you get to the green buoy that indicates the beginning of the drying stretch of the channel to the quay. When closing the

Hurst Castle and lighthouse. The 26m-high lighthouse was built in 1867

Stick closely to the channel, as drying mudbanks flank either side of it

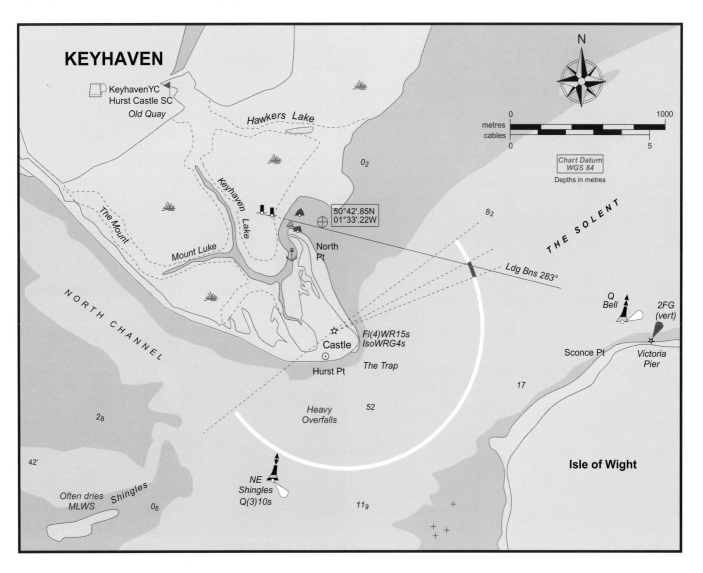

Hurst Castle is a conspicuous landmark that stands on Hurst Point, and which can be easily identified on approach from both the Western and Eastern Solent

quay the best water is to port by the ferry jetty. At the top of Spring tides there is about 2.5m of water at Keyhaven's quay but, owing to the unpredictable bottom, drying out is not a good idea.

The speed limit of four knots within the channel must be observed at all times. With its unlit entrance and fairway a night approach would be unwise.

BERTHING

There is space to anchor in about 3m of water just inside Keyhaven's entrance at North Point. Another popular anchorage in favourable conditions is outside the harbour, about halfway between the entrance and the fort, although this is mainly used while waiting for the tide. When anchoring here, the Hurst Tower light should bear between 210° and 230°. It is also possible to tie up alongside the quay for a short stay at High Water. For berthing availability and advice, contact the Keyhaven River Warden on Tel: 01590 645695 or VHF Ch37.

Berthing fees: Overnight stays alongside the quay, for any size of vessel: £12. Moorings: from £8-£14 per night, depending on the size of vessel and the location of the mooring. Anchoring: You are only allowed to anchor inside the spit and an overnight stay costs between £7-£13, depending on the size of vessel.

On High Water Springs, there is about 2.5m of water at Keyhaven's quay

The Gun Inn is well known for its real ale and extensive whisky collection

Useful information – Keyhaven

The channel up to Keyhaven is shallow and flanked by mudbanks. It is a pretty place to explore, however, if you have a boat that draws less than 1.75m

FACILITIES
Water is available from the tap by the warden's office, while West Solent Boatbuilders caters for most repair needs and is equipped with a 9.5-ton crane and a 25-ton slip. It also runs a small chandlery near the quay. There is no fuel available here although you can get fuel in cans from Milford-on-Sea, but this is a good half-hour's walk away and there are no public transport services.

Keyhaven Yacht Club (Tel: 01590 642165), which is adjacent the quay, welcomes visitors from other clubs and has its own showers, as well as a bar and lounge that overlook the river.

PROVISIONING
The village of Milford-on-Sea fulfils most shopping needs, but is a good 30-minute walk away along winding lanes.

The High Street incorporates most of the essential shops, including a Spar convenience store, a post office and a chemist. There is also an HSBC bank in Milford-on-Sea, which has a cashpoint.

EATING OUT
The attractive Gun Inn (Tel: 01590 642391) at Keyhaven serves local fish and shellfish and is famous for its real ales and extensive malt whisky collection. There are also a couple of good pubs and restaurants in Milford, among which are the Red Lion (Tel: 01590 642236) on the High Street and the White Horse (Tel: 01590 642360) on Keyhaven Road, which has a reputation for great homemade food.

ASHORE
Keyhaven is a conservation area and bird sanctuary, offering plenty of interesting shore-side walks. Situated towards the seaward end of the shingle spit is Hurst Castle (see p17 or Tel: 01590 642344). Now owned by English Heritage, the castle is open during the summer from 1000–1730 and from 1000–1600 during the winter months. A ferry (Tel: 01590 642500) runs regularly from Keyhaven to Hurst Castle or, alternatively, you can walk to it across the spit. It is about a 30-minute walk, and you will need to wear a pair of strong shoes to cope with all the shingle underfoot.

TRANSPORT
Buses: There are no buses between Keyhaven and Milford-on-Sea. Wilts and Dorset (Tel: 01590 672382) runs regular bus services between Milford, Lymington and Christchurch.

Trains: The nearest train station is Lymington, which is about three to four miles from Milford-on-Sea.

Taxis: J Hall, Milford-on-Sea (Tel: 01590 644896); Galleon Taxi Services, New Milton (Tel: 01425 622222).

USEFUL INFORMATION
Keyhaven River Warden: VHF Channel 37; Tel: 01590 645695.

Boatbuilders/engineers: West Solent Boatbuilders: Tel: 01590 642080.

Police: Tel: 999; Tel: 0845 045 4545.

Coastguard: Lee on Solent: Tel: 023 9255 2100; VHF Channel 16.

Hospital: Lymington Hospital: Tel: 01590 66300.

Doctor: Milford Medical Centre: Tel: 01590 643022.

Dentist: Tel: 01590 679888.

Tourist Information: Tel: 01590 689000.

Yarmouth is becoming a very desirable and useful destination indeed, offering 24-hour access and good amenities

Yarmouth

Yarmouth harbour entrance: 50°42'.42N 01°30'.05W

The most western harbour on the Isle of Wight, Yarmouth is not only a convenient passage stopover but has also become a very desirable destination in its own right, with virtually all weather and tidal access, although strong northerly to northeasterly winds can produce a considerable swell. The pretty harbour and town offer plenty of fine restaurants and amenities and are within easy reach of many of the Isle of Wight's tourist attractions.

NAVIGATION

Charts: Admiralty Charts: SC5600, 2021, 2035; Imray: C3, C15, 2200; Stanfords: 11, chartpacks 24 & 25, L9, L10
Tides: Double High Waters occur at or near Springs. Otherwise the stand lasts for about 2 hours. Predictions

refer to the first High Water when there are two, but other times to the middle of the stand.
HW Springs are 1 hour 5 minutes before and Neaps 5 minutes after HW Portsmouth. LW Springs are 25 minutes before and Neaps 30 minutes before LW Portsmouth. MHWS: 3.0m; MHWN: 2.6m; MLWN: 1.6m; MLWS: 0.8m.

Approaches: From the west, Black Rock, which is clearly marked by a green conical buoy (Fl G 5s), and the shoal water north of the outer east-west pier are the only dangers. From the east, apart from the unlit historic wreck buoy (Y SPM, position

Keep north of the Black Rock buoy

Yarmouth's 685ft pier is easily identifiable from some distance. The Grade II-listed pier was built in 1876 and is the longest wooden pier in Britain

50°42'.58N 01°29'.67W) and the obvious yacht club moorings east of the pier, there are no hazards. Probably the biggest concern in this area is the Wightlink car ferry, which runs every 30 minutes between Lymington on the mainland and Yarmouth.

The tide runs strongly at half flood and ebb, so in your final approach make sure you do not get swept either side of the narrow entrance.

Pilotage: Yarmouth is easily located by its pier, church tower and the constant stream of Wightlink ferries. At night, the pier-head lights (2FR) and the floodlit ferry dock can be clearly identified. From east or west, the East Fairway buoy (Fl R 2s) and West Fairway buoy (Fl G 2s) respectively will bring you to waypoint 50°42'.58N 01°30'.01W, about 400m north of the entrance waypoint 50°42'.42N 01°30'.05W.

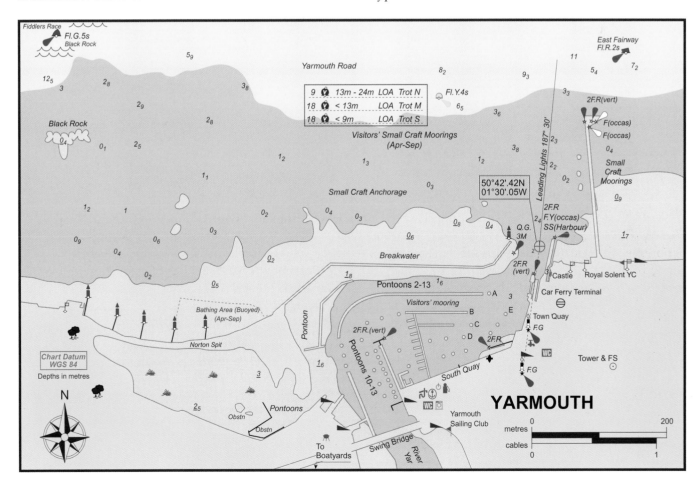

The leading beacons are 2 W ♦ on B/W masts and leading lights FG 9m 2M on the quay bearing 188°. The western breakwater is QG 3M and the eastern short ferry pier 2FR vertical lights.

Once past the breakwater, the majority of the visitors' moorings lie to starboard. The speed limit is six knots in the approaches and four knots within the harbour. It is often very busy, so entering under sail is not advised.

BERTHING

The extremely helpful harbourmaster launch (VHF Ch 68) patrols the harbour entrance and will direct you to available pontoon berths or piles. There are three types of visitors' moorings: fore and aft piles, alongside pontoon berths with shore access by dinghy or water taxi, and walk-ashore pontoons. On weekends during the summer months the harbour is frequently full, in which case 'Harbour Full' signs are shown at the end of the Wightlink ferry jetty and on the dolphin at the western side of the entrance. At night, the Wightlink sign is illuminated. A red flag is also flown on the pier-head. To contact the harbourmaster, Tel: 01983 760321 or VHF Ch 68.

Berthing fees: Prices vary depending on boat size, but an overnight stay for a 10m (33ft) yacht berthing on the walk-ashore pontoons is £26, while the other visitors' moorings inside the harbour cost £16. For short stays of up to four hours, the price for a 10m (33ft) yacht is £10.50 and £7 respectively. Fifteen of the walk-ashore pontoon berths can be prebooked, although payment is required in

The main hazard near Yarmouth is the half-hourly Wightlink ferries

On entering the harbour you will be greeted and directed to an available berth

advance. Three trots of moorings outside the harbour are available from March to October. To the north of these is an anchorage. All the moorings are served by the water taxis (VHF Ch15).

Yarmouth offers a variety of visitors' moorings, including walk-ashore berths, fore-and-aft piles and pontoon berths that are serviced by the water taxis

Useful information – Yarmouth

The Bugle Coaching Inn (above left) is situated in the centre of the original market square. A supermarket, deli and chandlers are all close by

FACILITIES

The walk-ashore pontoons all have electricity and water points, although you will need to supply your own hose. Water is also available beside the harbour office on the South Quay, as well as on the Town Quay. Petrol and diesel are available at the fuel pump, which is next to the harbour office. Gas, ice, showers (£1.20/token) and laundry facilities are all available at the harbour office, where the harbourmaster Bryn Bird and his staff will provide you with daily weather forecasts displayed on a plasma screen. Two computers with internet facilities are also available in the harbour office and the harbour has an Ocean Wave Wi-Fi system, so for a charge you can get online from your boat.

A sewage pump-out facility is available on the south quay. Scrubbing piles are at the north section of the inner harbour, although you need to book ahead of time if you want to use them. The harbour maintains a 5-ton crane for lifting smaller vessels. Local boatyards and marine businesses will carry out large lifts and provide repair services. In addition to these, there are a couple of chandleries nearby, some of which also sell gas and ice (for contact details, see p27). For sail repairs, go to the Saltern Sail Company at Saltern Wood Quay.

PROVISIONING

As well as a good number of specialist marine companies, this compact town also has an adequate range of shops for provisioning, including small delicatessens and a mini supermarket. A chemist and post office are located on Quay Street, while a doctor's surgery can be found on Station Road (see p27 for contact details). Lloyds TSB in the Square has a cash machine, as does the post office and the Bureau de Change. Bear in mind that out of season many shops close early on Wednesdays.

EATING OUT

There is no shortage of good restaurants and pubs in Yarmouth although they can get very busy during the height of summer, so it's best to book ahead of time. If you really want to treat your

The harbour can get very busy peak season

The formal George Hotel contrasts with the less formal Blue Crab

Useful information – Yarmouth

If you don't want to go into Yarmouth harbour, there are three trots of visitors' moorings available to the north of the harbour's breakwater

crew try the George Hotel (Tel: 01983 760331) in Quay Street, which is renowned for some of the best food on the island. Alternatively, situated not far from the George, in the Square, the Bugle Coaching Inn (Tel: 01983 760272) provides a choice of two restaurants and three bars. Offering a wide variety of beers, it seems very popular with yachtsmen, as does the Kings Head (Tel: 01983 760351) in Quay Street.

If you like seafood and a lively atmosphere then Salty's (Tel: 01983 761550) is the place to go. On the Rocks (Tel: 01983 760505) on Bridge Road and the Blue Crab (Tel: 01983 760014) on the High Street are also good for seafood, but for those who are simply after good pub-grub the Wheatsheaf (Tel: 01983 760456) in Bridge Road is an obvious choice.

If you don't fancy walking too far from the boat you can always go to Shenanigans (Tel: 01983 760054), which can be found conveniently close to the ferry terminal. With its excellent Solent

views, the Royal Solent Yacht Club's (Tel: 01983 760256) bar and restaurant welcomes visiting yachtsmen.

ASHORE

Yarmouth is an ideal base for an extended stay, with easy access to beaches and numerous places of interest. Besides the old town hall and the 16th century church, Yarmouth Castle (Tel: 01983 760678) is a major attraction in the town. It was constructed in 1547 by order of King Henry VIII after the French sailed into the Solent in 1545 and sank the Mary Rose. Well-preserved, the great hall, master gunner's parlour, kitchen and gun platforms are open to the public. Climbing the battlements is certainly worth while, as they offer spectacular views of the harbour and Solent. The castle is open 1000–1800 from 29 March to 30 September and 1000–1700 from 1-31 October.

Just a 15-minute walk from the harbour is Fort Victoria Country Park (Tel: 01983

760283). Incorporating an aquarium, a planetarium, Britain's biggest model railway and Seabed Heritage Exhibition, there is plenty to do and see here. Open 1000–1800 from Easter to the end of October.

Another great day out, especially if you have children on board, is a trip to the Needles Park at Alum Bay

(open 1000–1700 from Easter to early November, Tel: 0870 458 0022). Set in an area of outstanding natural beauty, the park offers an array of activities, including a chairlift ride over the impressive coloured sand cliffs of Alum Bay. You can also watch how traditional sweets are made at the Isle of Wight Sweet Manufactory,

An art gallery and a range of shops can be found on the High Street

The Royal Solent YC welcomes visiting sailors to its bar and restaurant

tasting them afterwards, or witness the skills of the Alum Bay glassmakers. Regular bus services run between here and Yarmouth.

Yarmouth is well-placed for exploring the West Wight on foot, by bicycle or on horseback (Come Riding: Tel: 01983 752502). For more details, contact the Tourist Information Office (Tel: 01983 813813) on the Quay. There are plenty of walks, cycleways and bridle-paths on either side of the River Yar to Freshwater, to Alum Bay and the Needles, or Freshwater Bay and Tennyson Down, where you can observe the abundance of wildlife that inhabit the estuary's peaceful waters and rural surroundings. For those who are feeling less energetic you can always go on one of the daily coach tours around the island or, alternatively, hire a car.

TRANSPORT
Buses: Southern Vectis (Tel: 01983 760012). Services 7/7A/42/43/47 run from Bridge Road to all island destinations. Note, however,

The George in Quay Street is adjacent to Yarmouth's 16th century castle and is well known for its excellent cuisine

several routes operate during the summer only.
Rail: Island Line (Tel: 0845 7484950) runs a service between Ryde Pierhead and Shanklin, via Sandown.
Taxis: Norton Taxis (Tel: 01983 759955); Rayners Taxis (Tel: 01983 752784).
Ferries: Wightlink ferries (Tel: 0870 582 7744) run every half hour between Yarmouth and Lymington on the mainland at peak travel times. From here there are regular train services to Poole and London.
Cycle hire: Harveys: Tel: 01983 785555.

OTHER INFORMATION
Harbourmaster: VHF Ch 68 Tel: 01983 760321.
Royal Solent Yacht Club: Tel: 01983 760256.
Yarmouth Sailing Club: Tel: 01983 760270.
Water taxi: VHF Ch 15 Tel: 01983 759910.
Chandleries: Harwoods: Tel: 01983 760258; Harold Hayles: Tel: 01983 760373; Buzzard Marine: Tel: 01983 760707.
Marine engineers: Buzzard Marine: Tel: 01983 760707; Harold Hayles: Tel: 01983 760373; Yarmouth Marine Service: Tel: 01983 760521;

Isle of Wight Outboards: Tel: 01983 760466.
Sail repairs: Saltern Sail Company: Tel: 01983 760120.
Police: Tel: 999; Tel: 0845 045 4545.
Coastguard: Lee on Solent Tel: 023 9255 2100/ VHF Channel 16.
Hospital: St Mary's Newport, Tel: 01983 524081.
Doctor: Station Road, Tel: 01983 760434.
NHS Direct: Tel: 0845 4647.
Dental helpline: Tel: 01983 537424.
Tourist information: Tel: 01983 813813.

Many permanent Yarmouth residents moor their boats on the River Yar, which winds its way south from the harbour to Freshwater

Extensive shoals lie to the east and west of the entrance to Lymington, but the only real hazard is the car ferries that operate from the town

Lymington

Lymington harbour entrance: 50°44'.37N 01°30'.54W

Lymington is an attractive old market town situated at the western end of the Solent, just three miles from the Needles Channel. Despite the fact that the river is monopolised by the regular ferries plying to and from the Isle of Wight, it is well sheltered and accessible at all states of the tide, and is a popular destination with yachtsmen.

NAVIGATION

Charts: Admiralty Charts: SC5600, 2021, 2035; Imray C3, C15, 2200; Stanfords: chartpack 24, chartpack 25, L9
Tides: Double High Waters occur at or near Springs, while on other occasions there is a stand lasting for about two hours. Predictions refer to the first High Water when there are two and to the middle of the stand at all other times.
HW Springs are 1 hour 10 minutes before and HW

Neaps 5 minutes after HW Portsmouth. LW Springs and LW Neaps are both 20 minutes before LW Portsmouth. MHWS: 3.0m; MHWN: 2.6m; MLWN: 1.4m; MLWS: 0.7m.

Approaches: Apart from the extensive shoals to the east and west of the harbour entrance and the regular Lymington to Yarmouth car ferry, there are no other real hazards to look out for. Owing to the frequency of the ferries, the fairway is fairly restricted, especially if the outbound ferry is crossing the inbound, so keep to the outside of the fairway. Better still, time your entry with the inbound ferry and follow it in. If you are approaching from the west, it pays to time your arrival on the flood, bearing in mind the strong tides through Hurst Roads.

Pilotage: By day, the Lymington river can be easily identified by the conspicuous yacht club starting platform, which lies to the east of the entrance. The regular

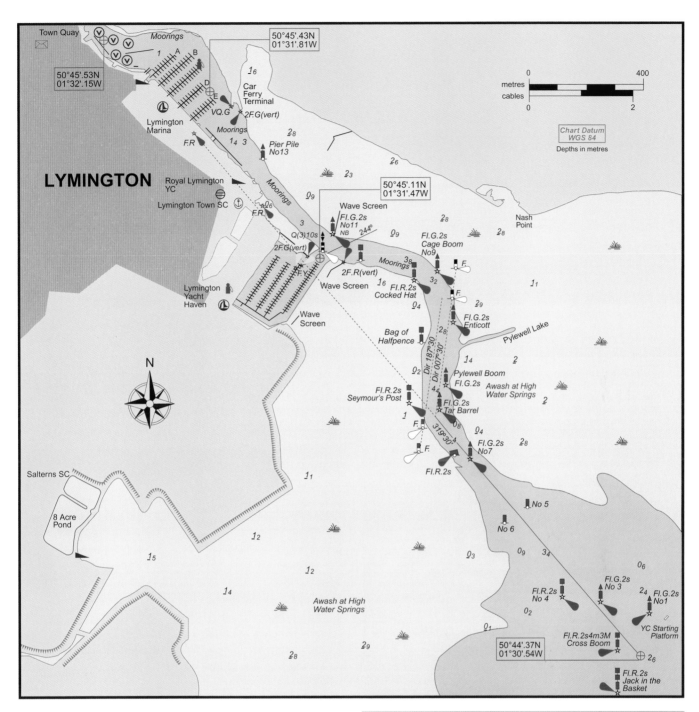

LYMINGTON

Town Quay

50°45'.53N
01°32'.15W

Moorings

50°45'.43N
01°31'.81W

Car Ferry Terminal

Lymington Marina

2F.G(vert)

VQ.G

F.R

Moorings

Pier Pile No13

Royal Lymington YC

Lymington Town SC

F.R.

Moorings

50°45'.11N
01°31'.47W

Wave Screen

Fl.G.2s No11 NB

244°

Q(3).10s

2F.G(vert)

F.Y

2F.R(vert)

Wave Screen

Fl.R.2s Cocked Hat

Moorings

Fl.G.2s Cage Boom No9

F.

Fl.R.2s

Fl.G.2s Enticott

Pylewell Lake

Nash Point

Lymington Yacht Haven

Wave Screen

Bag of Halfpence

Dir 187°.30

Dir 007°.30

Pylewell Boom

Fl.G.2s

Awash at High Water Springs

Fl.R.2s Seymour's Post

Fl.G.2s Tar Barrel

319°30.4

F.

F.

Fl.G.2s No7

Fl.R.2s

Salterns SC

8 Acre Pond

N

No 5

No 6

Awash at High Water Springs

Fl.R.2s No 4

Fl.G.2s No 3

Fl.G.2s No1

Fl.R.2s4m3M Cross Boom

50°44'.37N
01°30'.54W

YC Starting Platform

Fl.R.2s Jack in the Basket

0   400
metres
cables
0   2

Chart Datum WGS 84

Depths in metres

Wightlink ferries, which run between Lymington and Yarmouth on the Isle of Wight, will also help you identify the entrance. At night, the No1 starboard post (FL G 2s) is just west of the starting platform. The waypoint 50°44'.20N /01°30'.30W brings you to a position about 400m south-east of the platform. From this waypoint the FR leading lights bear 319° and the channel is clearly marked by starboard (Fl G 2s) and port-hand (Fl R 2s) beacons. After approximately half a mile on a course of 319° you will come to Tar Barrel Beacon (Fl G 2s), at which point you need to turn to starboard, coming on to a course of 007°. This will bring you on to the inbound ferry transit, which is identified by black and white leading marks. The channel turns to port at the No 9 Cage Boon beacon (Fl G 2s), from where the entrance to Lymington Yacht Haven bears approximately 280°. Harper's Post ECM (Q [3] 10s

The black and white leading marks identify the inbound ferry transit

New ferries to be introduced in 2008 will be 4m (13ft) longer and 0.8m (2ft 6in) wider than this existing ferry, creating even less room for manoeuvring

5m 1M) and two FY leading lights bearing 244° from waypoint 50°45'.12N 01°31'.42W mark the entrance to the Yacht Haven. Continuing further up river, you will pass the Royal Lymington YC to port and the ferry terminal to starboard before reaching Lymington Marina on your port-hand side. Beyond the marina the river bends sharply

to the left, after which the Town Quay, with its floating jetty and pontoon, and the visitors' buoys come into view. A six-knot speed limit applies in the harbour at all times.

Anchoring is not permitted in the river; however, with two large marinas, the Town Quay and numerous visitors' buoys, you have several options as to where to berth.

Lymington Yacht Haven

Yacht Haven entrance: 50°45'.11N 01°31'.47W

The closest marina to the Solent, Lymington Yacht Haven is a popular destination with yachtsmen and enjoys full tidal access. Its on-site boatyard provides a range of services from engine repairs to a hoist and pressure wash.

BERTHING

Although it has no allocated visitors' berths, it usually can accommodate visiting yachts in the summer when resident berth holders are away. For berthing availability and information, Tel: 01590 677071/VHF Channel 80.

Berthing fees: The peak rate is £2.95 per metre per day; a short stay of up to four hours is half the daily rate.

Useful information – Yacht Haven

FACILITIES
Lymington Yacht Haven offers an extensive array of facilities, including toilets and showers, which are open 24 hours a day, and a coin-operated launderette. Water and electricity are on the pontoons while gas refills can be obtained from either the fuel dock or the Nick Cox Yacht Chandler (Tel: 01590 673489) at the site entrance. Large skips are located close to each of the three bridgeheads for domestic refuse, with waste oil tanks adjacent to these. Fuel, diesel and two-stroke oil are available from the fuel station (situated on the sea wall in front of the marina office), 24 hours a day.

Security at the marina is of a high standard with a patrol in operation between 1800-0800, seven days a week, as well as CCTV cameras that

are monitored regularly. On site services include riggers and electronic engineers.

There is also a bar-cum-bistro, the Haven Bar & Bistro (Tel: 01590 679971), next to the marina reception, which serves breakfast, lunch and dinner on a daily basis from 0800 to 1015.

The Yacht Haven is a 10 to 15-minute walk from the town centre and for that reason is often quieter than Lymington Marina. However, a water taxi service (VHF Ch 10; Tel: 07972 170438) between the Yacht Haven and the Town Quay runs on weekends from May to September. The pick-up and drop-off point is situated at the fuel pontoon.

PROVISIONING
Nick Cox Yacht Chandler sells basic food provisions and is situated at the marina.

Lymington Marina

Marina entrance: 50°45'.43N 01°31'.81W

Situated roughly half a mile up river of the Yacht Haven, still on the port-hand side, lies Lymington Marina. It is easily accessible at any state of the tide.

BERTHING

Lymington Marina offers between 60 and 70 visitors' berths. For berthing availability, contact the marina on VHF Ch 80 or Tel: 01590 673312.
Berthing fees: £2.76 per metre per day (£0.83 per foot per day). A short stay is half the daily rate.

FACILITIES

Among the facilities available are impressive ablution and laundry amenities, water and electricity on the pontoons and a floating fuel dock that sells diesel, petrol and oil. A hard-standing area and a 75-ton hoist make this a convenient place for a winter lay-up. Five minutes' walk away from the town's High Street, the marina office provides gas and ice. You would also need to get your electricity cables and water hoses here.

PROVISIONING

For details of where to provision, eat out and things to do ashore, see Useful information on p32.

Lymington Marina has numerous visitors' berths and good facilities

Lymington Town Quay

Alongside quay: 50°45'.53N 01°32'.15W

The Town Quay's walk-ashore pontoons are a convenient place to berth

The Town Quay, with its walk-ashore jetty and nearby fore-and-aft moorings and pontoons, is a popular choice for many family cruisers. It can accommodate up to 150 vessels (maximum LOA 12m [39ft 4in] on the walk-ashore pontoons – 1.6m draught Low Water Springs). Contact the harbourmaster on Tel: 01590 672014 for availability.

The Dan Bran pontoon, which is situated to starboard of Lymington Yacht Haven, is available for events and rallies with a minimum of six boats and can also be booked through the harbour office (Tel: 01590 672014).

Berthing fees: 10m (33ft) yacht: £13.50 per night; four-hour short stay (which is only available up until 1600): £6.

FACILITIES

Water is available on the jetty, but visitors must supply their own hoses. Showers and toilets are available between April and November and are free of charge. There is also a waste disposal facility. There are two large chandleries nearby – Yachtmail (Tel: 01590 672784) on Captain's Row and Force 4 (Tel: 01590 673698) on Bath Road. The Lymington Harbour water taxi is based on the Town Quay and can be contacted on VHF Ch10 or Tel: 07972 170438.

PROVISIONING

For details of where to provision, eat out and things to do ashore, see Useful information on p32.

Useful information – Lymington

The Royal Lymington YC is one of two yacht clubs on the river

The Ship Inn on the Town Quay is highly recommended

PROVISIONING

With its picturesque cobbled streets, shopping in this pretty Georgian/Victorian town is very pleasurable. There are several **supermarkets** to choose from, the closest and most convenient one being Tesco Metro on the High Street. Alternatively, Waitrose can be found a little further away at the top of the High Street, with Marks & Spencer in St Thomas Street. Opposite Tesco is the **Lymington Larder** (Tel: 01590 676740), which sells a selection of farmhouse cheeses, patés, continental hams as well as chutneys and mustards. Most of the mainstream **banks**, some with cashpoints, are also situated in the High Street, as is the Lymington **post office**.

If you are in need of a **chemist** go to either Boots on the High Street or Moss in St Thomas' Street. Besides these more practical shops, there are also several clothes boutiques, antiques and gift shops to browse around. If you find yourself in Lymington over the weekend don't miss the lively street market, which is held every Saturday in the High Street.

EATING OUT

When it comes to restaurants and cafés you are spoilt for choice in Lymington. If you are moored at the Yacht Haven and don't feel like making the 15-minute walk into town, the **Haven Bar and Bistro** (Tel: 01590 679971), with its splendid views of the Solent, provides an alternative to eating aboard. It has a good, varied menu and puts on a daily barbecue during the summer. The **Lymington Town Sailing Club** (Tel: 01590 674514), which welcomes visiting yachtsmen, has its own restaurant, while the **Royal Lymington Yacht Club** (Tel: 01590 672677) is rather smarter and only accommodates visitors belonging to clubs with reciprocal arrangements.

If you like bistro-style food then **Graze** (Tel: 01590 675595) is a popular choice. Based on Gosport Street, this privately run, 40-seater restaurant serves fresh food cooked to order at fairly reasonable prices. The **Bluebird Seafood Restaurant** (Tel: 01590 676908) on Quay Street comes highly recommended for its fresh fish and shellfish, which are

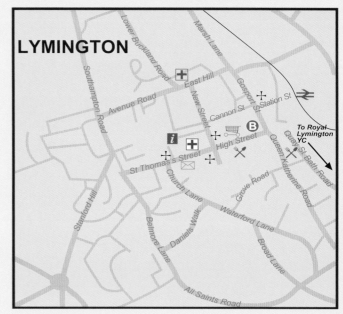

caught locally and vary from season to season.

For a good Indian, try **Lal Quilla** (Tel: 01590 671681) at the bottom of the High Street. Open seven days a week for lunch and dinner, it also has a takeaway service. **Caffè Uno** (Tel: 01590 688689) serves freshly prepared pasta at very reasonable prices. The **Roundhouse** (Tel: 01590 679089) on St Thomas' Street offers Mediterranean food with an Italian slant. The **Stanwell House Hotel** (Tel: 01590 677123), which overlooks the High Street, incorporates a modest restaurant that specialises

exclusively in seafood.

Among the pubs to be recommended is the **Ship Inn** (Tel: 01590 676903, VHF Ch10), situated right on the Town Quay. More bar/restaurant than pub, it especially welcomes visiting yachtsmen, and even offers showers if you are eating there. The **Bosun's Chair** (Tel: 01590 675140), a pub that is very proud of its fine ales, is situated at the foot of Station Street.

Other popular choices with yachtsmen are the **Chequers Inn** (Tel: 01590 673415) on Ridgeway Lane, which serves great food in congenial surroundings, the Angel Inn (Tel: 01590 672050) on the High Street and the Kings Head (Tel: 01590 672709) on Quay Hill. The Mayflower (Tel: 01590 672160), close to Lymington Yacht Haven, has good views over the river and a large garden.

Besides an abundance of pubs and restaurants, only a few of which have been mentioned above, Lymington also has a good selection of cafés and coffee shops, providing a pleasant way to while away the time. Both the Coffee Mill (Tel: 01590 676874) on New Street, off the High Street, and Tres Bon Sandwich Bar and Restaurant (Tel: 01590 673064) serve breakfast, lunch and teas.

ASHORE

There is a full range of things to do in Lymington and its surrounding area. In Lymington itself, you could begin by visiting the St Barbe Museum and Art Gallery (Tel: 01590 676969) on New Street. Through various activities, pictures and artefacts, the museum depicts the history of the New Forest, as well as exhibiting works by local artists and sculptors. The museum is open Monday to Saturday, 1000–1600.

For recreational pursuits, the local open-air sea baths (Tel: 01590 674865) lie adjacent to Lymington Yacht Haven or, alternatively, the Lymington Recreation Centre (Tel: 01590 670333) in North Street, Pennington, has a 25m indoor pool as well as a teaching pool. If that's too energetic for you, give the

small cinema (Tel: 01590 676939) at the Community Centre a call to find out what film is being shown.

The horticulturists among you may enjoy a trip to Spinners Garden (Tel: 01590 673347) at Boldre, Lymington, where its woodland garden, packed full of azaleas, magnolias, Japanese maples and various other rare shrubs, overlooks the Lymington River valley. It is open during the summer season from Tuesday to Saturday, 1000–1700.

If you prefer a good walk, the Solent Way footpath provides an invigorating stroll to and from Hurst Castle. For more details on Hurst Castle, see p17 & p21.

With the New Forest on its doorstep, small villages and towns such as Brockenhurst and Lyndhurst are only a bus, train or taxi ride away from Lymington. A fun day out is to hire bikes and cycle along the forest tracks in beautiful scenery. Lymington also has direct transport links with Beaulieu, where a trip to the National Motor Museum and Beaulieu Abbey is well worth while (see p44).

TRANSPORT

Trains: Lymington's railway station can be found on Station Street, just off Gosport Street. Direct train services run from here to Poole and London. For train times, contact National Rail Enquiries (0845 7484950).
Buses: Wilts and Dorset Bus Company (Tel: 01590 672382) operate direct bus services to Brockenhurst, Lyndhurst, Beaulieu,

Lymington is a lively and bustling town, with plenty to see and do

The Bluebird restaurant on the cobbled Quay Street is recommended

The Angel Inn dates back to the 13th century when it was a coaching inn

The charming streets offer a wide selection of pubs, cafés and shops

Useful information – Lymington

The visitors' moorings lie close to the Town Quay, and up to 150 boats can be accommodated between here, the walk-ashore jetty and the pontoons

Southampton and Bournemouth.

Air: Lymington is conveniently situated between two airports, at Bournemouth (Tel: 01202 364000) and Southampton (Tel: 0870 040 0009).

Ferries: Wightlink (Tel: 0870 582 7744/01590 673301) runs a car and passenger service between Lymington and Yarmouth. For Hurst Castle and Yarmouth Ferry, Tel: 01590 642500.

Taxis: Allports Taxi (Tel: 01590 679792); Lymington and Grosvenor Taxis (Tel: 01590 672842/670670).

Car hire: There are no car hire companies in Lymington itself, the nearest one being Meadens of Sway (Tel: 01590 683684) about 2½ miles away in Sway.

Cycle hire: Again, none in Lymington, but there are several in nearby Brockenhurst – Balmer Lawn Bike Hire: Tel: 01590 623133; Country Lanes Cycle Centre: Tel: 01590 622627; Cyclexperience: Tel: 01590 623407.

USEFUL INFORMATION

Lymington Harbourmaster: Tel: 01590 672014.

Lymington Yacht Haven: VHF Ch 80/Tel: 01590 677071.

Lymington Marina: VHF Ch 80/Tel: 01590 647405.

Royal Lymington Yacht Club: Tel: 01590 672677.

Lymington Town Sailing Club: Tel: 01590 674514.

Lymington Water Taxi: VHF Ch 10/Tel: 07972 170438.

Operates between the moorings and the Town Quay and the Yacht Haven and the Town Quay.

Chandleries: Nick Cox Yacht Chandler: Tel: 01590 673489; Force 4 Chandlery: Tel: 01590 673698; Yachtmail: Tel: 01590 672784.

Marine services: Greenham Regis, Electronics: Tel: 01590 671144; Tinley Electronics: Tel: 01590 610071; Ocean Rigging: Tel: 01590 676292; Hood Sailmakers: Tel: 01590 675011.

Police: Tel: 999; Tel: 0845 045 4545.

Coastguard: Lee on Solent: Tel: 023 9255 2100.

Lymington Hospital: Tel: 01590 677011.

Doctor: Tel: 01590 672953.

Dentist: (private practice) Tel: 01590 679888.

NHS Direct: Tel: 0845 4647.

Tourist Information: Tel: 01590 689000.

The Mayflower's garden offers good views towards the river

The Newtown River is managed by the National Trust and one of the Solent's most popular anchorages

Newtown River

Newtown River entrance: 50°43'.69N 01°24'.90W

During the Middle Ages Newtown was a thriving and busy commercial harbour. However, it was attacked in 1377 by the French who, by burning it to the ground (after which the town's prosperity never recovered), turned it into probably the most unspoiled anchorage in the Solent today. The Newtown River estuary is now a nature reserve owned by the National Trust. Its only downside is its popularity, so try to time your visits on weekdays or, better still, out of season.

NAVIGATION

Charts: Admiralty Charts: SC5600, 2021, 2035, 2036; Imray: C3, C15, 2200; Stanfords 11, chartpack 24, chartpack 25, L10

Tides: Double High Water is at or near Springs; at other times there is a stand which lasts about two hours. Predictions refer to the first High Water when there are two, otherwise they apply to the middle of the stand. The flood is seven hours making for a strong ebb.

HW Springs are 1 hour 5 minutes before and Neaps

A lit port-hand entrance buoy provides a useful reference at night

The leading beacons assist with locating the entrance to Newtown River

The anchorage at Newtown is the most unspoiled in the Solent and an idyllic spot to spend a day or two, particularly mid-week or out of season

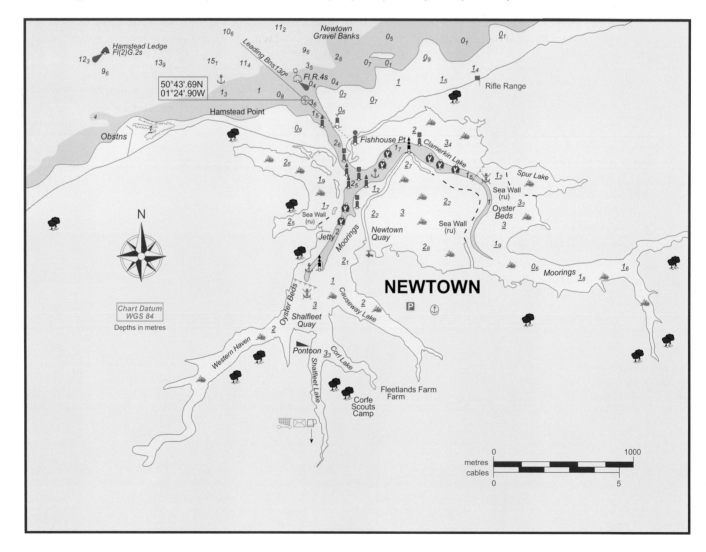

5 minutes after HW Portsmouth. LW Springs are 25 minutes before and Neaps 30 minutes before HW Portsmouth. MHWS: 3.0m; MHWN: 2.6m; MLWN: 1.6m; MLWS: 0.8m.

Approaches: From the east, keep north of the Salt Mead buoy (Fl [3] G 10s) and at least half a mile from the island's shore to clear the Newtown Gravel Banks. Hamstead Ledge (Fl [2]G 5s) provides a good approach from the west.

Pilotage: The entrance is narrow and difficult to spot from seaward. From the waypoint 50°43'.85N 01°22'.0W, the conspicuous TV mast bearing 150° provides the initial approach. Having picked up the lit port-hand buoy (Fl R 4s), steer 130°. This can be confirmed by the leading beacons – the front RW banded beacon, which has a Y topmark, should be kept in line with the red circle on the white rear beacon. However, when you are within 200m of the Y beacon, it is better to keep the beacons open as the best water is to starboard. Once abeam of the Y beacon, the narrow entrance opens up and you should steer a few degrees to starboard and head directly for the middle of the two shingle spits that mark the entrance. The gap is very narrow but the spits are steep-to, with deep water in between. For newcomers the best time to enter is about High Water -4 hours, on the flood, while the mud flats are still visible.

Entering the Newtown River at night for the first time is quite demanding. However, the lit port-hand entrance buoy (Fl R 4s) makes it easier, as does the reflective red and green tape on the port and starboard piles. However, if entering the harbour at night, it is safer to do so on a rising tide.

Once inside, the channel is marked with red and green withies. Where it divides into the Clamerkin Lake to the east and Newtown River to the west, the marks can appear quite confusing, so tread carefully and study the chartlet. If you are taking the westerly branch to Shalfleet, don't cut in to starboard as there is a hard, drying bank. When manoeuvring inside the harbour, keep a close watch on your echosounder, although most of the bottom is soft mud and is easy to back off if you do run aground. Make sure you observe the speed limit of five knots.

MOORING/ANCHORAGE

There is a row of 20 marked visitors' moorings in the main arm of the river leading up to Shalfleet Quay and six in Clamerkin Lake. White buoys indicate visitors' moorings, while the red buoys are used by local boats.

You can anchor just inside the entrance or in Clamerkin Lake. Be careful, however, to avoid the oyster beds on either side and do not anchor beyond the boards showing 'Anchorage Limit'. The holding ground is excellent, but on a crowded summer weekend strong winds and unpredictable eddies can make for some close quarters sparring. The harbourmaster's launch is usually on hand to give advice, although he cannot be contacted on VHF.

Berthing fees: A short stay on a mooring costs £3-£5 while overnight ranges from £8-£10. Rafting on the moorings is only allowed with the permission of the harbourmaster. Please note that these prices may be subject to a slight change according to inflation. Anchoring in the river is free of charge. However, most vessels make a voluntary donation (£5) to the National Trust to help the organisation maintain this gem of a location.

The main anchorage is in Clamerkin Lake, or just inside the river's entrance

Useful information – Newtown River

The National Trust looks after the Newtown River Estuary and is grateful for all donations

FACILITIES

There are no proper facilities for yachtsmen here, which is no bad thing as the intrinsic charm of the Newtown River would undoubtedly be lost by their introduction. You can, however, get water from the end of the footbridge at Newtown Quay (accessible three hours either side of High Water) and both fuel and gas, plus limited basic food provisions are available from the garage at Shalfleet (Tel: 01983 531315), which is situated to the east of the village on the main road. The town of Yarmouth (see p22-27), which lies three miles to the west, is more convenient if you need to stock up on marine supplies.

Several lovely walks start from the banks of the Newtown River

PROVISIONING

If you go past the Shalfleet church and left at Warlands Lane you will find the Shalfleet post office and shop. For more serious provisioning, head to Yarmouth or Cowes.

EATING OUT

A dinghy trip to Shalfleet Quay (which is not accessible two hours either side of Low Water Springs), followed by a very pleasant 15-minute riverside walk brings you to the excellent New Inn (Tel: 01983 531314). Dating back to the 17th century, its flagstone floors, scrubbed tables and open log fires create a congenial atmosphere. Specialising in seafood and serving various real ales, it was awarded the Good Pub Guide Isle of Wight Dining Pub of the Year 2007. In peak season, it is best to book in advance.

ASHORE

With only a handful of cottages, it is hard to imagine that Newtown was once a thriving port with flourishing salt works and oyster beds. On the road to Shalfleet and Newport the old town hall still stands and serves as a reminder of the town's former importance. Built in 1699, it is now owned by the National Trust and, with its round-headed windows and stone dressings, is well worth a visit. The old town pump, found on the right-hand side as you head away from the quay, has also been preserved. A quiet haven for wildlife, the Newtown Estuary offers several lovely walks, one of which is the Hamstead Trail, which starts from the banks of the Newtown River and crosses via the small hamlet of Wellow to the southern shore at Brook Bay.

Barbecues are very popular on the western entrance spit although, in order to preserve the rare plants, they should only be held below the High Water mark. Likewise, to protect the important bird nesting area, landing on the eastern spit is forbidden.

TRANSPORT

Buses: Southern Vectis (Tel: 01983 827000). operates an hourly service from Shalfleet to Yarmouth.
Taxis: Norton Taxis (Tel: 01983 759955); Rayners Taxis (Tel: 01983 752784).

OTHER INFORMATION

Harbourmaster: Tel: 01983 531424; no VHF.
Police: Tel: 0845 045 4545.
Coastguard: Lee on Solent: Tel: 023 9255 2100.
Hospital: St Mary's Newport: Tel: 01983 524081.
Doctor: Tel: 01983 760434.
NHS Direct: Tel: 0845 4647.
Dental helpline: Tel: 01983 537424.
Tourist office (Yarmouth): Tel: 01983 813813.
The National Trust: Tel: 01983 741020.

The Beaulieu River

Beaulieu River entrance: 50°46'.90N 01°21'.72W

Meandering through the New Forest, the Beaulieu River is by far the most romantic harbour on the mainland side of the Solent. A few miles upstream from the mouth of the river lies Buckler's Hard, an historic 18th century village where shipwrights skilfully constructed warships for Nelson's fleet.

NAVIGATION
Charts: Admiralty Charts: SC5600, 2021, 2036; Imray: C15, 2200; Stanfords: 11, chartpacks 24 & 25, L9, L10

Tides: Double High Water occurs at or near Springs, with the second High Water being 1 hour 45 minutes after the first. On other occasions the stand lasts for about two hours.
HW Springs are 40 minutes and Neaps 10 minutes before HW Portsmouth. LW Neaps are 10 minutes before and Springs 5 minutes after LW Portsmouth. MHWS: 3.7m; MHWN: 3.0m; MLWN: 1.7m; MLWS: 0.5m.

Approaches: From the east, keeping the Lepe Spit SCM (Q[6]+LFl 15s YB) to starboard, steer towards the yellow spherical racing buoy (Fl 4s; March – October; position: 50°46'.59N 01°21'.46W) in order to stay well clear of the shallows off Stone Point, until you get to the

The Beaulieu River winds inland to Buckler's Hard. The channel is well marked, and if you stay close to the moorings, you will pass through deep water

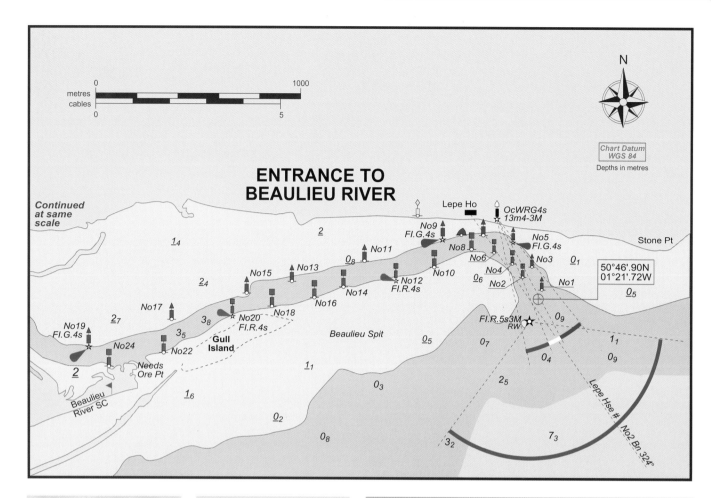

ENTRANCE TO BEAULIEU RIVER

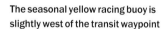
The seasonal yellow racing buoy is slightly west of the transit waypoint

On entering the river, leave the Beaulieu Spit dolphin 40m to port

transit waypoint 50°46'.57N 01°21'.37W. On a western approach, to avoid the shallows you need to leave the yellow spherical racing buoy (March – December) at position 50°46'.15N 01°22'20W to port, steering a course towards the transit waypoint as above.

Pilotage: With its prominent Millennium Beacon (position 50°47'.08N 01°21'.81W) and sector light Oc WRG 4s 13m 4/3M (Vis G 321° – 331°; W 331° – 337°; R337° – 347°) as well as the old white boathouse, the mouth of the Beaulieu River is easily identified both at day and night. Owing to the bar and shifting sands, the entrance can be dangerous and should not be attempted until two hours either side of Low Water. Beware that there are patches drying to 0.3m approximately 95m south of the Beaulieu Spit. From the transit waypoint 50°46'.57N 01°21'.37W the leading marks, bearing 324°, must be aligned carefully to avoid the shoal water (which to the west can be as low as 0.1m) either

The Millennium Beacon clearly identifies the entrance to the Beaulieu River

side. The front mark is the No 2 port beacon, while the rear is the eastern side of Lepe House. The Beaulieu Spit dolphin Fl R 5s 3M (Vis 277° – 037°) should be kept about 40m to port.

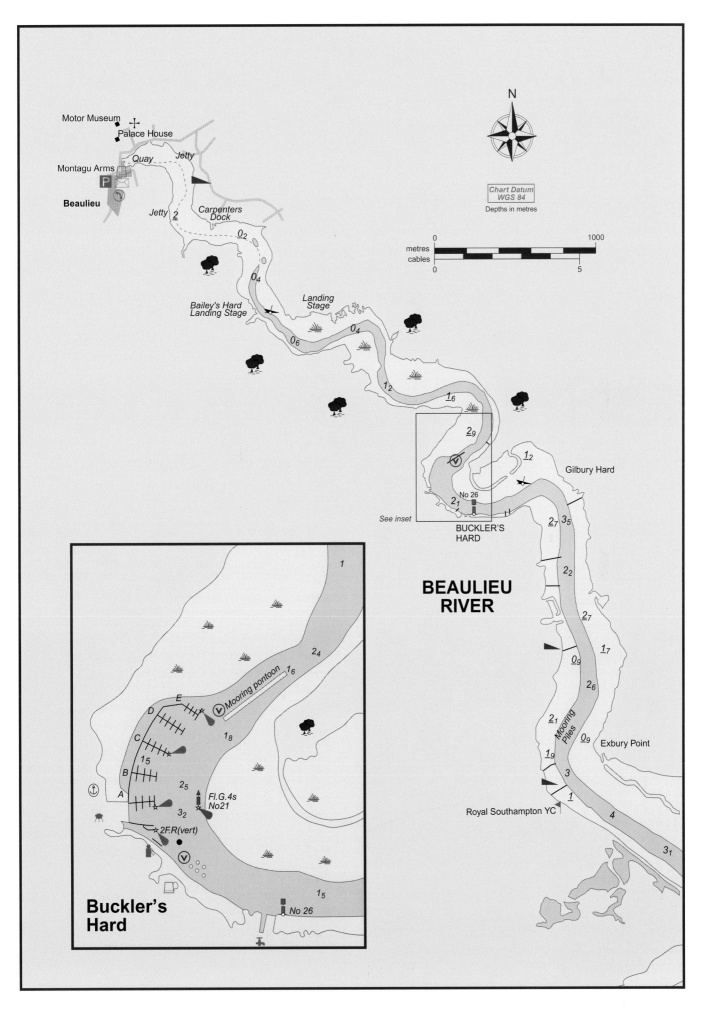

Motor Museum

Palace House

Montagu Arms

Quay   Jetty

P

Beaulieu

Jetty   2

Carpenters
Dock

0₂

0₄

Bailey's Hard
Landing Stage

Landing
Stage

0₆   0₄

1₂

1₆

2₉

1₂

Gilbury Hard

No 26

2₁

See inset

BUCKLER'S
HARD

2₇   3₅

2₂

**BEAULIEU
RIVER**

2₇

1₇

0₉

2₆

2₁   0₉   Exbury Point

1₉

3

1

4

Royal Southampton YC

3₁

Mooring Piles

N

*Chart Datum
WGS 84*

Depths in metres

0				1000

metres
cables

0				5

Buckler's Hard inset:

1

2₄

1₆   Mooring pontoon

E

D

C   1₈

15   B

A   2₅

Fl.G.4s
No21

3₂

2.F.R(vert)

1₅

No 26

**Buckler's
Hard**

Looking south-west down the Beaulieu River. The marina at Buckler's Hard welcomes visitors, and is a good place to stop if you want to explore ashore

In the river, the channel is marked with numbered red and green beacons, of which numbers 12 and 20 are lit with Fl R 4s and 5, 9 and 19 with Fl G 4s. Once past the No 19 starboard beacon, the channel turns north-west and is identified by withies. Following the line of mooring buoys should keep you in the channel, although due care needs to be taken at night to avoid the moored yachts. Buckler's Hard and its marina are a few miles upstream. The river's five-knot speed limit must be observed.

The entrance is well marked with port and starboard-hand marks

BERTHING

Owing to the large quantities of moorings in the river, the only recognised anchorage is in the first reach on the south side of the channel, opposite Gull Island. Here there is good holding ground on mud, but it can be uncomfortable in strong easterly winds. There are also four white visitors' mooring buoys. There are no visitors' buoys past Gull Island, although vacant ones may be used with the harbourmaster's permission (Tel: 01590 616200). Visitors are welcome to enter the marina (dredged to 1.8m below

Mean Low Water Springs) at any time. Alternatively, moor fore and aft to the piles below the marina or berth alongside the river pontoon, which has recently been installed above the marina.

Berthing fees: Overnight fees in the marina currently range from £30.50 for yachts up to 12m (39ft 4in) in length to £45.50 for yachts up to 18m (59ft) LOA. A short stay in the marina, which is only applicable up to 1530, costs from £12.50. Visitors' river pontoon moorings cost from £10 per day, while anchoring in the river costs £5.

The river is packed with moorings, particularly around Buckler's Hard

The marina usually has room for visitors and is accessible to most boats

Useful information – Beaulieu River

Buckler's Hard has a long association with shipbuilding and if you are interested in maritime history is a fascinating place to visit

FACILITIES

Buckler's Hard offers a comprehensive range of facilities to yachtsmen, including showers, toilets and a coin-operated launderette ashore, while rubbish skips are situated near the landing points. Diesel, unleaded petrol, fresh water and ice are all obtainable from the fuel pontoon, which is manned until sunset. Buckler's Hard Garage (BHG Marine, Tel: 01590 616479) is open six days a week throughout the summer, and provides superb outboard engine repair facilities.

If you need to have your keel cleaned, then a scrubbing grid can be booked for £22 through the harbour office, as can the yacht valet service, which is available mid-week only. A good presence of marine engineers and riggers, along with a Renner mobile boat hoist and a hard-standing area, make Buckler's Hard an obvious place to have repairs carried out, although bear in mind that as this is one of the more desirable ports on the South Coast, it doesn't necessarily offer the most competitive prices.

The Agamemnon chandlery is situated conveniently close to the marina, next door to the shower block. Members of affiliated yacht clubs are made welcome at the Royal Southampton Yacht Club, which has a small offshoot at Gins Farm.

PROVISIONING

Buckler's Hard does not cater for serious provisioning but the village store, situated just behind the Maritime Museum, provides all the essential groceries as well as incorporating an off-

The Montagu Arms Hotel in nearby Beaulieu is recommended

licence. Alternatively, you can go by dinghy (depending on the state of the tide) or walk (about 2½ miles) to the nearby village of Beaulieu where you will find a few more village shops, including a bakery and a post office.

EATING OUT

For a good pub meal in a warm and friendly atmosphere, you need only walk a short distance along the river-bank to the Master Builder's House Hotel (Tel: 01590 616253), where the Yachtsman's Bar and Gallery is a popular choice with visiting sailors. Once the home of Henry Adams, the most celebrated of the master shipwrights at Buckler's Hard, the bar now displays an impressive list of the 60 wooden men-of-war and merchant ships built at the yard from 1698 to 1818.

For something a little smarter and more sophisticated, the hotel's Riverview Restaurant and Terrace provides the answer. As its name suggests, it offers a delightful setting for lunch or an evening meal and serves an extensive choice of wines, among which are those from the Beaulieu Estate. If the Master Builder's House Hotel is full, which it often is in the summer, you

Useful information – the Beaulieu River

could always go a bit further afield to Beaulieu where the Montagu Arms Hotel (Tel: 01590 612324) provides restaurant and bar meals. Its bistro, Monty's, can also be recommended and has reasonable prices.

The Captain's Cabin Café (Tel: 01590 616293), which is amalgamated with the village store at Buckler's Hard, serves a selection of hot and cold snacks.

ASHORE

As Buckler's Hard is renowned for its shipbuilding history, its Maritime Museum (Tel: 01590 616203) is certainly worth a visit. Here you can learn about the life of Henry Adams, the master shipbuilder who, even in the 18th to early 19th century, lived to the ripe old age of 92 years. Among the displays are models of the ships built for Lord Nelson, the

most notable of which was the *Agamemnon*, allegedly Nelson's favourite vessel.

You can also see exhibits relating to Sir Francis Chichester who made Buckler's Hard his home port, and in 1967, on board *Gipsy Moth IV*, was the first person to circumnavigate the globe singlehandedly. A few metres up from the Master Builder's House Hotel, cottages have been authentically reconstructed to give a realistic insight into the life and times of the village and its residents during the 1700s.

Rich in birdlife, the Riverside Walk between Buckler's Hard and Beaulieu should not be overlooked. Starting at the back of Agamemnon Boatyard you can stroll along the tree-lined path, taking in the views across the river and saltmarshes which are now

There are many waterside properties with private jetties

inhabited by an abundance of wildfowl including shelduck and waders.

If you do get as far as Beaulieu, make sure you visit the National Motor Museum (Tel: 01590 612345). Even if you aren't a car-lover you will still be impressed by some of the world's most famous vehicles. Alternatively, you may be interested in seeing the ruins of Beaulieu's ancient monastery, established by French monks over 800 years ago, or visiting Palace House where 'Victorian' staff will give you an insight into what life was like during that period. For details on any of the Beaulieu attractions, Tel: 01590 612345.

The nearby Exbury Gardens (Tel: 023 8089 1203) are also worth a visit, particularly during the Spring when the woodland gardens created by Lionel Nathan de Rothschild are ablaze with vibrant colours. Open March to November, 1000-1730.

TRANSPORT

There is no public transport from Buckler's Hard to Beaulieu.

Taxis: Marchwood Motorways is a local firm (Tel: 023 8084 2134).

Rail: Beaulieu Road or Brockenhurst train stations are about six miles from Buckler's Hard and provide fairly frequent South-West Trains services to London. For details, contact National Rail Enquiries: Tel: 0845 748 4950.

Buses: The No 112 bus runs via Beaulieu (the bus stop is in front of the garage) between Lymington and Hythe. Wilts & Dorset Bus Company: Tel: 01590 672382.

Cycle hire: Country Lanes Cycle Hire, Beaulieu: Tel: 01590 611029.

OTHER INFORMATION

Harbourmaster: Tel: 01590 616200.

Marine services: Buckler's Hard Boatbuilders: Tel: 01590 616214; BHG Marine: Tel: 01590 616249.

Lymington Hospital: Tel: 01590 677011.

Police: Tel: 0845 0454545.

Coastguard: Lee on Solent: Tel: 023 9255 2100.

Doctor: Tel: 01590 672953.

NHS Direct: Tel: 0845 4647.

Dentist: Tel: 01590 679888.

Tourist Information: Lymington office: Tel: 01590 689000. New Forest office: Tel: 023 8028 2269.

The historic Beaulieu Abbey and Palace House at the head of the river

The surrounding New Forest is renowed for its herds of wild ponies

Chapter two
Central Solent

The central Solent is a busy but exciting area to sail in. With Cowes as the hub of British yachting and Southampton a magnet for large container vessels and high-speed ferries, cruising between these two harbours needs constant vigilance. An Area of Concern (AOC) dominates this region to improve the safety for commercial ships, and you are advised to pay close attention to the enforced restrictions. See p47 for details.

Hazards along the Isle of Wight coast are mainly close inshore and are avoided by staying in reasonable soundings. If sailing along the shore from Osborne Bay to Cowes, the rocks off Norris Castle can easily catch you out. The popular anchorage in Osborne Bay is well sheltered from the prevailing wind and out of the main tidal stream, but watch out for the rocks at its eastern end and the drying patches some 150m offshore to the west.

On the mainland side, Horseshoe Spit, east of the Beaulieu River's entrance, runs south of Stansore Point, but is clearly marked by the Lepe Spit SCM. Extending well offshore, Calshot Spit can be a trap to newcomers, especially as you may have to stay close to its eastern edge to keep clear of the main fairway and its AOC.

Being one of the few 'mid-channel' hazards in the Solent, the Bramble Bank lies roughly halfway between Cowes and Southampton Water. It is easily misjudged despite being well marked by Hill Head and East Knoll buoys to the north, East Bramble ECM, West Knoll green conical buoy and the Brambles post to the south. Cricket matches are sometimes played on this bank at Low Water Springs. Approximately a mile north of the East Bramble ECM and north-west of Lee Point are two buoyed areas for jet skiing and water-skiing, both of which you may want to avoid.

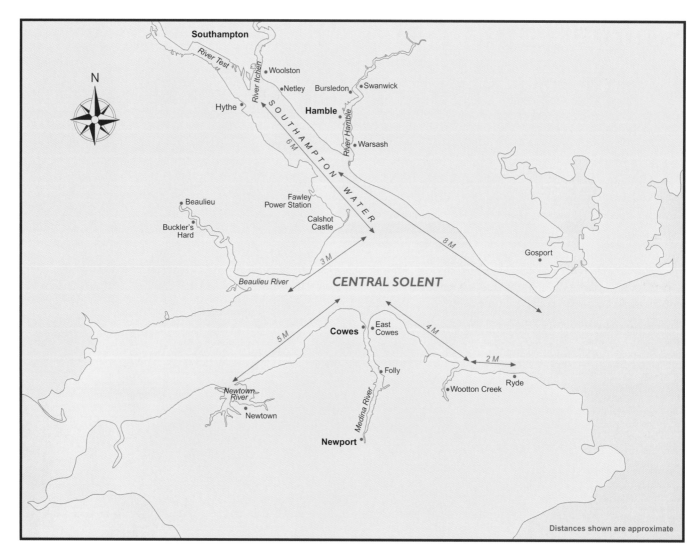

Cricket at Low Water on the Bramble Bank is now a long held tradition. Here, the late Uffa Fox plays against the Parkhurst Prison Officers' team

Southampton Water – rules of the road

Southampton Water and the area surrounding its entrance is a busy shipping area, and it is important to obey the rules of the road that relate to it – not only to avoid the hefty fines imposed should you contravene them, but also for your own safety. The principal deep-water channels used by shipping are clearly marked with buoys and lights, and should be avoided at all times. If you do need to cross the channels, then you should do so at right angles, so as to spend as little time in the fairway as possible. Whatever you do, try to avoid crossing in front of a ship – many travel at deceptively fast speeds and require several miles to slow down or take avoiding action. Many also suffer from restricted visibility, so may not be able to see you.

In order to improve safety, both for commercial ships and leisure craft, an Area of Concern (AOC) has been set up at the entrance to Southampton Water, which is used by large vessels bound to or from the port. Many pleasure boats often cut across this 'area' and so, to reduce the risk of collision, vessels over 150m LOA, when entering the AOC, are given a Moving Prohibited Zone (MPZ), which extends 1,000m ahead of the craft and 100m on either beam. Craft under 20m (66ft) LOA are prohibited from entering this zone. The Vessel Traffic Service (VTS), operated by Southampton on VHF Ch 12 and Ch 14, controls the shipping throughout the Solent, with the exception of Portsmouth Harbour and its approaches north of a line from Gilkicker Point to Outer Spit buoy, which is regulated by QHM Portsmouth on VHF Ch 11. If near the AOC, listen out on VHF Ch 12 for the regular broadcasts transmitted by Southampton VTS.

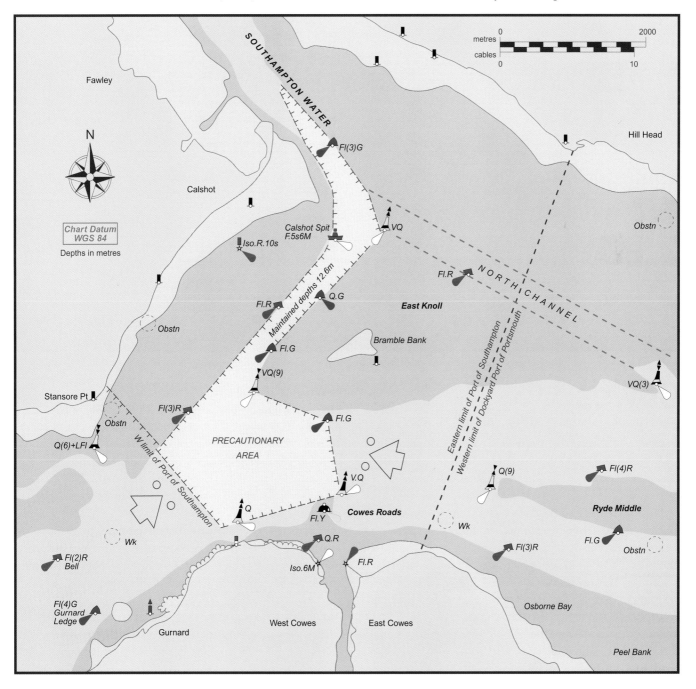

Cowes is seen by many as the hub of the Solent, and the navigable Medina River, which bisects it, winds up to Newport, the island's administrative capital

Cowes

Cowes harbour entrance: 50°46'.08N 01°17'.93W

Situated virtually at the centre of the Solent, Cowes is best known as Britain's premier yacht racing centre and offers every facility to yachtsmen. Although not all the yacht clubs welcome visitors, the town boasts an array of pubs, restaurants, cafés and shops as well as many places of interest at which to while away a few hours.

For the non-racing cruiser it is probably best to avoid the mayhem of Cowes Week, which is held every year at the beginning of August, unless you want to experience the vibrant atmosphere and don't mind burning a large hole in your pocket. At the top of the Medina River, which winds inland from Cowes, lies the town of Newport, the capital of the Isle of Wight, which can only be reached by deep-draughted yachts on favourable tides.

NAVIGATION

Charts: Admiralty Charts: SC5600, 2793, 2036; Imray: C3, C15, 2200; Stanfords: 11, chartpacks 24 & 25, L11

Tides: Double High Water occurs at or near Springs, otherwise the stand lasts for up to two hours; the times given represent the middle of the stand. The west-going Spring tide can run at up to four knots across the harbour entrance.

HW Springs are 15 minutes before and Neaps 15 minutes after HW Portsmouth. LW Neaps are 20 minutes before and Springs the same as LW Portsmouth. MHWS: 4.2m; MHWN: 3.5m; MLWN: 1.8m; MLWS: 0.8m.

Approaches: The eastern and western approaches to Cowes are fairly straightforward. From the east, Old Castle Point needs to be kept at least 400m off, staying outside the yellow racing spherical buoy (Fl Y 4s/March

The 18th century Norris Castle overlooks the Solent to the east of Cowes

Cowes and the Medina lie opposite the entrance to Southampton Water

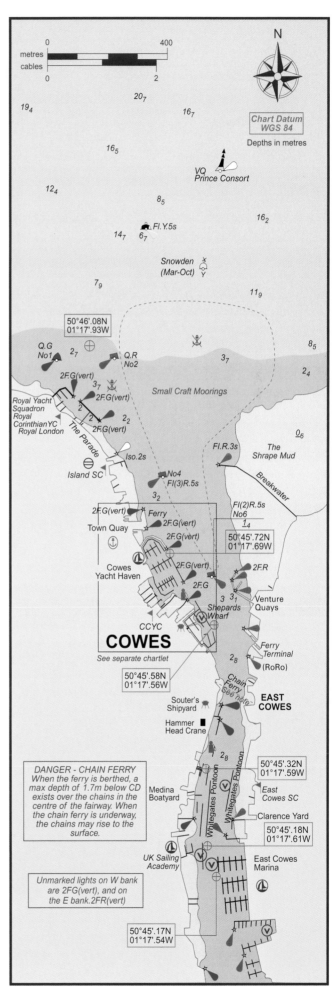

– December/waypoint 50°46'.15N 01°16'.64W). From here aim for the Cowes Roads Trinity House buoy (Fl Y 5s) to avoid the Shrape mud shallows to port. From the west, the inshore Grantham Rocks between Egypt Point and the SHM QG entrance buoy need to be given a good offing. If you are coming from the north be aware that there is a Restricted Entry Area north-east of the line between Gurnard NCM in the west and the Prince Consort NCM in the east, enabling large vessels to turn easily. A mile further to the north of Prince Consort buoy lies the Bramble Bank, which dries to 1.2m and catches out many deep-keeled yachts. To make sure you avoid it, keep west of the green conical West Knoll buoy.

Pilotage: From the waypoint 50°46'.23N 01°17'.99W, a course of 167° puts you in mid-channel between the No 1 starboard-hand (QG) and the No 2 port-hand (QR) fairway

West Cowes, viewed from the east. The Royal Yacht Squadron is housed in Cowes Castle, which is particularly distinctive amid the 20th century architecture

buoys. Use the main channel but keep close to the western shore as the Red Funnel car and high-speed passenger ferries take up a good deal of room – on leaving the harbour there is just enough space between the moorings and the port-hand mark to keep out of their way. On the east side of the fairway are two further port-hand marks – No 4 (Fl [3] R5s) and No 6 (Fl [2] R5s – further to the east of No 4 buoy). To starboard, the RYS Haven, the Trinity Landing and the Jubilee Pontoon, along with the outer limits of Cowes Yacht Haven and the fuel jetty between the marina and Shepards Wharf, are clearly lit at night (2FG [vert]). Likewise all the port and starboard jetties and pontoons between the chain ferry and the National Power Jetty are marked with 2FR (vert) and 2FG (vert)

lights respectively, making the channel easy to identify at night. Vessels should keep a sharp look-out for the Red Funnel car ferries and the Red Jet high-speed catamarans, particularly in the busy Town Quay area.

Upstream, beyond the National Power Jetty, the channel starts to narrow and shoals rapidly. Between the Medham beacon (VQ [3] 5s) and the South Folly beacon (QG 3m 1M) the depth is at times only about 1m, so for the best water stay as close as possible to the starboard-hand moorings.

There is a six-knot speed limit in the channel and the harbourmaster advises all yachts to use their engines, especially when approaching the chain ferry.

The Medina River offers several options for berthing, all with varying degrees of facilities for yachtsmen.

A chain ferry south of Shepards Wharf links East and West Cowes

The fuel jetty 100m south of the chain ferry is the easiest place to get fuel

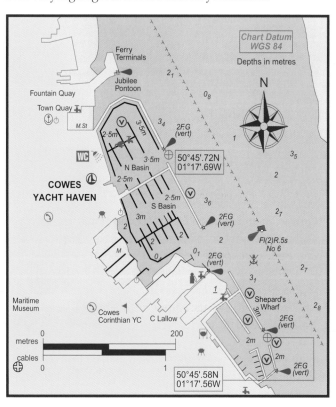

Cowes Harbour Commission

The Cowes Harbour Commission has, in the past few years, been busy increasing the number of its visitors' moorings. A pontoon called Trinity Landing, with shore-side access, has replaced the old swinging moorings just inside the harbour entrance alongside the Esplanade. The outside of the pontoon should only be used for quick pick-ups and drop-offs, but the inside can be used for overnight stays. Water and electricity are available. A section of Trinity Landing is reserved for the private use of members of the Royal London Yacht Club. Another area out of bounds to members of the public is the Royal Yacht Squadron's new yacht haven, just north of the pontoon.

The Town Quay, which lies immediately south of the ferry terminal, is only suitable for small vessels, such as RIBs and motor boats measuring less than 9m (30ft) LOA.

Another recent addition to Cowes is Venture Quays on the eastern side of the river, in front of the large shed that bears the Union Flag. Venture Quays offers pontoon berths with water and electricity, but no walk ashore access. The harbour taxi service runs to Shepards Wharf, where there are toilet/shower facilities available to Venture Quay users.

A short distance up river of the chain ferry on both sides of the river lie the Waitegates visitors' moorings. Occasionally, the harbourmaster can find you a vacant resident's berth among the swinging moorings east of the

Trinity Landing has access ashore and can be used for pick-ups and drop offs

main channel, and during special events such as Cowes Week and the Round the Island Race, extra moorings are laid to the east and west of the river-mouth.

To contact Cowes Harbour Control, call VHF Ch 69 or Tel: 01983 293952.
Berthing fees: Town Quay and Trinity Landing: Short stays (max 4 hours, 1000-1600): Monday to Thursday: £0.75 per metre; Friday to Sunday: £0.90 per metre. Overnight: £1.60 per metre. Waitegates Visitors' Moorings & Venture Quays: Overnight: £1 per metre. Short stay (up to 4 hours): up to 12m (42ft): £5; 12-15m (42-50ft): £6; over 15m (50ft): £10.

Cowes Yacht Haven   Yacht Haven entrance: 50°45'.72N 01°17'.69W

Cowes Yacht Haven provides lots of visitors' berths and is close to the town

Cowes Yacht Haven is the most central marina at Cowes and is extremely popular with cruising yachtsmen who come here to experience the atmosphere of Britain's yachting headquarters. It is open 24 hours a day and, with few permanent moorings, is dedicated to catering for visitors and events. At peak times it can become very crowded, with multiple rafting being the order of the day. For events such as Cowes Week, Round the Island Race and various other regattas, you need to book in advance and prices during Cowes Week are definitely

geared to the serious racers. On the whole it offers good protection, although there is often a swell in north to northeasterly winds and passing traffic can make the outside moorings quite rolly at times. To find out about berthing availability, contact Cowes Yacht Haven on VHF Ch 80 or Tel: 01983 299975.
Berthing fees: Peak season, Friday to Saturday: £2.85 per metre per day, Sunday to Thursday: £2.20 per metre per day. A short stay of up to four hours costs £0.90 per metre from April to October.

FACILITIES

With a 30-ton hoist and a comprehensive list of nearby services ranging from engineers and sailmakers to chandlers and electricians (see p58), Cowes Yacht Haven is a convenient place to be if something goes wrong with your boat. Other facilities include water and electricity on the pontoons, waste disposal units at strategic points throughout the marina, and showers, toilets and a token-operated launderette ashore. The marina also offers wireless internet access. Fuel (diesel and LPG) can be obtained at the fuel jetty at Lallows Boatyard, which is about 50m south of the marina (see p52 for details).

Shepards Wharf
Marina entrance: 50°45'.58N 01°17'.56W

Two hundred yards upstream of the Yacht Haven, on the starboard-hand side, is Shepards Wharf. This marina has several visitors' pontoon berths. For availability, contact Cowes Harbour Control on VHF Ch 69; Tel: 01983 293952.

Berthing fees: April to September: £1.80 per metre per day; October to March: £1.45 per metre per day. Multihulls are charged slightly more. Short stay (up to four hours): 8m (26ft): £2.80; 9-12m (30-39ft): £3.90; 12-15m (39-49ft): £5; over 15m (49ft): £6.

FACILITIES
Facilities are limited at Shepards Wharf, but water and electricity are available, as are showers and toilets. There is also a working boatyard on site that provides a range of services, including a 40-tonne boat hoist, crane, dry-sail storage and maintenance. A chandlery, sailmaker and marine engineer are also based at the yard.

Fuel can be obtained from the Lallows Boatyard fuel jetty or the Marine Support Bunkering fuel barge (VHF Ch69/ Tel: 01983 200716/Mobile: 07860 297633) further up river.

Lallows Boatyard
Fuel pontoon: 50°45'.63N 01°17'.64W

Established in 1867, Lallows Boatyard is one of the oldest yards in Cowes. It is situated on the west bank of the River Medina between Cowes Yacht Haven and Shepards Wharf. Offering both traditional and modern boatbuilding skills, its facilities include slipping, storage and engineering as well as a joinery shop. Another useful service is its fuel pontoon, selling diesel and LPG. Lallows can be contacted on Tel: 01983 292112.

Medina Yard
Medina Yard pontoon: 50°45'.32N 01°17'.59W

Medina Yard is on the west bank of the Medina River, between the chain ferry and the UK Sailing Academy. It is located on the site of the former FBM shipbuilding yard, which was acquired to launch the British America's Cup team GBR Challenge in 2003, and was subsequently converted into a thriving boatyard that boasts the largest travel hoist on the Isle of Wight. Thanks to the large Medina Yard signs on the pierheads and on the white hoist in the main yard, it is very easy to spot. Although it has no dedicated visitors' berths, it will allow visitors to berth alongside its well-protected pontoon if space permits. Contact the yard before arrival on Tel: 01983 203872.
Berthing fees: Overnight stay, yachts up to 10m (33ft): £2.30 per metre; 10-16m (33-52ft): £2.70 per metre.

FACILITIES
Water and electricity are available at the yard, but the nearest fuel point is the Marine Support Bunkering barge (VHF Ch69/Tel: 01983 200716/Mobile: 07860 297633), which is immediately to the south of the yard.

The yard has the capacity to lift and store vessels of up to 60 tonnes with a maximum 6m (20ft) beam. It can also offer undercover storage for most yachts up to 25 tonnes.

Across the road from the yard is Marine Bazaar (Tel: 01983 298869), a second-hand chandlery, while just outside the main gate, on Pelham Road, is a convenience store. Cowes town centre is only a seven-minute walk away. For more information on provisioning, eating out and things to do ashore see p55-58.

The UK Sailing Academy is essentially a sea school, but does welcome visitors if space permits

UK Sailing Academy UKSA's outer pontoon: 50°45'.18N 01°17'.61W

The United Kingdom Sailing Academy, which is located upstream of the chain ferry on the starboard side of the river, has a large outside pontoon on which visitors are allowed to berth as and when space permits. It is only about a 15-minute walk from the centre of Cowes, although Cowes Harbour Water Taxi (VHF Ch 77/ Tel: 07050 344818) also services the moorings.

For details and berthing availability, contact the UK Sailing Academy on Tel: 01983 294941.

Berthing fees: Approximately £3.30 per metre per night (£1 per foot) or £6 for a short stay of up to four hours.

FACILITIES

Facilities include water and electricity on the pontoons, as well as showers, toilets and a bar. For diesel or petrol you need to go to the Marine Support Bunkering fuel barge (VHF Ch 69/Tel: 01983 200716/Mobile: 07860 297633), which is situated just to the north.

East Cowes Marina Just off A and B pontoons: 50°45'.17N 01°17'.54W

With full tidal access and the capacity to accommodate approximately 150 visiting boats, East Cowes Marina is situated in a relaxed setting about half a mile above the chain ferry. For berthing arrangements, call East Cowes Marina on VHF Ch 80 or Tel: 01983 293983.
Berthing fees: Summer rates: £2.70 per metre per night; winter rates: £1.40 per metre per night. Summer short stay (maximum four hours): £7; winter short stay (maximum four hours): £4.

FACILITIES

Facilities include shore power, water, gas, good shower, toilet and laundry amenities, as well as a barbecue and marquee during the season. There is also a good chandlery behind the marina, Wi-Fi internet access, and rubbish and waste oil disposal facilities. There is no fuel available in the marina; however, The Marine Support Bunkering fuel jetty (VHF Ch69/Tel: 01983 200716) is conveniently situated on the western side of the river, south of the chain ferry. The Cowes Harbour Water Taxi (VHF Ch 77/Tel: 07050 344818) provides a regular service to Cowes and back (£3 return).

East Cowes Marina is very spacious, and has good facilities available

PROVISIONING

Besides the on-site chandlery which sells essential items, the nearest shops to the marina are in East Cowes, which is about a 10-minute walk away. For more serious provisioning you need to go to Somerfield on York Avenue (opposite East Cowes Town Hall) or Alldays on Well Road. The latter also incorporates an Abbeylink cash machine and post office, while a Lloyds Pharmacy can be found on Ferry Road.

The yacht clubs of Cowes

ROYAL YACHT SQUADRON

The Royal Yacht Squadron (RYS) is the most well known of the yacht clubs in Cowes, and one of the most influential, too. Formed in 1815 as the Yacht Club, membership was originally open to owners of boats with a displacement of over 10 tons. It was granted 'Royal' status by King George IV in 1820, who became a member in 1817. The club was originally located at the Thatched House Tavern in St James's, London, but from 1858 has been based at the historic Cowes Castle. Since then it has been instrumental in setting up many of the major events held in the Solent. Tel: 01983 292191.

ROYAL LONDON YC

The Royal London Yacht Club was originally set up in London in 1838, but moved to a pair of Georgian houses on the Parade in Cowes in 1872. Like the RYS, the club has been actively involved in organising Solent yacht racing from the start, and also helped establish a universal yacht measurement system. Tel: 01983 299727.

COWES CORINTHIAN YC

The Cowes Corinthian YC, south of the Yacht Haven, is one of Cowes' newer clubs, and was set up in 1952 by FR 'Tiny' Mitchell, an International Finn sailor. Tel: 01983 296333.

The Island Sailing Club is the most popular club for visiting yachtsmen

ROYAL CORINTHIAN YC

The Royal Corinthian was founded in 1872 at Erith in Kent, and now has two branches – one at Cowes and another at Burnham-on-Crouch in Essex. Its present clubhouse in Cowes was originally a fishermen's beer house, but was bought by FG 'Tiny' Mitchell for use as a yacht club in 1948. It now has over 800 members. Tel: 01983 293581.

EAST COWES SAILING CLUB

This club, on Clarence Road, East Cowes, was set up in 1912 and caters for all types of boating activities. It organises weekly evening races during the Spring and Summer months and is also keen to promote youth training. Tel: 01983 531687

COWES COMBINED CLUBS

The Cowes Combined Clubs (CCC) was established in 1964 primarily to organise the racing at Cowes Week. Prior to this, each of Cowes' yacht clubs organised their own day's racing, which often proved a logistical nightmare. Ten member clubs make up the CCC, with representatives of each involved in planning the racing programme.

ISLAND SAILING CLUB

This is the largest sailing club in Cowes, and was formed in 1889 to organise racing for smaller boats. Located at the southern end of Cowes Parade, the club is host to the annual Round the Island Race, and welcomes visiting yachtsmen to its bar and restaurant. Tel: 01983 296621.

GURNARD SAILING CLUB

A mile or so west of Cowes is Gurnard Bay, on the shore of which stands Gurnard Sailing Club. This club is the Isle of Wight's leading dinghy club, and currently has over 1,000 members. Established in 1931, it received a National Lottery grant in 1996, with which its current clubhouse was built. Tel: 01983 295169 .

ROYAL OCEAN RACING CLUB

Although the Royal Ocean Racing Club is based at St James's Place in London, the prestigious club has a long history with Cowes, and currently has accommodation for its members at the Disrespect. Many of the club's major events, such as the Fastnet Race and Commodores' Cup start from Cowes. Tel: 020 7493 2248.

The Sir Max Aitken Museum

The Sir Max Aitken Museum is housed in the Prospect, the famous pink building on Cowes High Street. Son of the first Baron Beaverbrook, Sir Max was a man of great prominence: newspaper magnate, fighter pilot in the Second World War and Conservative MP were just some of his many achievements. He was also a keen racing yachtsman and contributed enormously to ocean yacht racing as well as founding the London Boat Show. He succeeded his father as Baron Beaverbrook on his father's death in 1964, but a few days later disclaimed the title on the basis that he wished there to be only one Lord Beaverbrook in his lifetime.

In 1947 Sir Max acquired the Prospect, an 18th century sailmaker's loft. It was here that he entertained many important guests before creating the Prospect Museum Trust in 1979. He died in 1985, but his personal compilation of nautical artefacts are a permanent reminder of this distinguished man.

Among the museum's memorabilia are an impressive collection of maritime paintings including works by Bakhuyzen, Luny, Monamy and Whitcombe, and some original Giles cartoons. There is also an array of items relating to sailing vessels from Nelson to modern times, including a gaff from King George V's racing yacht *Britannia*, which spans the entire length of the museum. Also on display is a cradle made for the son of Napoleon Bonaparte as well as one designed by Uffa Fox for Sir Max Aitken's daughter.

The museum is open for guided tours and special events. For details of opening times, see p58.

The museum is a cornucopia of maritime history and well worth a visit

Useful information – Cowes

PROVISIONING
Cashpoints can be found at all the major banks along Cowes High Street, while post offices are located on Terminus Road or, a bit further away, on York Street. Somerfield supermarket is also based on the High Street and there is a Co-op on Terminus Road. There are two chemists in close proximity to one another – Day Lewis on the High Street and Moss on Birmingham Road.

Internet facilities can be found at the Plaza Ice Cream Parlour and Internet Café (Tel: 01983 249600) on the High Street or at Cowes Internet Café (Tel: 01983 247774) on Shooters Hill. Both are open from 0900.

Besides some excellent chandleries (see under 'Useful Information' on p58), electronic and electrical shops, there are a number of specialist photographers based in Cowes, including the world-famous Beken of Cowes, which has been capturing images of yachting since 1888. The company now sells spectacular pictures of current and past racing yachts from its shop on Birmingham Road. Cowes also boasts a huge selection of fashionable clothing shops

Useful information – Cowes

The smart China China restaurant and the quirky but very popular Eegons café caters for all tastes

for sailors, among which are Musto, Fat Face, Chatham Clothing and Crew Clothing.

EATING OUT

As a centre for yachting, it is hardly surprising that there is a plethora of pubs and restaurants in this small town. Opposite the entrance to Cowes Yacht Haven, the Anchor Inn (Tel: 01983 292823) claims to be the oldest and most traditional pub in Cowes, and offers a broad range of fine ales and bar meals. The Pier View pub (Tel: 01983 294929), which is also in the High Street, is popular with younger sailors.

The former Globe pub on the Parade is now a large Chinese restaurant and bar called China China (Tel: 01983 298198). Also on the Parade and close to the Trinity Landing moorings is Lugleys (Tel: 01983 299618), which offers fabulous views across the Solent. The Union Inn (Tel: 01983 293163) is tucked away in Watch House Lane just off the High Street. Situated about 1½ miles up the river and with its own pontoon for berthing is the famous Folly Inn (Tel: 01983 297171). Recommended in the Good Food Guide, this pub is extremely popular in the summer, specialising in local fish as well as home-made casseroles and grills.

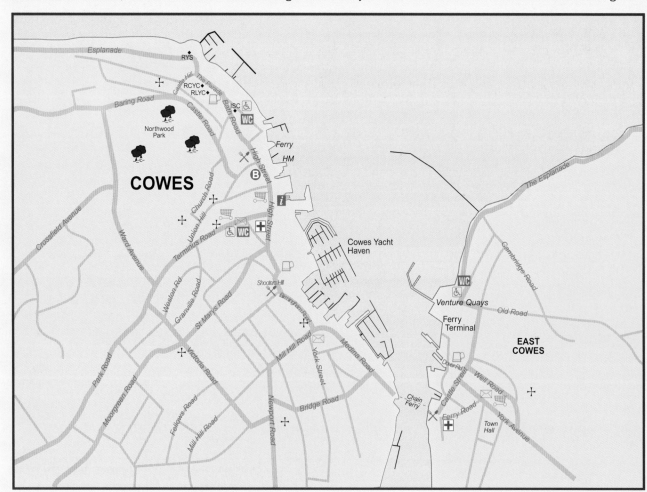

Cowes is packed with good pubs, restaurants and bars. If you're missing a piece of sailing equipment, too, there's several good chandlers

If you need somewhere to go for breakfast or want to have a packed lunch made up for you, then Tiffins (Tel: 01983 292310) is an obvious choice. Conveniently located on the High Street, at the entrance to Cowes Yacht Haven, its filled baguettes are justifiably renowned. The 'Wicked' Espresso Bar (Tel: 01983 289758) on Shooters Hill can also be recommended for its packed lunches and Lavazza coffee. For an eccentric atmosphere then Eegon's Café (Tel: 01983 291815) on the High Street is definitely the place to go , although as it calls itself a 'smile zone' it is probably best to avoid it if you are ever feeling a bit worse for wear after a good night out.

For a bistro-style atmosphere and high-quality reasonably priced food you would be hard pushed to better the Red Duster (Tel: 01983 290311) on the High Street. Also on the High Street (about halfway along) is Murrays Seafoods (Tel: 01983 296233) which, as its name implies, offers excellent seafood dishes. Café Mozart (Tel: 01983 293681) on the High Street is an inexpensive licensed restaurant and tea shop.

For a cheerful crew outing go to Tonino's (Tel: 01983 298464), just up Shooters Hill. This restaurant serves good Italian food in convivial surroundings. In true Cosmopolitan style, Baan Thai Restaurant (Tel: 01983 291917) in Bath Road and Bahar Tandoori (Tel: 01983 200378) on the High Street also come highly recommended. In the summer, especially during Cowes Week, it is worth booking a table in advance. Despite all this choice, if all you feel like is fish and chips then go to Corries Cabin (Tel: 01983 293733).

The Island Sailing Club (Tel: 01983 296621) is probably the most popular and welcoming club in Cowes among visiting yachtsmen and has a splendid restaurant and bar.

Besides the Lifeboat (Tel: 01983 292711), which is on Britannia Way in the heart of East Cowes Marina, the majority of restaurants are situated in West Cowes (see 'Useful Information' for details of the water taxi and chain ferry). There is, however, the Pizza Oven (Tel: 01983 200433) opposite the Floating Bridge in East Cowes which offers a takeaway and delivery service.

ASHORE IN COWES

Between Cowes and Newport and the surrounding area, there are enough attractions to suit everyone. Cowes itself is home to several museums, one of which is the Cowes Maritime Museum (Tel: 01983 823433) on Beckford Road. The museum, which houses two of Uffa Fox's famous boats, *Avenger* and *Coweslip*, is open Mondays, Tuesdays and Fridays 0930–1730; Wednesdays 1100–1900; Saturdays 0930–1630, and admission is free of charge.

Situated on the Parade is the Isle of Wight Model Railways Exhibition & Museum (Tel: 01983 280111), which conveys 100 years' development of toy and model trains. It is open daily (except for Sundays in winter) from 1100–1640.

Useful information – Cowes

Red Funnel operates a regular car ferry service between Southampton and East Cowes. There is also a high-speed foot-passenger service available

Not too far away from here, in the old Ratsey & Lapthorn sailmakers' loft on the High Street, is the Sir Max Aitken Museum (Tel: 01983 292191). The museum opens from May to the end of September, Tuesday to Saturday 1000–1600. For more details, see p55.

TRANSPORT

Buses: Southern Vectis (Tel: 01983 292082) operates local buses between Newport and Cowes, as well as to other towns and villages on the Isle of Wight.

Ferries: Red Funnel (Tel: 0870 444 8898) runs a daily car ferry service every 50 minutes to an hour and a high-speed foot passenger service every 30 minutes between Cowes and Southampton.

Taxis: Alpha Cars: Tel: 01983 280280; Gange Taxis: Tel: 01983 281818; Taxi Rank: Tel: 01983 297134.

Car hire: Solent Self Drive: Tel: 01983 282050.

Bicycle hire: Offshore Sports: Tel: 01983 290514; Mobile Cycle Hire: Tel: 01983 294910.

OTHER INFORMATION

Harbourmaster: VHF Ch 69/Tel: 01983 293952.

Cowes Yacht Haven: VHF Ch 80/Tel: 01983 299975.

East Cowes Marina: VHF Ch 80/Tel: 01983 293983/280503.

Water taxis: Cowes Harbour Taxi: VHF Ch 77/Tel: 07050 344818; Sally Water Taxi: VHF Ch 06; Tel: 07831 331717.

Chain Ferry: VHF Ch 69/Tel: 01983 293041

Yacht clubs: The Royal Yacht Squadron: Tel: 01983 292191; the Royal London YC: Tel: 01983 299727; the Royal Corinthian YC: Tel: 01983 293581; the Island

SC: Tel: 01983 296621; the Cowes Corinthian YC: Tel: 01983 296333

Fuel: Lallows Boatyard: Tel: 01983 292112; Marine Support Bunkering: VHF Ch 69; Tel: 01983 200716; Mobile: 07860 297633

Chandlers: Aquatogs: Tel: 01983 295071; Kevin Mole Outboards: Tel: 01983 299599; Marine Bazaar: Tel: 01983 298869; Pascall Atkey & Son: Tel: 01983 292381; East Cowes Marina: Tel: 01983 293983.

Boatyards/Repair services: Adrian Stone Yacht Services (Cowes Yacht Haven): Tel: 01983 297898; Cowes Yacht Haven: VHF Ch 80; Tel: 01983 299975; Lallows Boatyard: Tel: 01983 292112; Victory Marine Services: Tel: 01983 200226; Eddie Richards: Tel: 01983 299740; Emblem Enterprises, Tel: 01983 294243.

Electrical Engineers: Cowes Yacht Haven: Tel: VHF Ch 80; Tel: 01983 299975; DG Wroath (Cowes Yacht Haven): Tel: 01983 281467; RHP Marine: Tel: 01983 290421.

Sail repairs: Ratsey & Lapthorn: Tel: 01983 294051; McWilliams (Cowes Yacht Haven): Tel: 01983 281100; Solent Sails: Tel: 01983 280014.

Police: Tel: 999; Tel: 01983 528000.

Coastguard: Lee on Solent Tel: 023 9255 2100.

Hospital: St Mary's, Newport: Tel: 01983 524081.

Cowes Health Centre: Tel: 01983 294902.

East Cowes Health Centre: York Avenue: Tel: 01983 295611.

NHS Direct: Tel: 0845 4647.

Dental helpline: Tel: 01983 537424.

Tourist office: Cowes: Tel: 01983 813813.

The Medina River beyond Cowes is navigable on the right tide all the way to Newport. It's a beautiful river and somewhere to retreat to avoid the Cowes' bustle.

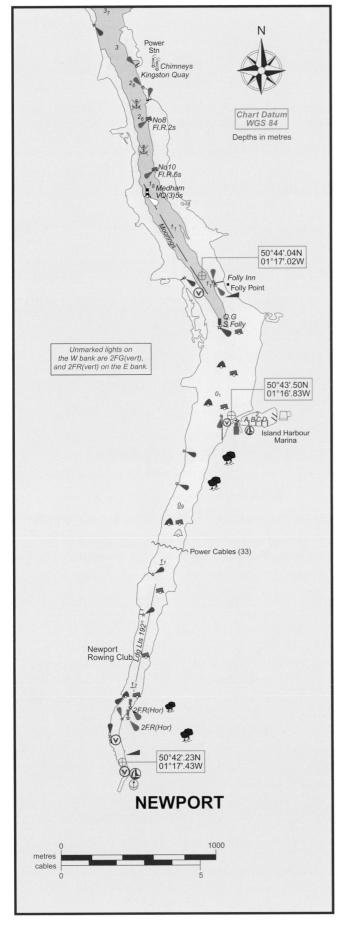

Folly Reach

Visitors' pontoon: 50°44'.04N 01°17'.02N

There are visitors' pontoons on the west bank of the River Medina, just north of Folly Point. However, these berths get extremely busy during the summer weekends due to their close proximity to the popular Folly Inn. Access to the pub is either by dinghy or via the Folly Launch (VHF Channel 69/Tel: 07887 725922).

For berthing availability, particularly during the summer weekends, contact Cowes Harbour Control on VHF 69/Tel: 01983 293952.

Berthing fees: £1 per metre per day. Short stay up to four hours (1000-1600), Monday to Thursday: £0.55 per metre; Friday to Sunday: £0.65 per metre.

FACILITIES

The pontoons are not equipped with water and electricity, although these supplies can be obtained from the Folly Inn pontoon (Tel: 01983 297171). The Folly Inn also provides showers while a nearby retirement park sells essential but basic provisions.

PROVISIONING

If you are in need of a chemist, post office, bank or supermarket, then head for Newport. For more details, and for information on eating out, see p62-63.

Visiting yachts can berth alongside the pontoons on the River Medina

The well-known Folly Inn is very popular with yachtsmen during the summer

A view of the Medina River as it winds its way up to Newport. The river is packed with moorings and the nearby Island Harbour Marina provides good facilities

Island Harbour Marina

Holding pontoon: 50°43'.50N 01°16'.83W

Set in beautiful rolling farmland about half a mile south of the Folly Inn, and two miles upstream of Cowes, Island Harbour Marina offers around 200 berths for permanent berth holders and visiting yachts. Protected by a lock that is operated daily from 0800–2100 during the summer and from 0800–1730 during the winter, the marina is usually accessible for about four hours either side of High Water for boats with a draught of 1.5m (4ft 9in). The deep-water channel is distinctly marked by port-hand withies and there is a holding pontoon outside the lock to starboard. Entrance to this lock is controlled by the obvious red and green traffic lights and mooring ropes tend to be provided once you are inside, which makes life easier for yachtsmen. Facilities were updated and improved in 2007 and the marina has much to offer the cruising yachtsman.

BERTHING

For information on berthing and depths in the approach channel, contact Island Harbour Marina on VHF Ch 80 or Tel: 01983 822999.

Berthing fees: Overnight, Friday to Sunday: £2.80 per metre; overnight, Monday to Thursday: £2.30 per metre.

Useful information

FACILITIES
All the visitors' berths benefit from **water** and **electricity**. There are **toilets**, **showers** and a **laundry** room ashore as well as an on-site **chandler** and **boatbuilder** offering a variety of services from haul-out and antifouling to mechanical and electrical repairs.

PROVISIONING
Island Harbour Marina is ideal if you are after a quiet, picturesque setting, but if you want to be in the heart of a bustling town then this is not the place to come to. Newport offers an array of shops and is a 30-minute walk along the river's edge. On the other hand, you may want to take a taxi (see under Transport on p63). Conveniently, however, there is a licensed restaurant on site (The Bistro, Tel: 01983 532698), which also sells essential provisions and newspapers.

EATING OUT & THINGS TO DO ASHORE
For eating out and ideas for what to do ashore in Cowes and Newport, see p52-56 and p62-63.

If you don't mind drying out alongside, visitors can berth on the pontoons on either side of the river in Newport Harbour, near the 18th century warehouses

Newport Yacht Harbour

Newport Visitors' Quay: 50°42'.23N 01°17'.43W

If you sail about four miles up the River Medina from Cowes and you are willing to dry out alongside, you will eventually come to the ancient port of Newport, which is well protected in all conditions and acts as an ideal base for exploring the Isle of Wight. Located 1½ miles south of the Folly Inn, Newport is reached via a well buoyed and partially lit drying channel (about two hours either side of High Water Portsmouth you can find a depth of approximately 2m), which favours the western bank. Moving south of Folly Point, two pairs of fixed green lights are positioned on the western bank at the Cement Mills site, while at Dodnor, a further pair of fixed green lights signify the end of a small jetty that protrudes from the western bank. Power lines have a 33m (108ft) clearance. Upstream, the shallow patches are marked with seven port-hand and three starboard-hand buoys. The approach to Newport Harbour can be easily identified by large white beacons on the east bank, which show pairs of horizontal red lights at night. When these beacons are lined up they should bear 192°, leading you to the harbour entrance. A first time night entry is not recommended and the speed limit of six knots must be adhered to. The visitors' pontoons, suitable for bilge-keelers or multihulls, are on the eastern side of the harbour, while single-keeled boats should lie south of the pontoons against the quay. The harbour dries out five hours after High Water to reveal a firm, level mud bottom. There is only 1.3m two hours

before High Water and up to three hours after High Water. At High Water Springs the depth is approximately 2.5m; at High Water Neaps it is approximately 1.85m.

The harbourmaster can be contacted on VHF Ch 69 or Tel: 01983 525994 to answer any queries on mooring availability, tide times, etc.

Berthing fees: During the summer season, from 1 April to 31 October, mooring charges for yachts between 6m (20ft) and 9m (30ft) are £11 per day and £13 per day for yachts between 9m (30ft) and 12m (39ft). In winter, from 1 November to 31 March, there is 50% discount on summer rates. A short stay, which must not exceed four hours, costs £4 for vessels under 7m (23ft) and £4.50 for those over 7m (23ft). No discounts are given out of season.

Most single-keeled yachts berth alongside the quay on the western side

Useful information – Newport

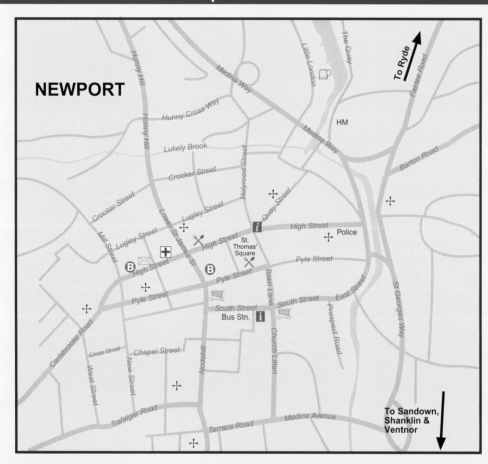

NEWPORT

ideal setting to dine alfresco in the summer but bear in mind that during the height of the season there is live traditional music most nights. Another popular choice is the Wheatsheaf Hotel (Tel: 01983 523865). With friendly service and good quality food, it also caters for children, designating a specific area for families.

For something more sophisticated, Joe Daflo's (Tel: 01983 532220) on the High Street could be a good option. Besides having a huge selection of beers, wines and cocktails, it also serves good food and doesn't skimp on the portions. Olivo (Tel: 01983 530001), the Italian restaurant in St Thomas' Square, provides everything from coffee to home-cooked daily specials.

An attractive setting for lunch is God's Providence House (Tel: 01983 522085) in St Thomas' Square. With Georgian bow windows and an impressive oak staircase, it serves traditional English

FACILITIES

The visitors' pontoons are equipped with water and electricity, with ablution and laundry facilities on the quayside. Other services include four slipways around the harbour, a hand-operated crane and a plentiful supply of dry berths for winter storage. Fenderboards to use against the quayside berths are available from the harbourmaster's office.

PROVISIONING

As Newport is the capital and county town of the Isle of Wight it incorporates more than enough shops for the average yachtsman's needs. All the major banks, most of which have cash machines, are situated in the High Street, St James' Street or St James' Square. Other essential shops

such as the post office and chemists are also located on the High Street, while the supermarkets are spread out around the town: Sainsbury's is on Foxes Road, Safeway is on South Street, Somerfield is on Pyle Street and Marks & Spencer is on Church Litten. Internet access is provided at Lord Louis Library (£1.20 for 30 minutes/£2 for an hour) in Orchard Street or Computer Plus in Scarrots Lane (£0.50 for 15 minutes plus £0.03 per minute after that or £1.50 for an hour).

Newport was once renowned for its markets, and still has a flourishing one every Tuesday and a Farmers' market each Friday.

EATING OUT

A cheerful and relaxed pub is situated on Little London Quay overlooking Newport

Harbour. Decked out in a nautical style, Bargeman's Rest (Tel: 01983 525828) serves real ales and good home-cooked food, including fresh crab and lobster when available. The terrace is an

Newport's Guildhall is home to the Museum of Island History

A variety of interesting boats are on display at the Classic Boat Museum

food, including home-made steak pudding and apple pie.

ASHORE
Newport has its fair share of museums, including the Museum of Island History (Tel: 01983 823366), which is housed in the Guildhall on the High Street and illustrates the island's history from the time of the dinosaurs right up to present day. Opening times are Monday to Saturday 1000–1700 and Sundays 1100–1530. Newport also lays claim to the Island's only arts centre, Quay Arts (Tel: 01983 822490), which is open Monday to Saturday 0930–1700. Enclosed in the 18th-century warehouses along the Harbour, it comprises four art galleries, a theatre-cum-cinema and a contemporary craft shop.

The Classic Boat Museum (Tel: 01983 533493) is also there and houses a collection of sailing and powerboats

of both local and national importance. Among these are an 1887 Bembridge lifeboat, an airborne lifeboat that was dropped to aircrew shot down during World War II, and several Uffa Fox designs. The museum is open daily from late March to late October, 1000–1630, and on Tuesdays and Saturdays, 1030–1530, from early November until late March.

Several historic places of interest can be found in the area. Newport Roman Villa (Tel: 01983 529720) on Cypress Road exhibits well-preserved baths that are complemented by fully restored living rooms and a Roman garden. It is open from 2 April to 31 October, Monday to Saturday, 1000–1630 and 1200–1600 on Sundays in July and August.

Situated on a high ridge two miles south-west of Newport is Carisbrooke Castle (Tel: 01983 522107), which dates back to Norman

times, although the original site was Saxon. It was here that King Charles I was imprisoned before being taken to London for his trial and subsequent execution in 1649. Open daily from 1000–1800 in the summer and from 1000–1600 in the winter, it also includes a museum founded in 1898 by Queen Victoria's youngest daughter, Princess Beatrice.

Queen Victoria was a regular visitor to the Isle of Wight, residing at Osborne House (Tel: 01983 200022), a country retreat that she and Prince Albert built between 1845 and 1850. Designed in an Italian style, the house now belongs to the English Heritage and is open from 1 April to 30 September, 1000–1700 and between 1000–1600 during October.

Newport caters well for evening entertainment, too, offering a couple of cinemas (Cineworld Tel: 0871 220 8000) and several theatres, two of which are the Apollo Theatre (Tel: 01983 527267) on Pyle Street and the Medina Theatre (Tel: 01983 527020) in the Mountbatten Centre on Fairlee Road.

For an unusual experience you could always go on the Ghost Walk, which takes place every Wednesday at 2000, departing from the Wheatsheaf in St Thomas' Square. To find out more, contact the tourist information centre on Tel: 01983 813813.

TRANSPORT
Buses: Southern Vectis (Tel: 01983 827000) operates regular buses between

Newport and Cowes and to other towns and villages on the Isle of Wight.
Ferries: Red Funnel (Tel: 0870 444 8898/023 8033 4010) runs a daily car ferry service every 50 minutes to an hour and a high-speed foot-passenger service every 30 minutes between Cowes and Southampton.
Taxis: Amar Taxis: Tel: 01983 522968; Prices Taxi Rank: Tel: 01983 522084.
Car hire: Ford Rental (Newport) Tel: 01983 523441. Solent Self Drive (Cowes): Tel: 01983 282050.

OTHER INFORMATION
Island Harbour Marina: VHF Ch 80; Tel: 01983 822999.
Newport Harbour: VHF Ch 69; Tel: 01983 525994.
Folly Waterbus: VHF Ch 77; Tel: 07974 864627.
Folly Launch: VHF Ch 69; Tel: 07887 7725922.
Cowes Harbour Water Taxi: VHF Ch 77; Tel: 07050 344818.
HM Customs and Excise: Tel: 01983 293132
Fuel: See 'Other Information' on p58.
Chandlers/repairs: Richardsons Yacht Services Ltd (Island Harbour Marina): Tel: 01983 821095; Pascall Atkey & Son: Tel: 01983 292381.
Police: Tel: 999; Tel: 01983 528000.
Coastguard: Lee on Solent: Tel: 023 9255 2100.
Hospital: St Mary's Newport: Tel: 01983 524081.
Doctor: Tel: 01983 522150.
Dental helpline: Tel: 01983 537424.
Tourist Information Office: Tel: 01983 813813.

Southampton Water

A cable west of West Bramble buoy: 50°47'.20N 01°18'.82W
A cable east of East Bramble buoy: 50°47'.23N 01°13'.48W

Southampton Water comprises three navigable rivers – the rivers Test, Itchen and Hamble – that provide a wealth of facilities for cruising yachtsmen

At the head of the six-mile stretch of Southampton Water lies the city of Southampton. Founded in around 70AD, when the Romans first built a town on the banks of the River Itchen, the city has always held an important place in maritime history and each year hosts what is considered to be one of Europe's finest on-the-water boat shows.

Boasting several major marinas with comprehensive facilities, Southampton Water over recent years has become increasingly accommodating to visitors and is well protected in all but strong southeasterly winds.

NAVIGATION

Charts: Admiralty Charts: SC5600, 2036, 2041; Imray: C3, C15, 2200; Stanfords: 11, chartpack 24

Tides: Southampton is a standard port. Double High Waters occur at Springs, about two hours apart, while at Neaps there is a long stand. When there are two High Waters predictions are for the first, otherwise they refer to the middle of the stand.

MHWS: 4.5m; MHWN: 3.7m; MLWN: 1.8m; MLWS: 0.5m.

Approaches: The approaches are controlled by the port of Southampton and all craft should heed the priority given to commercial traffic by the Vessel Traffic Services (VTS) VHF Ch 12. There is no right of way for sail, and particular care should be taken around the Area of Concern (see p47), which covers the main channel from the Cowes Prince Consort North Cardinal buoy to the Hook buoy in Southampton Water. Any vessel over 150m in length in this channel must be given a 'moving prohibited zone' of 1,000m ahead and 100m on either beam. The turning point in the area of the West Bramble West Cardinal buoy and the Calshot Spit light (Fl 5s) is particularly restricted.

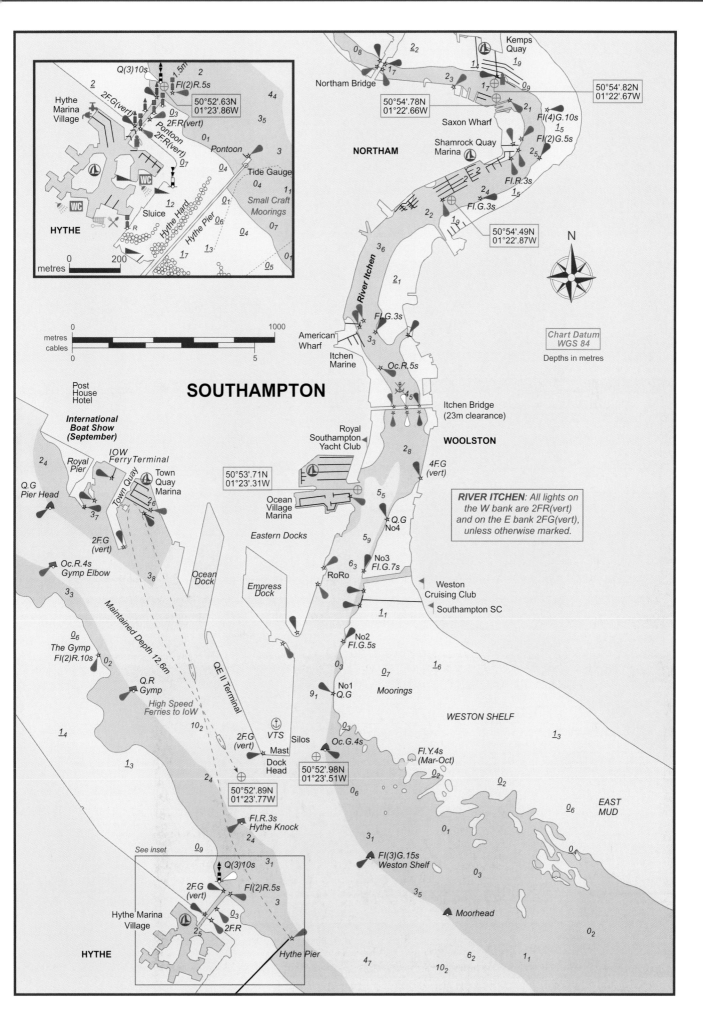

HYTHE

Q(3)10s
Hythe
Marina
Village
2F.G(vert)
Fl(2)R.5s
50°52'.63N
01°23'.86W
1.5m
2F.R(vert)
Pontoon
2F.R(vert)
Pontoon
Tide Gauge
Small Craft
Moorings
Hythe Hard
Hythe Pier
Sluice
R
WC
WC
metres
0   200

metres   0 ──────────────── 1000
cables   0 ──────────────── 5

Post
House
Hotel

International
Boat Show
(September)

IOW
Ferry Terminal
Royal
Pier
Town
Quay
Marina
Town Quay
Q.G
Pier Head
2F.G
(vert)
Oc.R.4s
Gymp Elbow

SOUTHAMPTON

American
Wharf
Itchen
Marine
Fl.G.3s
Oc.R.5s
Royal
Southampton
Yacht Club
50°53'.71N
01°23'.31W
Ocean
Village
Marina
Eastern Docks
Ocean
Dock
Empress
Dock
QE II Terminal
Maintained Depth 12.6m
High Speed
Ferries to IoW
Q.R
Gymp
The Gymp
Fl(2)R.10s
2F.G
(vert)
VTS
Mast
Dock
Head
Silos
50°52'.89N
01°23'.77W
Fl.R.3s
Hythe Knock
See inset
Q(3)10s
2F.G
(vert)
Fl(2)R.5s
Hythe Marina
Village
2F.R

HYTHE

Hythe Pier

NORTHAM

Kemps
Quay
Northam Bridge
50°54'.82N
01°22'.67W
50°54'.78N
01°22'.66W
Saxon Wharf
Fl(4)G.10s
Fl(2)G.5s
Shamrock Quay
Marina
Fl.R.3s
Fl.G.3s
50°54'.49N
01°22'.87W
River Itchen

N

Chart Datum
WGS 84
Depths in metres

Itchen Bridge
(23m clearance)

WOOLSTON

4F.G
(vert)

RIVER ITCHEN: All lights on
the W bank are 2FR(vert)
and on the E bank 2FG(vert),
unless otherwise marked.

Q.G
No4
No3
Fl.G.7s
RoRo
Weston
Cruising Club
Southampton SC
No2
Fl.G.5s
No1
Q.G
Moorings
WESTON SHELF
Oc.G.4s
Fl.Y.4s
(Mar-Oct)
Fl(3)G.15s
Weston Shelf
Moorhead

EAST
MUD

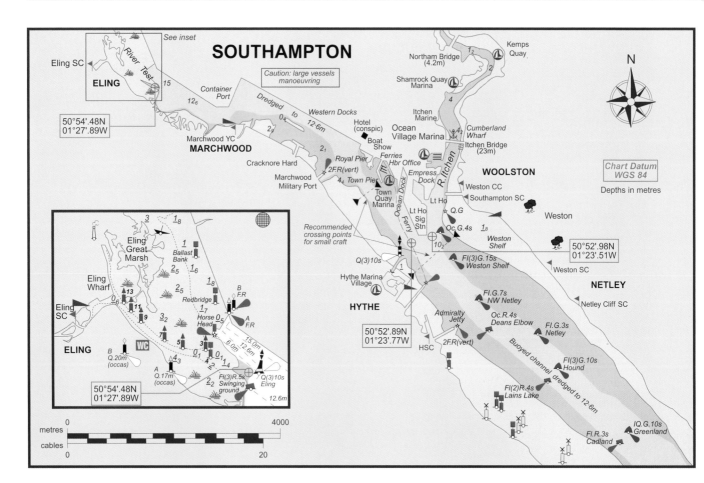

Southampton is a good place to change crew as it is serviced by ferries from the Isle of Wight and Continent and has good train links and an airport nearby

This port-hand mark identifies the end of the hazardous Calshot Spit

Fawley Power Station's chimney marks the entrance to Southampton Water

Southampton Water is a fairly large area so there is plenty of room for sailing without encroaching too much on the main shipping channel. However, yachts are advised to keep just outside the buoyed lit fairway and, if possible, cross the channel at right angles at either (a) abeam Fawley chimney, (b) at Cadland/Greenland buoys, (c) abeam Hythe or (d) abeam the Town Quay.

Pilotage: The entrance to Southampton Water is clearly marked by Calshot Radar Tower on its western bank along with Fawley Power Station and chimney. There is reasonable water on both sides of the main channel until

the Weston Shelf buoy (Fl [3] G 15s) where the depth shallows. Waypoint 50° 52'.71N 01°23'.26W brings you to the starboard-hand mark Weston Shelf Buoy (Fl [3] G 15s). Approximately a quarter mile north-east of the waypoint, Southampton Water divides at Dock Head into two rivers – the River Test to port and the River Itchen to starboard. The split can be easily identified by the conspicuous Signal Station and tall grain silos at Dock Head where due care should be taken to avoid the large vessels that are in the process of manoeuvring.

With no fewer than six marinas in the Southampton area, visitors should not have a problem finding a berth.

Southampton Water is dominated by commercial shipping, so it is important to pay close attention to the rules and regulations when sailing in this area

Hythe Marina Village

Hythe Marina Entrance: 50°52'.63N 01°23'.86W

Situated on the western shores of Southampton Water, Hythe Marina Village is approached by a dredged channel leading to a lock basin. The lock gates are controlled 24 hours a day throughout the year and visitors are welcome so long as space is available. There is a waiting pontoon to the south of the approach basin. For access through the lock gates, contact the marina on VHF Ch 80. Traffic flow through the lock is controlled by lights: three fixed green = go; three fixed red = stop and two fixed green over white = free flow. During free flow you should only proceed into or out of the marina with permission from the lock office (VHF Ch80/Tel: 023 8020 7073). **Berthing fees:** An overnight stay for boats up to 12.5m (41ft): £3.00 per metre; boats over 12.5m (41ft): £3.80 per metre. Short stay of up to four hours: £8.

This marina is the first one you come to on entering Southampton Water

Useful information

On approach, contact the marina office to gain access through the lock

FACILITIES

With the capacity to accommodate yachts of up to 17m (56ft) LOA the marina offers petrol, diesel and calor gas as well as water and electricity on the pontoons. It can also provide wireless internet access. Each basin has its own toilet and shower block (the use of heads is strictly forbidden here, although it does offer a toilet pump-out facility) as well as rubbish disposal. Ice is available from the lock office and there are laundry facilities at 'C' basin. Besides a 40-ton boat hoist there is

a hard-standing area for any necessary repairs as well as a small chandlery next to the fuel berth (open 0800–1700), which is on your port-hand side after passing through the lock.

PROVISIONING

Essential items and newspapers can be bought at Londis in the Marina Village Centre, with other shops including chemists and hairdressers nearby. Hythe village is about a five-minute walk away. Here you will find a Waitrose supermarket and a post office in the High Street.

EATING OUT

The marina village incorporates two restaurants: the Italian La Vista (Tel: 023 8020 7730) and the Salt Bar and Kitchen pub (Tel: 023 8084 5594).

Hythe itself has an assortment of eating places, including three pubs/restaurants on the High Street – the Seashell Lounge Bar & Restaurant (Tel: 023 8084 7188), the Lord Nelson (Tel: 023 8084 2169), and Hobbits Restaurant Bar (Tel: 02380 848524), as well as an Indian restaurant, Forest Spice (Tel: 023 8084 2315),

Above: The Lord Nelson is in Hythe

on Pylewell Road, which has a good takeaway menu.

ASHORE

Forming an integral part of the New Forest Waterside,

Useful information – Hythe Marina Village

Hythe once had its own prosperous maritime industry. A shipyard on the south side of the village built small craft for the Royal Navy during the Napoleonic Wars. It was also home to famous inhabitants such as Lawrence of Arabia and Sir Christopher Cockerell, who invented the hovercraft.

From the marina you can explore the inland villages and small towns of the New Forest or catch a ferry to Southampton's Town Quay from where the West Quay Shopping Centre is some three minutes away. The ferry departs from the end of Hythe Pier, which was built in Victorian times and accommodates the world's oldest working pier train.

For more information on what to do and see in Southampton, see p74-77.

TRANSPORT
Buses: The Solent Blue Line (Tel: 023 8061 8233) Bluestar service operates regular buses between Hythe ferry pier and Southampton throughout the week. It also runs shuttle services to Portsmouth, Eastleigh, Winchester, Hedge End and Hamble, and scenic tours of the New Forest.
Taxis: AA Taxis: Tel: 023 8086 4210; Totton & Waterside Cab Co: Tel: 023 8084 2134.
Ferries: Ferries run daily between Hythe Pier and Southampton every half hour – Tel: 023 8084 0722.

Hythe Pier opened in 1881 and is home to the oldest working pier train

OTHER INFORMATION
Hythe Marina Village: VHF Ch 80; Tel: 023 8020 7073.
Colin Bridle Marine Services: Mob: 07850 934496/ Tel:01425 615688.
Hospital: Southampton General Hospital: Tel: 023 8077 7222.
Police: Tel: 999; Tel: 023 8033 5444.

Coastguard: Lee on Solent: Tel: 023 9255 2100.
Hythe Medical Centre: Tel: 023 8084 5955.
NHS Direct: Tel: 0845 4647.
Dentist: Southampton Dental helpline: Tel: 023 8033 8336.
Tourist Information Centre: Tel: 023 8028 2269.

The River Itchen branches off Southampton Water at Dock Head

River Itchen

Entrance to the River Itchen: 50°52'.98N 01°23'.51W

Leaving the Signal Station to port and the green conical buoy (Oc G4s) to starboard, you come to the entrance to the River Itchen. Ocean Village Marina appears shortly after the Empress Dock on the port-hand side, opposite No 4 Beacon (QG). Between the marina and the Itchen Bridge (which has a height clearance of 24m) the best water is to starboard. Above the bridge, which is marked by 2FR (vert), 2FG (vert) and a FW (indicating the main channel), the channel swings slightly to port and then to starboard, favouring the west bank. If possible, keep the midstream unlit moorings to starboard, sticking to the fairly steep-to docks to port. Opposite No 5 bn (Fl G 3s) lies Shamrock Quay Marina. Above Shamrock Quay Marina, the river starts to shallow, although there is still a little over 2m until you reach the Northam Bridge.

Ocean Village

Marina entrance: 50°53'.71N 01°23'.31W

The entrance to Ocean Village is to port just before the Itchen bridge. As soon as you have entered, tie up against the dock office pontoon to enquire about berthing availability (unless you have contacted staff ahead of time). This marina has no dedicated visitors' berths but will do its best to find you somewhere to overnight. Able to accommodate large yachts and Tall Ships, the marina is renowned for hosting the starts of major international events and can be accessed 24 hours a day. To contact Ocean Village Marina for more information, call VHF Ch 80 or Tel: 023 8022 9385.

Berthing fees: These may be subject to a slight increase. A short stay of up to four hours is a flat rate of £8.50; for yachts up to 12.5m (41ft) LOA, charges are £3 per metre per night; yachts between 12.6m (41ft 4in) and 20m (65ft 6in) are charged £3.80 per metre per night and yachts of 20.1m (66ft) and over pay £4 per metre per night.

The Royal Southampton Yacht Club overlooks Ocean Village Marina

Useful information

FACILITIES

The marina offers a range of amenities including water and electricity on the pontoons, toilets, showers and a launderette and wireless internet access. For repairs, go to nearby Shamrock Quay (see p71), which has boat lifting and hard-standing facilities. To fill up with fuel call Itchen Marine (Tel: 023 8063 1500), which is situated 300m upstream of the Itchen Bridge between Ocean Village and Shamrock Quay on the port-hand side. Alternatively, Hythe Marina has a fuel pontoon.

The Royal Southampton YC (Tel: 023 8022 3352) overlooks the marina and welcomes members from affiliated clubs. Open every lunchtime and evening, it has a bar, buffet and dining room, although it only serves evening meals from Wednesday to Saturday.

PROVISIONING

You'll find a Tesco Metro Express at Ocean Village Marina for general groceries. For more serious provisioning, however, catch a bus into Southampton where there is an Asda supermarket opposite the Marlands Shopping Centre. Alternatively, there is a Marks and Spencer at the West Quay shopping centre.

There is a NatWest bank close to the marina, with a cash machine, but for all other major high street banks again take a bus into the city centre. Internet cafés can be found in the Bargate Centre and West Quay. With plenty of shops, restaurants and cinemas on the complex, Ocean Village is definitely not the place to visit if you are looking for a quiet spot.

At Ocean Village there is a restaurant/bar called Banana Wharf (Tel: 023 8033 8866), which serves a varied menu of Oriental cuisine with a tropical twist, as well as traditional dishes such as pasta and pizza.

For more information about where to eat and what to do ashore in Southampton, see p74-77.

Shamrock Quay

Shamrock Quay Marina: 50°54'.49N 01°22'.87W

Shamrock Quay offers excellent facilities to yachtsmen. Upstream of the Itchen Bridge on the port-hand side, it used to be part of the Camper & Nicholsons' yard, taking its name from the J-Class yacht *Shamrock V* which was constructed on the site in 1931 as a challenger for the America's Cup. The marina is easily accessible 24 hours a day, but it's worth noting that some of the inside berths can get quite shallow at Low Water Springs. It is best to arrive at slack water as the cross tide can be tricky when manoeuvring in close quarters. Should you require assistance, the dockmaster is on hand 24 hours a day.

For berthing information, contact the marina on VHF Ch 80 or Tel: 023 8022 9461.

Berthing fees: Overnight, 12.5m (41ft): £3 per metre; overnight, 12.6m (41ft) and above: £3.80 per metre per night. Short stay (up to four hours): flat rate of £8.

Useful information

Shamrock Quay has a travel hoist capable of lifting boats up to 63 tons

The chandlery at the marina is well stocked and should serve most needs

FACILITIES

A selection of marine engineers, riggers, sailmakers, electronic and electrical experts (ask at the dock office for information) along with hard standing and a boat lifting service make this the ideal place if your boat needs overhauling. Other facilities include water and electricity on the pontoons plus showers, toilets and a coin-operated launderette ashore. Gas and ice can be obtained on site, and a well-stocked chandlery is conveniently close to the pontoons. You can get rid of waste oil in front of Building 2, while there are rubbish bins at the top of each pontoon access ramp. The dock office is manned 24 hours a day, but if you find it is locked, the duty dockmaster can be contacted on either VHF Ch 80 or Tel: 07740 806038. The marina is hot on security, enforcing a 24-hour security system with coded gates and CCTV.

Unfortunately, there is no fuel berth here, but about 300m before the Itchen Bridge, on your starboard-hand side, as you are heading back down the River Itchen, is Itchen Marine (Tel: 023 8063 1500), which does supply fuel as do Hythe Marina and Kemp's Marina.

PROVISIONING

The marina office sells basic provisions, sweets and snacks, cleaning supplies and toiletries, but the closest shop for essential items would be the Tesco Metro Express in Ocean Village.

A bit further afield, you will find a Marks and Spencer at West Quay and an Asda supermarket opposite the Marlands Shopping Centre. Southampton's centre is approximately 1½ to two miles away and takes about 30 to 40 minutes to walk to or, alternatively, you can get a bus from nearby Northam Road or a taxi from the marina office. As to be expected in a major city, you will find all the necessary banks, post offices, chemists, supermarkets and so forth here. If you don't want to venture into Southampton, catch a bus or take a taxi to Portswood, which is not a particularly attractive suburb but it does have a Waitrose supermarket, a post office and a couple of chemists and is quieter than the city centre.

EATING OUT

The marina has its own pub, the Waterfront (Tel: 023 8063 2209), which offers good bar meals at reasonable prices. Otherwise you could try the neighbouring restaurant Taps (Tel: 023 8022 8621). The Yellow Welly Café (Tel: 023 8022 3535) sells sandwiches, baguettes and cakes.

For details of restaurants in Southampton, see p74.

Saxon Wharf is geared up towards superyachts and boats up to 80m LOA, but it does have a good range of marine services ashore suitable for smaller craft

Saxon Wharf   Saxon Wharf marina entrance: 50°54'.78N 01°22'.66W

Situated next to Shamrock Quay, Saxon Wharf is geared up to accommodate superyachts and larger vessels. It is equipped with 80m (263ft) marina berths and heavy duty pontoons.

Contact Saxon Wharf on VHF Ch 80 or Tel: 023 8033 9490 for more details.

Berthing fees: Visitors' fees for an overnight stay are £3 per metre per night for yachts up to 12.5m (41ft) and £3.80 per metre per night for yachts of 12.6m (41ft) and over. A short stay of up to four hours costs a flat rate of £8.

FACILITIES

With a 200-ton boat hoist and several marine specialists such as Southampton Yacht Services (SYS), Saxon Wharf repairs and restores big boats, whether it is a quick lift-out or a full-scale refit project. There is plenty of storage space ashore and a round-the-clock security system.

As the development is part of the Shamrock Quay complex, it shares its laundry facilities with Shamrock Quay Marina, although it does have its own shower block. The marina also has Wi-Fi internet access.

Kemps Quay   Kemps Quay's outer pontoons: 50°54'.82N 01°22'.67W

At the head of the River Itchen on the starboard-hand side is Kemps Quay. A family-run business, it is a friendly yard and has a pleasant, old-fashioned feel. However, its semi-industrial environs mean that it is not located in the most attractive of areas and is quite far from the city centre. Out of 200 berths, 50 are deep water berths, the rest being half-tide, drying out to soft mud. You can only enter the marina about 3½ hours either side of High Water – its restricted access reflected in the lower prices. For berthing information and availability, contact Kemps Quay on Tel: 023 8063 2323.

Berthing fees: £0.72 per foot per day (approximately £2.40 per metre) or £1.90 per foot per week (approximately £6.25 per metre).

FACILITIES

Water, electricity, toilets and showers are all available here. There is also an 8-ton hoist, hard standing and repair and maintenance services.

PROVISIONING

A nearby BP garage sells bread and milk while a five-minute bus ride takes you to Bitterne, where you will find, among other shops, Safeways and Sainsburys.

There is an 8-ton travel hoist at Kemps Quay as well as hard standing

The River Test

Entrance to the River Test: 50°52'.89N 01°23'.77W

To enter the River Test leave the Signal Station to starboard, keeping the dock walls to starboard and the red navigation buoys to port. You will soon come to Town Quay Marina on your starboard-hand side, but once past this the river is dominated by the large container docks to starboard and the industrial docks to port. However, in contrast to these surroundings, about four miles upstream of the entrance to the Test lies the rural haven of Eling. The Test has a maintained depth of 12.6m from Hythe

Pier (50°52'.49N 01°23'.60W) right the way up to the Eling Channel, but note that the shoal area on its western bank is foul. Once past the Marchwood Sea Mounting Centre (50°53'.76N 01°24'.96W), it is possible with the right tide to take a slight short cut from the deep-water channel through the Marchwood Channel (50°53'.88N 01°25'.21W), which starts just south of the Cracknore buoy (Oc R 8s). Keeping on a bearing of 298° for just under a mile will bring you back into the main channel. Just west of the Eling ECM, small craft moorings lead you into the Eling Channel. Once past the No 13 starboard-hand mark, the Eling basin opens up sharply to port.

Eling

Start of Eling Channel: 50 54'. 48N 01 27'.89W

The village of Eling is a quiet backwater, famous for its tide mill, which is one of only five productive tide mills left in the world (see p75). At a quick glance at the chart, it would seem that this harbour is restricted to small, shallow-draught craft that are able to take the ground. Those with a deep draught may prefer to pick up one of Eling Sailing Club's deep-water moorings at the mouth of the Eling Channel and use their dinghy for the last ¾ mile to the haven. The club welcomes visitors and, besides the moorings, will also accommodate visiting yachts on one of its two pontoons or alongside the scrubbing-off berth or drying wall. A charge of £5 for using any of these moorings will be payable as from 2008 and this should be paid at the club bar or put in the club's

'honesty box'. For berthing availability and/or more information, contact Eling Sailing Club on Tel: 023 8086 3987 or the moorings master on Tel: 023 8086 3846.

Visitors are permitted to use the club's facilities (water and toilets), but not its electric shore power connection. There are several good pubs in the village and the Heritage Centre next to the tide mill has a coffee shop.

Town Quay Marina   Marina entrance: 50°53'.66N 01°24'.27W

Beyond the cruise liner dock, on the starboard side, lies the small Town Quay Marina which, close to the city centre, is a popular spot with local boat owners. When approaching the marina, which is accessible at all states of the tide, keep out of the way of the fast ferries, which frequently shuttle between Southampton and the Isle of Wight. The marina entrance is between two floating wavebreaks (2FR [vert] and 2FG [vert]) that can appear continuous from seaward. Unfortunately, the marina does not have any visitors' berths any more, but can offer annual berths.

FACILITIES
Besides 24-hour CCTV security, there are all the usual facilities at Town Quay Marina, including water and electricity, showers, toilets and a launderette, as well as rubbish disposal and a nearby chandlery. For fuel, go to Hythe Marina or Itchen Marine (Tel: 023 8063 1500) on the River Itchen, situated just upstream of the Itchen bridge on the port-hand side. The marina is also within walking distance of West Quay shopping centre and the town. For more details on Town Quay Marina, Tel: 023 8023 4397.

Useful information – Southampton

PROVISIONING

The nearest grocery store to Town Quay Marina is Waitrose, which is in the West Quay shopping centre. For other essential items, try the newsagent on the High Street. Alternatively, there is a Marks and Spencer in West Quay and an Asda opposite the Marlands Shopping Centre. The city centre is a few minutes' walk from the Town Quay and all of the major shops, banks, post offices and chemists can be found here. A free bus shuttle service to the city centre and railway station runs every 10 minutes from just outside the Red Funnel ferry terminal, which is next to the Town Quay Marina.

EATING OUT

Numerous bars and restaurants can be found near the Town Quay, ranging from Cuccini's (Tel: 023 8033 5045), which has a very lively atmosphere and serves tapas-type food, to La Margherita (Tel: 023 8033 3390). Both offer good value for money. Southampton has several other recommended eating places. The Olive Tree (Tel: 023 8034 3333) on Oxford Street is more sophisticated, with a wide selection of wines and memorable haute cuisine. Next door is the Oxford Bar Restaurant (Tel: 023 8022 4444), which also serves good food in convivial surroundings. A cheap and cheerful Italian is La Lupa (Tel: 023 8033 1849) on the High Street. For a more wine-bar-type atmosphere, choose Bouzy Rouge (Tel: 023 8022 0545) in East Bargate or Wild Orchid (Tel: 023 8063 9040) in Vernon Walk, which is just off London Road. For excellent fish and chips, try Harry Ramsden's (Tel: 023 8023 0678) in the West Quay shopping centre.

ASHORE

The annual Southampton International Boat Show, which takes place in mid-September at the Mayflower Park, entices an enormous number of visitors each year. If in the vicinity make sure you secure a berth with one of the marinas well in advance. Reputed to be Europe's most impressive on-the-water show, it is well worth a visit.

The sinking of the *Titanic* during her maiden voyage from Southampton in 1912 continues to attract a good deal of attention. An exhibition at the Maritime Museum (Tel: 023 8063 5904) at Town Quay conveys a fascinating account of what really happened told through the voices of some of the survivors, as well as through the people of Southampton whose lives were affected by the tragic disaster in which 1,500 people drowned. By means of a panoramic model of the docks as well as informative video presentations, the museum also gives a detailed account of the history of the port of Southampton since 1838. Open Tuesdays to Fridays 1000–1700, Saturdays 1000–1600 and Sundays 1400–1700, admission is free of charge.

As the Solent was one of the most significant places in the world for aircraft innovation, the Solent Sky Aviation Museum (Tel: 023

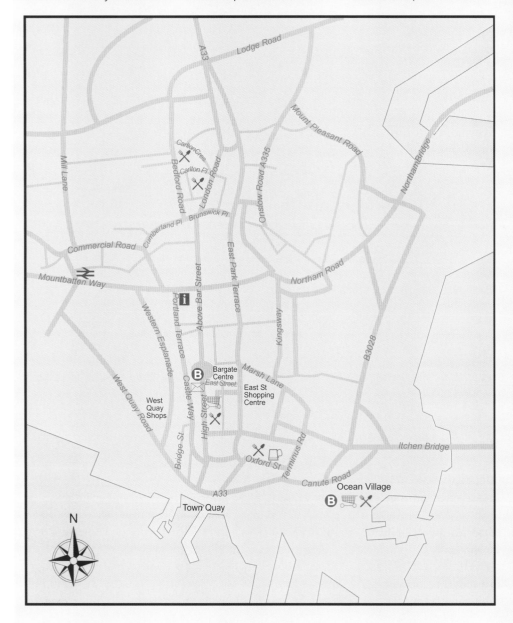

The annual Southampton Boat Show draws thousands of visitors throughout its 10-day duration, and is well worth a visit if you are in the area

8063 5830) on Albert Road South is well worth visiting. Here you can sit at the controls of a supersonic jet or visit the flight deck of a giant flying boat. The museum commemorates the work of RJ Mitchell, who pioneered the legendary Second World War Spitfire fighter aircraft. It is open from Tuesday to Saturday 1000–1700 and Sunday from 1200–1700.

The **Medieval Merchant's House** (Tel: 023 8022 1503) on French Street is another interesting place to visit, having been restored and furnished to look exactly as it would have done in 1290. It opens in the summer 1000–

1800 from Friday to Sunday and on Bank Holidays.

The **Southampton City Art Gallery** (Tel: 023 8083 2277) in the Civic Centre on Commercial Road houses a collection spanning six centuries and boasts some of the finest 20th century works of art outside London. Open Tuesday to Saturday from 1000–1700 and Sunday from 1300–1600.

As Southampton was severely bombed in the Second World War, it is no longer a picturesque city. However, a short bus ride (of about 20 minutes) takes you to places like **Lyndhurst**, 'the capital of the New Forest'.

This quaint little town, filled with cafés and restaurants, is surrounded by beautiful forest walks. Peak season it can get rather crowded and its one-way system causes a good deal of congestion.

En route to Lyndhurst is **Eling Tide Mill** (Tel: 023 8086 9575), allegedly the only surviving tide mill in the UK to produce wholemeal flour. Established over 900 years ago, it is open all year round from Wednesday to Sunday and Bank Holiday Mondays 1000–1600.

Adjacent to this is the **Totton & Eling Heritage Centre** (Tel: 023 8066 6339), which conveys the history

of the area from the Bronze Age through to the present day. Admission is free. It is open from Wednesday to Sunday 1000–1630 during the summer months and 1030–1600 in the winter.

Southampton offers plenty to do in the evening, too. Besides its restaurants, the nearby **Ocean Village** has a range of facilities on offer, including a Cineworld **cinema** (Tel: 0871 200 2000) and the **Harbour Lights Picture House** (Tel: 08707 551237), which screens non-mainstream films.

For a complete night out, look no further than **Leisure World** on West Quay Road. As

Useful information – Southampton

Left: The Royal Victoria Country Park overlooks Southampton Water and is home to a heritage centre, miniature railway and delightful woodland walks.
Above: The "Father of English Hymnody", Isaac Watts, who was born in Southampton

the South's most successful multi-purpose entertainment complex, it features a 13-screen Odeon cinema (Tel: 0871 224 4007), a bowling alley and casino, as well as several bars, restaurants and two nightclubs. For live entertainment, the Mayflower theatre on Commercial Road provides a colourful setting for performances ranging from West End musicals through to ballet and opera. To find out what's on, Tel: 023 8071 1800/1811.

A theatre more established for classical and contemporary plays is the Nuffield (Tel: 023 8031 5500) on University Road.

For more suggestions on what to do in the area, see under the Hamble on p88.

TRANSPORT

Trains: Southampton's railway station is about a 15-20 minute walk from Town Quay and Ocean Village and has direct links to London Waterloo, Poole, Weymouth, Portsmouth and Brighton. For train times, fares, etc, contact National Rail Enquiries on Tel: 08457 484950.

Buses: Various bus companies provide frequent services throughout the city as well as to the surrounding areas. Contact Solent Blue Line: Tel: 023 8061 8233; First Hampshire and Dorset: Tel: 023 8022 4854; Stagecoach South: Tel: 0845 1210170; National Express Coaches: Tel: 08705 808080.

Ferries: Red Funnel (Tel: 0870 444 8898) runs a high-speed foot-passenger ferry service between Southampton and the Isle of Wight every half hour

throughout the day, as well as an hourly car ferry service. White Horse Ferries (Tel: 023 8084 0722) operates a half-hourly service between Southampton and Hythe Pier, providing links with the New Forest and surrounding area.

Airports: Southampton Airport (Tel: 0870 040 0009) caters for flights to and from several key UK and European destinations and its terminal is situated less than 50m from Southampton Airport (Parkway) Station. From here there are up to four trains per hour to Southampton Central

A memorial in East Park is dedicated to the *Titanic*'s heroic engineering staff

West Park is a good place to stretch your legs

(a seven-minute journey away) and then on to London Waterloo (which takes approximately 70 minutes). A rail-air coach service provides a connection between Heathrow Airport (Tel: 0870 000 0123) and Woking Station, which in turn has an hourly train service to and from Southampton. Gatwick Airport (Tel: 0870 000 2468) is about a one hour, 40-minute drive from Southampton while Bournemouth Airport (Tel: 01202 364000) is about 40 minutes away by car .

Taxis: Radio Taxis: Tel: 023 8066 6666; Shirley Cabs: Tel: 023 8039 3939; West Quay Cars: Tel: 023 8022 3450.

Car hire: Avis Rent-a-car: Tel: 0870 608 6361; National Car Rental: Tel: 0870 191 0556; Europcar: Tel: 023 8033 2973.

Cycle hire: AA Bike Hire (Gosport Lane, Lyndhurst): Tel: 023 8028 3349.

OTHER INFORMATION

Harbourmaster: Tel: 023 8033 0022.

Southampton Harbour Patrol: VHF Channel 12, 16.

Hythe Marina: VHF Ch 80; Tel: 023 8020 7073.

Ocean Village Marina: VHF Ch 80; Tel: 023 8022 9385.

Shamrock Quay Marina: VHF Ch 80; Tel: 023 8022 9461.

Kemps Quay: Tel: 023 8063 2323.

Saxon Wharf: Tel: 023 8033 9490.

Town Quay Marina: Tel: 023 8023 4397.

Itchen Marine (fuel): Tel: 023 8063 1500.

Royal Southampton Yacht Club: Tel: 023 8022 3352.

Chandleries: Shamrock Chandlery: Tel: 023 8063 2725; Kelvin Hughes: Tel: 023 8063 4911.

Marine services: Shamrock Quay Marina: Tel: 023 8022 9461; the Sadler Group (boat repair facilities): Tel: 023 8023 4777; the Rig Shop: Tel: 023 8033 8341.

Police: Tel: 999; Tel: 023 8058 1111.

Coastguard: Lee on Solent Tel: 023 92 552100.

Hospital: Southampton General Hospital: Tel: 023 8077 7222.

Doctor: Tel: 023 8033 6676.

NHS Direct: Tel: 0845 4647.

Dentist: Southampton Dental helpline: Tel: 023 8033 8336

Tourist Information: Southampton Tourist Information: Tel: 023 8083 3333; New Forest Information Centre: Tel: 023 8028 2269.

Many cruise ships, such as the *Queen Mary 2*, visit Southampton

A high-speed ferry service operates between Southampton and Cowes

The River Hamble is the boating capital of Southampton Water and home to five marinas, numerous boatyards and a wide range of marine services

River Hamble

Hamble River entrance: 50°50'.15N 01°18'.64W

The River Hamble is renowned internationally as a centre for yachting and boatbuilding. With five marinas and several boatyards, it accommodates over 3,000 boats and is a constant hive of activity during the summer. Due to its popularity and the lack of designated visitors' berths, mooring in peak season can be difficult so it is advisable to contact the marinas or harbourmaster slightly ahead of time.

Once in the river, you will be spoilt for choice by the number of charming pubs and restaurants lining the water's edge.

A south cardinal lies at the entrance to the River Hamble off Hamble Point

NAVIGATION

Charts: Admiralty: Charts: SC5600, 2036; Imray: C3, C15, 2200; Stanfords: 11, chartpack 24

Tides: Double High Water occurs at or near Springs, while at other times there is a stand of about two hours. Predictions are for the first High Water if there are two, otherwise they refer to the middle of the stand.

At Warsash, near the entrance to the Hamble River, HW Springs are 10 minutes after and HW Neaps 20 minutes after HW Southampton. LW Neaps are 10 minutes after and LW Springs the same as LW Southampton. MHWS: 4.5m; MHWN: 3.8m; MLWN: 1.9m; MLWS: 0.8m.

A 6-knot speed limit should be adhered to when navigating the river

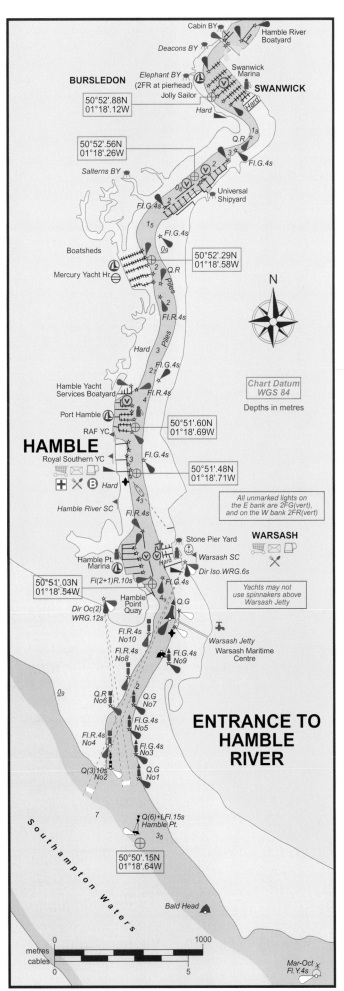

Approaches: From the east there are no real hazards except for the extensive but gentle shoaling from Lee Point to the entrance on your starboard-hand side. There is, however, plenty of room to sail outside the North Channel shipping lane. From the west, after rounding Lepe Spit SCM (Q [6] + LFl 15s) to port and keeping clear of Calshot Spit (Fl 5s), stay to the outside edge of the main channel. Cross over to the eastern side, heading for the Hamble Point SCM (Q [6] + LFl 15s) and retaining a distance from commercial vessels. If approaching from Southampton, do not cut inside No 2 ECM (Q [3] 10s) for fear of getting caught on the Hamble Spit.

Pilotage: Hamble Point south cardinal mark (position 50°50'.15N 01°18'.66W) is best left close to port. A course of 002° brings you to the No 1 QG pile from where the channel is clearly marked with port and starboard piles that are all lit. Once through the entrance keep to the starboard side of the river, between the moorings.

At night, from the Hamble Point SCM, a Dir light on the shore west of Hamble Point (Oc [2] WRG12s W351°–353°) at 352° leads you into the entrance. Between the No 5 beacon (FlG 4s) and the No 7 beacon (QG) alter course to 028° to bring you into the W sector of the Dir light (Iso WRG 6s 5m 4M) on the Warsash shore. Abeam the No 11 buoy (QG), alter course due north to enter the river between the visitors' pontoon (Fl [2 + 1] R 10s) and the No 13 starboard-hand mark (FL G 4s). Remember to keep to starboard to avoid vessels leaving the river. In addition, if navigating the river at night, watch out for the unlit mooring piles.

Despite the River Hamble having 3,000 berths or more spread between several major marinas and the Harbour Authority's facilities, you may still encounter difficulties finding a berth in the summer, even mid-week. The volume of traffic on summer weekends can be so great that it is recommended that engines should be used in the river and one of the regulations is that spinnakers must not be flown north of the Warsash jetty.

The Warsash Maritime Centre is a useful starboard entrance landmark

Warsash

Midstream visitors' pontoon: 50°51'.07N 01°18'.54W

The Hamble harbourmaster, situated in the conspicuous black and white striped building at Warsash on the eastern shore of the river, has several midstream visitors' piles and pontoons as well as a couple of jetties. You can't reserve a berth ahead of time as all places are on a 'first come first served' basis, but staff at the harbourmaster's office will usually manage to find you a place. For berth allocation, call 'Hamble Harbour Radio' on VHF Ch 68 or Tel: 01489 576387; Mob: 07718 146380, 07718 146381 or 07718 146399.

Berthing fees: A short stay of a maximum of four hours (between 0900 and 1600) for a yacht of up 12m (39ft) on a pontoon berth costs £6; yachts over 12m: £8. An overnight stay from 1600 to 1700 the next day: £2 per metre. For the midstream pile berths, the rates are £1.50 per metre for an overnight stay (1600–1700 the next day), while for a short stay of up to four hours between 0900 and 1600, yachts up to 12m LOA are charged £4 and those over 12m £6.

The distinctive black and white building is the harbourmaster's office

Fuel can be obtained from the adjacent Stone Pier fuel pontoon

Useful information

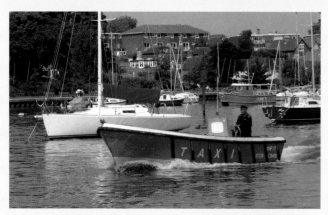

The unmistakeable river taxi runs between Warsash and Hamble Quay

FACILITIES

Facilities include water (no hoses supplied) and electricity on the pontoon, and toilets, as well as scrubbing piles next to the harbourmaster's slipway. There are plenty of marine services and chandleries in the area (see under 'Other Information' on p90). Gas and fuel can be obtained from the Stone Pier fuel pontoon, just past the harbourmaster's jetty. If you end up on one of the midstream moorings, you can get to either shore of the river by calling the river taxi on Tel: 023 8045 4512; mobile 07720 438402 or VHF Ch 77 (although you are encouraged to use a mobile).

Warsash Sailing Club (Tel: 01489 583575) welcomes members from affiliated clubs and offers shower and toilet facilities.

PROVISIONING

A short walk from the harbourmaster's office up Shore Road and beyond the unusual Edwardian clock tower on the crossroads brings you to Warsash Road, with a Co-op on the left and, a little further on, a One Stop incorporating the village post office on the right. Both these stores have cash machines. Not far from Warsash Road, in Dibles Road, is Warsash Nautical Books (Tel: 01489 572384), which has a good selection of local charts and nautical publications.

EATING OUT

Warsash boasts three pubs, one of which is the Rising Sun (Tel: 01489 576898) on the village quay. Although it serves good food and offers superb views, it is more expensive than the other two pubs on Warsash Road. The first one you come to is the Ferry Man (Tel: 01489 573088) and the second, opposite One Stop, is the Silver Fern (Tel: 01489 572057). Neither of these pubs has a particularly cosy atmosphere, but they do offer food at fairly good prices. Alternatively, there is an Indian restaurant on Shore Road, the Chon Chona (Tel: 01489 573110), which has a takeaway service, or Rumours (Tel: 01489 573720) on Brook Lane, which serves an Italian/American evening menu in pleasant surroundings. At lunchtimes it offers lighter snacks, such as deep-filled baguettes and baked potatoes, which you can take away if you prefer. On Bridge Road in Sarisbury Green is a sandwich bar called Chives (Tel: 01489 577875), which sells sandwiches, baked potatoes and salads at very reasonable prices. It is too far away to walk to easily, so take advantage of its free delivery service. Warsash SC welcomes yachtsmen from affiliated yacht clubs to its bar and restaurant, provided it is not too busy. It does lunchtime food from Tuesday to Sunday and evening food on certain race nights during the summer.

The 230-berth Hamble Point Marina is situated close to the entrance of the Hamble River and has extensive facilities, including a 75-ton boat hoist

Hamble Point Marina

Marina entrance: 50°51'.03N 01°18'.54W

Situated practically opposite Warsash, this is the first marina you will come to on the western bank of the River Hamble. The entrance is to port of the visitors' pontoons, opposite the harbourmaster's office. Accommodating yachts up to 20m (66ft) in length, it offers easy access to the Solent. As with all the berths in the Hamble, be careful when manoeuvring at certain states of the tide and if possible try to avoid berthing when the tide is ebbing strongly. Contact the marina office ahead of time on VHF Ch 80 or Tel: 023 8045 2464, as there are no dedicated visitors' berths here and availability is subject to how many resident berth holders are away at the time. The marina does, however, have an events pontoon that will accommodate several visiting yachts.

Berthing fees: These fees may be subject to a slight increase but are currently set at £3 per metre per night for yachts up to 12.5m (41ft) LOA and £3.80 per metre per night for yachts of 12.6m (41ft 3in) and over. A short stay of up to four hours is charged at a flat rate of £8.50.

Useful information

FACILITIES

With plenty of marine services on hand as well as boat lifting facilities, hard standing and undercover storage, Hamble Point Marina is an ideal place if you need to winter your boat or have extensive repairs carried out. There is an on-site chandlery, which supplies calor gas, while electricity and water are installed on the pontoons. Fuel is available from the nearby Port Hamble Marina.

Staff at Hamble Point Marina are extremely helpful and will supply you

with weather and tourist information. Ice can be purchased at the dock office. The ablution facilities and a launderette are situated behind the Ketch Rigger

Good facilities can be found here

restaurant and can only be accessed with a code. Refuse skips are located at each bridge head, with bottle banks behind the restaurant. The marina also offers Wi-Fi internet access, and has 24-hour security cameras around the site.

PROVISIONING

The on-site chandlery provides the basics, such as bread, milk, sandwiches and snacks. The nearest convenience store is the Co-op in Hamble Village, a 15-minute walk away. For more information, see p84.

EATING OUT

The marina has its own bar and restaurant on site, the Ketch Rigger (Tel: 023 8045 5601), which serves lunchtime and evening meals as well as takeaway sandwiches.

Hamble Quay   Hamble visitors' quay: 50°51'.48N 01°18'.71W

Like Warsash, Hamble Quay comes under the jurisdiction of the harbourmaster. You are permitted to lie alongside the quay free of charge for one hour, but if you want to stay any longer than this, you have to get

permission from the duty harbourmaster. Note that the quay gets very crowded on weekends and the depth can drop to about 1.5m at Low Water Springs. To contact the harbourmaster for berth allocation, call 'Hamble Harbour Radio' on VHF Ch 68 or Tel: 01489 576387; Mobile: 07718 146380 or 07718 146381.

Berthing fees: A short stay between 0800 and 1600 for a 10m (33ft) yacht alongside the harbourmaster's jetty costs £7.50; overnight stay: £15; 24-hour stay: £22.50.

FACILITIES
Facilities are pretty basic at Hamble Quay, although you can get water here, dispose of your rubbish and use the nearby public toilets. For shopping, restaurants and places of interest, see p84 and p88-90.

Port Hamble Marina is a popular destination with visiting yachtsmen because it is so close to the village of Hamble-le-Rice

Port Hamble Marina
Marina fuel dock: 50°51'.60N 01°18'.69W

As the second marina on the western bank of the River Hamble, it is also the one closest to the picturesque Hamble village (correctly known as Hamble-le-Rice), therefore proving extremely popular with visiting yachtsmen. With no dedicated visitors' berths, it is advisable to book ahead on VHF Ch 80 or Tel: 023 8045 2741. The marina can be accessed at any state of the tide, 24 hours a day.
Berthing fees: £3 per metre per night or £8.50 for a short stay of up to four hours.

Useful information – Port Hamble Marina

FACILITIES

Like most of the marinas in the Solent, Port Hamble Marina offers a full range of facilities. Unleaded petrol and diesel are available from the fuel barge on the outside of 'B' pontoon from 0800–1800 during the summer months and from 0900–1700 during the winter. Having been developed from a former boatyard, there is also no shortage of marine expertise on site for any work you may need carried out. For a full list of contractors, or if you want to have your boat craned out of the water and put on the hard-standing area, ask at the marina office. They will also provide you with ice as well as take any urgent messages and update you on the latest weather forecast.

Behind the marina office is a chandlery, while toilets and showers are located underneath the office. The amenities are open 23 hours a day, being closed for one hour for cleaning. A coin-operated launderette can also be found on site and there is a 24-hour security system in place.

PROVISIONING

The chandlery stocks a small range of basic provisions. Fortunately, the Co-op supermarket in Hamble village is only a short walk away. This also has a cashpoint. Hamble village has several little shops, including a post office, a chemist and Bonne Bouche (Tel: 023 8045 5771), a delicatessen that supplies freshly filled baguettes as well as a great selection of cheeses, patés and hams, and serves delicious, freshly cooked breakfasts. There are two banks in the village, a NatWest and Barclays, although only Barclays, which is situated about a 5-minute walk away from the village centre, has a cashpoint. If you want to do a big shop, catch a bus or take a taxi to the large Tesco at Bursledon on Hamble Lane, which also has a cash machine.

EATING OUT

The marina has its own restaurant/bar, which is due to open in 2008. The village also has a selection restaurants, see p84.

Mercury Yacht Harbour   Just off D pontoon: 50°52'.29N 01°18'.58W

Mercury Yacht Harbour is the third marina on the western bank, tucked away in a picturesque, wooded site where Badnam Creek flows into the River Hamble. The marina can be accessed 24 hours a day and can accommodate yachts up to 24m (79ft) LOA. Contact the marina in advance as there are no allocated visitors' berths, although space can usually be found during the summer when many resident berth holders are away.

For more details and to check availability, call Mercury Yacht Harbour on VHF Ch 80 or Tel: 023 8045 5994.

Berthing fees: All fees are subject to a slight increase after 1 April 2008 and quotations are available from the dockmaster's office. A short stay of four hours for yachts of any length costs £8.50. For an overnight stay, yachts up to 15m (49ft) LOA will be charged £3 per metre and for those over 15m (49ft) £3.80 per metre.

Useful information – Mercury Yacht Harbour

The Bugle has been on this site for over 800 years and is recommended as a good place to have an evening meal

Below: The Victory Inn is also close by and is another good place to eat at, whether you are looking for decent pub grub or an à la carte dining experience

FACILITIES

Water and electricity are available on the pontoons, with toilets, showers and a coin-operated launderette ashore. Gas can be obtained from the on-site chandler, while ice is available at the dock office. As there is no fuel barge at this marina, refuel at Swanwick Marina or stop off at Port Hamble (the closest marina to Mercury) or Hamble Point Marina. Alternatively, you could get fuel from Stone Pier Yard, near the harbourmaster's office at the entrance to the River Hamble.

As with the two previously mentioned MDL marinas – Port Hamble and Hamble Point – Mercury Yacht Harbour is hot on security and its cameras operate day and night. Dock office staff are willing to help with any enquiries and will take urgent messages for you, too.

Other facilities include a boat hoist and hard-standing

area as well as chandlery, sailmakers and other marina experts (ask at the dock office for more information).

The dock office is manned around the clock but, if locked, the duty dockmaster is usually found patrolling the pontoons and can be contacted on VHF Ch 80 or Mobile: 07831 452445.

PROVISIONING

The on-site chandlery stocks a small amount of essential items, otherwise the nearest convenience store is the Co-op (with cash point) in Hamble Village, which is open seven days a week from 0700 to 2200. Bear in mind that the village is a good 20–25-minute walk away.

For serious provisioning, take a taxi or bus to the large Tesco supermarket on Hamble Lane, Bursledon. As mentioned before, Hamble village also has a couple of banks as well as a post office and a delicatessen.

EATING OUT

The Oyster Quay Bar and Restaurant (Tel: 023 8045 7220) at the marina serves good food and its balcony offers great views over the River Hamble.

Hamble village is home to three sailing clubs, all of which welcome visiting yachtsmen and serve food and drinks. (See under 'Other Information' on p90 for contact details.)

Besides these, there are plenty of restaurants to choose from here. Three pubs recommended are the Bugle (Tel: 023 8045 3000), which has been established on its present site for over 800 years, the Victory Inn (Tel: 023 8045 3105), which serves home-made food and has an à la carte menu, the King & Queen (Tel: 023 8045 4247) and the R Bar (Tel: 023 8045 4314), a wine bar and bistro on Hamble's High Street. Another good one to try is the Whyte Harte

(Tel: 023 8045 2108) on Hamble Lane heading out of the village which, set up in around 1563, is also steeped in history. Throughout the summer the pub puts on barbecues in its attractive walled garden.

For a good Italian menu go to La Dolce Vita (Tel: 023 8045 4567) in the Square, while for homemade lunches or teas don't miss the Village Tea Rooms (Tel: 023 8045 5583). For breakfasts, the Bonne Bouche (Tel: 023 8045 5771) delicatessen in the High Street comes highly recommended and is hard to beat.

The village also has a fish and chip shop (Tel: 023 8045 6711) and an Indian restaurant, the Cinnamon Bay (Tel: 023 8045 2285), which offers a takeaway service. This can be found next to Barclays Bank, which is about a five-minute walk out of the village along Hamble Lane.

Universal Marina

Between H and I pontoons: 50°52'.56N 01°18'.26W

Situated a little further up river from Mercury Yacht Harbour, but on the eastern shore, is Universal Marina. The marina is accessible at any state of the tide and has berths available for visitors. It can accommodate craft of between 6-25m (20-82ft) and offers both deep-water and semi-tidal berths. Accessible 24 hours a day, the marina can be contacted on VHF Ch 80 or Tel: 01489 574272.
Berthing fees: £2.85 per metre per night or a short stay of up to four hours is a flat rate of £8.

FACILITIES

A 50-ton boat hoist, a hard standing area along with an array of marine specialists make it easy to have repairs carried out on your boat. Other amenities are water and electricity on the pontoons, showers, toilets and laundry facilities ashore, wireless internet access, rubbish disposal and good security.

If you need diesel or petrol then the closest fuel berths can be found at Swanwick Marina, a little further upstream of Universal, or back at Port Hamble Marina.

The Café Lulworth provides breakfasts, lunches and dinners and is also a fully licensed bar.

PROVISIONING

One Stop is about a 15-minute walk away at Sarisbury Green and sells basic provisions. It also has a cashpoint.

Swanwick Marina is situated immediately to the south of the Bursledon bridge, and is accessible at any state of the tide

Swanwick Marina

Between C and D pontoons: 50°52'.88N 01°18'.12W

Situated on the east bank of the River Hamble next to Bursledon Bridge (which has a height clearance of 4m at Mean High Water Springs and 8m at Mean Low Water Springs), Swanwick Marina is accessible at any state of the tide and the dock master can be contacted 24 hours a day on VHF Ch 80 or Tel: 01489 884081. The marina has no allocated visitors' berths, but will accommodate visiting yachts (up to 20m [66ft] in length) when resident berth holders are away. It is advisable to call ahead of time to find out about berthing availability.
Berthing fees: £2.80 per metre per night. A short stay of up to four hours is £0.85 per metre.

Useful information – Swanwick Marina

The Jolly Sailor is a jolly place to spend the evening

FACILITIES
Water and electricity are available on the pontoons while calor, camping gas and ice can be acquired from the Aladdin's Cave chandlery in Deacon's Boatyard, which is just across the Bursledon bridge. Note that the Aladdin's Cave at Swanwick Marina only sells clothes, but the other one sells a wide range of chandlery. The toilets and shower block are situated below the dock office and are accessed by a security code. The launderette is also located here and is open from 0800 to 2000, although a key is available if you want to use it out of these hours. Rubbish disposal is straightforward,

with yellow rollerbins located at the end of each jetty for general domestic waste and specific drums and tanks for surplus engine oil and oil filters. A fuel berth opens on request at the dock office.

The office also supplies a daily weather forecast as well as selling milk. A full range of services are available on site, ranging from repairs and maintenance to engineers and sailmakers. Ask the marina staff for details. Open-air and undercover storage is also available.

PROVISIONING
The nearest store is the Swanwick post office in Swanwick Lane. Within easy walking distance of the

marina, it is open until 1730 Monday to Friday and until 1230 on Saturday; closed Sundays. About half a mile away at Sarisbury Green is a One Stop, which has a greater range of provisions than the post office and also has a cash machine. The closest large supermarket is Tesco, about a mile from the marina at the top of Hamble Lane.

EATING OUT
The marina's fully-licensed bar and restaurant, Velsheda's (Tel: 01489 885745) is situated next to the chandlery and is open seven days a week. Overlooking the river, it serves breakfast, lunch and dinner. A short row or walk

away is the celebrated Jolly Sailor (Tel: 023 8040 5557) pub in Bursledon on the west bank, made famous for being the local watering hole in the 1980s British television series *Howard's Way*. Not too far from the Jolly Sailor, in Lands End Road, Old Bursledon, is the Ferry Restaurant (Tel: 023 8040 2566), also serving good quality food at reasonable prices. On the eastern side and closer to Swanwick Marina are two pubs: the Spinnaker (Tel: 01489 572123) and the Old Ship (Tel: 01489 575646). The Riverside Chinese Restaurant (Tel: 023 8040 4100) comes highly recommended and is near the Spinnaker pub.

Elephant Boatyard

Elephant Boatyard pontoons: 50°52'.96N 01°18'.22W

On the opposite side of the river to Swanwick Marina is the Elephant Boatyard. Specialising in classic wooden yachts, it was founded in 1952 on the site of a yard that constructed the 74-gun HMS *Elephant* in 1786 as Nelson's flagship for the battle of Copenhagen in 1801. Although it has no allocated berths for visitors, it is worth giving the yard a call (Tel: 023 8040 3268), as it may have space on one of its pontoons, with the added advantage that it is far cheaper than the marinas. Try to avoid berthing on the fast ebbing tide, however, as it can prove tricky.

Berthing fees: Fees are 50p per foot or £1.28 per metre. Short stays are not encouraged as the yard does not want to become a quick stopover for yachts visiting the adjacent Jolly Sailor pub.

FACILITIES

Pontoons are equipped with electricity and water. A crane and yard repair facilities make it easy to have work carried out on your boat. The nearest fuel pontoon is at Swanwick Marina, although you should contact the marina ahead of time if you require diesel or petrol.

PROVISIONING

A One Stop convenience store with a cash machine can be found near Bridge Road in Lowford, about a 10-minute walk from the yard. Also based in Lowford is a post office, garage and hairdresser. The large Tesco supermarket at the top of Hamble Lane is about a 20-25 minute walk from here. See p84, p88-90 for more details of Hamble village.

A view towards the top of the River Hamble. In the foreground (left-hand side) is the Elephant Boatyard, with Deacons beyond and Swanwick Marina opposite

Deacons Boatyard

Deacons pontoon approach: 50°52'.99N 01°18'.20W

North of the Elephant Boatyard is Deacons Boatyard, which offers 140 pontoon berths and several swinging moorings. The yard has no specific visitors' berths, so the best bet is to make contact once you are in the River Hamble, as short-term berths are normally available.

The yard has no VHF channel but can be contacted on Tel: 023 8040 2253.

Berthing fees: £17 per night, plus VAT.

FACILITIES

Facilities at the yard comprise water, electricity, toilets and showers as well as good repair facilities. For fuel, head for Swanwick Marina, although you need to phone the marina's dock office before going alongside. There is a well-stocked Aladdin's Cave chandlery within the yard, as well as engineers, shipwrights, riggers, a 20-ton lifting dock, boat mover and brokerage office.

For details of where to provision, see above and p86.

Useful information – River Hamble

The Hamble – one of many
Solent harbours contributing to
the Second World War

The Priory Church of St Andrew the
Apostle in Hamble-le-Rice (left) dates
to 1109 when a group of Benedictine
monks were granted the land by the
Bishop of Winchester

ASHORE

A walk along the River Hamble is well worth while, if only to reflect on its past maritime history which began as far back as the ninth century when King Alfred's men sank as many as 20 Viking longships at Bursledon during the Battle of Brixdone. By the 14th century the Hamble had become a primary trading port and it is here that King Henry V's flagship *Grace Dieu* was constructed.

Throughout the 18th and 19th centuries several battleships were built on the Hamble, the most famous of which was the *Elephant* which, as mentioned on p87, was Nelson's flagship during the 1801 Battle of Copenhagen.

The Hamble's creeks and tidal inlets made it a popular smuggling haunt and it was home to one of Britain's most notorious 17th century pirates, Henry Mainwaring, who was later pardoned and knighted by King James I.

Nearby are plenty of interesting places to visit. The beautiful ruins of the 13th century Netley Abbey (Tel: 0845 3010008), allegedly haunted by Blind Peter the monk, was a favourite place with smugglers for stashing away rum, tea and other goods and is well worth seeing. It is owned today by English Heritage and admission is free of charge. The abbey is half a mile from the Royal Victoria Country Park (Tel: 023 8045 5157), which lies about two miles from the Hamble on the edge of Southampton Water. With large open spaces, a children's play area and a miniature railway, it is a great place to visit if you have young children on board. It was within this park that the first purpose-built military hospital was constructed,

designed with the input of Florence Nightingale and opened in 1856 by Queen Victoria. Today only the chapel remains in existence, the rest of the building having been destroyed by a fire in the 1960s. The park is open all year round.

Manor Farm Country Park, (Tel: 01489 787055) in Pylands Lane, Bursledon, is a working farm from the Victorian era, where you can participate in traditional farming activities. Great for children, there are specific activities laid on throughout the summer as well as picnic and play areas. The farm is open 1000–1700 each day from Easter through to October, while the park is open all year round during daylight hours.

Bursledon Windmill (Tel: 023 8040 4999) is reputed to be Hampshire's only working windmill. Over the years, the tower mill, built

between 1813 and 1814, has been carefully restored and produces stoneground flour milled from local wheat. It is open on Sundays and Bank Holidays throughout the year, 1000–1600.

On a favourable tide a dinghy trip up the River Hamble as far as Botley Village is a pleasant way to pass the time, especially if you stop off at the Jolly Sailor pub at Bursledon for a quick drink en route. The top of the river eventually divides: the main fork branching left to Botley, where the flour mills signify the end of the salt water. The right-hand fork leads to the Horse and Jockey (Tel: 01489 782654) pub at Curbridge, which you can get to at High Water.

The River Hamble is also known as the Strawberry Coast because of its thriving strawberry industry in the early 20th century. Although today this industry has much declined, the strawberries are still regarded as some of the best in Britain and there are plenty of 'pick-your-own' strawberry farms in the area: an alternative activity to while away a few hours on a fine afternoon some say.

The Hamble is a hive of activity during the summer, but even more so during Hamble Week, which takes place towards the end of June to the beginning of July (for details, Tel: 023 8045 7935). This is a week packed full of watersports and is combined with the Hamble Valley Food & Drink Festival (Tel: 0906 68 22 001).

The Bursledon Regatta tends to be held over a weekend either towards the end of August or at the beginning of September at the Elephant Boatyard and comprises sailing and rowing races, swimming and fancy dress competitions, as well as a torchlight procession afloat and fireworks.

There are also several used-boat shows held on the Hamble during the Southampton Boat Show: the Premier Used Boat Show (Tel: 01489 884075; 01489 884081) is held at Swanwick Marina, while Deacons Boatyard (Tel: 023 8040 2253) organises another show, as does Hamble Point Marina (Tel: 023 8045 2464). For more details of the Southampton Boat Show, see p74.

TRANSPORT

Buses: Many of the marinas are within easy reach of bus stops, with regular buses running between Warsash, Hamble, Swanwick, Bursledon and Southampton. Contact Solent Blue Line (Tel: 023 8061 8233) for details. FirstDay Explorer tickets provide unlimited daily travel on the whole of First Bus's network from Southampton to Portsmouth. To find out about bus times, Tel: 023 8022 4854.

Trains: There are train stations at Bursledon, Hamble, Netley, Hedge End and Botley providing links with Southampton and Portsmouth, from where train services run regularly to London. For information, Tel: 08457 48 49 50.

Ferries: From Southampton, which is only about 15-minutes away by car, you can catch a ferry to the Isle of Wight. Contact Red Funnel on Tel: 0870 444 8898. About a 30 to 40-minute drive away, you can catch

Bonne Bouche is highly recommended for its breakfasts

The Rising Sun pub in Warsash has superb views over the river

Despite the River Hamble being extremely popular in the summer, there is no shortage of marinas, moorings and boatyards to serve visiting yachtsmen

Useful information –River Hamble

Although the River Hamble heaves with boats and people peak season, it can also have its quieter spots

a cross-Channel ferry from Portsmouth. For timetables and fares, call P&O on Tel: 08716 646464 for details.

Airports: There are good UK, European and worldwide connections from Southampton Airport (Tel: 0870 040 0009), which is only about a five-minute walk from Southampton Parkway railway station. The Hamble is about a 70-minute drive from Heathrow Airport (Tel: 0870 000 0123) and about 1½ hours from Gatwick Airport (Tel: 0870 000 2468). There is also a small airport at Bournemouth (Tel: 01202 364000), which takes about 45 minutes to get to by car.

Taxis: Phipps Taxis: Tel: 0700 234 5678; Radio Taxis: Tel: 023 8066 6666.

Car hire: Peter Cooper Volkswagen (Hedge End): Tel: 01489 783434; Sixt Rent-a-Car: Tel: 0870 1567 567.

OTHER INFORMATION

Harbourmaster: VHF Ch 68; Tel: 01489 576387; Mobile: 07718 146380; 07718 146381; 07718 146399.

Hamble Point Marina: VHF Ch 80; Tel: 023 8045 2464.

Port Hamble Marina: VHF Ch 80; Tel: 023 8045 2741.

Mercury Yacht Harbour: VHF Ch 80; Tel: 023 8045 5994.

Universal Marina: VHF Ch 80; Tel: 01489 574272.

Swanwick Marina: VHF Ch 80; Tel: 01489 884081.

The Elephant Boatyard: Tel: 023 8040 3268.

Deacons Boatyard: Tel: 023 8040 2253.

River taxi: A ferry runs between Hamble and Warsash, while a river taxi covers the whole of the River Hamble. Contact the Hamble-Warsash ferry on Tel: 023 8045 4512; mobile 07720 438402 or VHF Ch 77 (you are encouraged to call

them on a mobile rather than the VHF).

Hamble River Sailing Club: Tel: 023 8045 2070.

The Royal Southern Yacht Club: Tel: 023 8045 0300.

The RAF Yacht Club: Tel: 023 8045 2208.

Warsash Sailing Club: Tel: 01489 583575.

Chandleries: Aladdin's Cave (Swanwick Marina – clothing only): Tel: 01489 555999; Aladdin's Cave (Deacon's Boatyard – full range of chandlery): Tel: 023 8040 2182; Hamble Point Marina: Tel: 023 8045 5058; Mercury Marina: Tel: 023 8045 4849; Port Hamble Marina: Tel: 023 8045 4858.

Sailmakers: Bank Sails: Tel: 01489 582444; Shore Sailmakers: Tel: 01489 589450; UK Sails: Tel: 01489 583583.

Marine services: Elephant Boatyard: Tel: 023 8040

3268; Deacon's Boatyard: Tel: 023 8040 2253; Hamble Yacht Services: Tel: 023 8045 4111; Marine Services: Tel 01489 885000; RK Marine (engine stockist): Tel: 01489 583585; Tel: 01489 583572; TS Marine: Tel: 01489 581030; Fairlie Restorations (Hamble): Tel: 023 8045 6336.

Police: Tel: 999; Tel: 08450 454545.

Coastguard: Lee on Solent: Tel: 023 9255 2100.

Hospital: Southampton General Hospital: Tel: 023 8077 7222.

Doctor: Tel: 023 8040 4671.

NHS Direct: Tel: 0845 4647.

Dentist: Dental helpline: Tel: 0845 0508345.

Tourist information office: Southampton (covers Hamble): Tel: 023 8083 3333; Hamble Valley Tourism (Walking Distance) Tel: 0906 6822001.

Chapter three
Eastern Solent

The eastern end is probably the most diverse of the three sections of the Solent. Here ports range from the large, modern marinas of Portsmouth through to the rural charm of Chichester and Langstone harbours. Bembridge, with its numerous deep-water berths, is also ever more popular with locals and visitors alike. However, less protected from the Isle of Wight, the eastern Solent can be more exposed than the other two areas in rough weather. You should avoid crossing Langstone and Chichester bars in strong onshore winds, particularly against the ebb on Spring tides.

Like the rest of the Solent, hazards in this part are all clearly marked on the charts. Among the sandbanks to

look out for are the East and West Pole sands on either side of the entrance to Chichester Harbour and the East and West Winner banks, flanking the channel to Langstone Harbour. All of these sandbanks extend a considerably deceptive distance from shore. Off Ryde, beware of the expansive Ryde Sand, too, which is most likely to catch out people cruising through the Solent from the east. Stay to the north of No Man's Land Fort, however, and you should encounter no difficulties.

Bembridge Ledge is one of the few rocky hazards in the eastern approach. Watch out, too, for the prominent Wootton Rocks just to the west of Wootton Creek. Although a passage between these rocks and Wootton

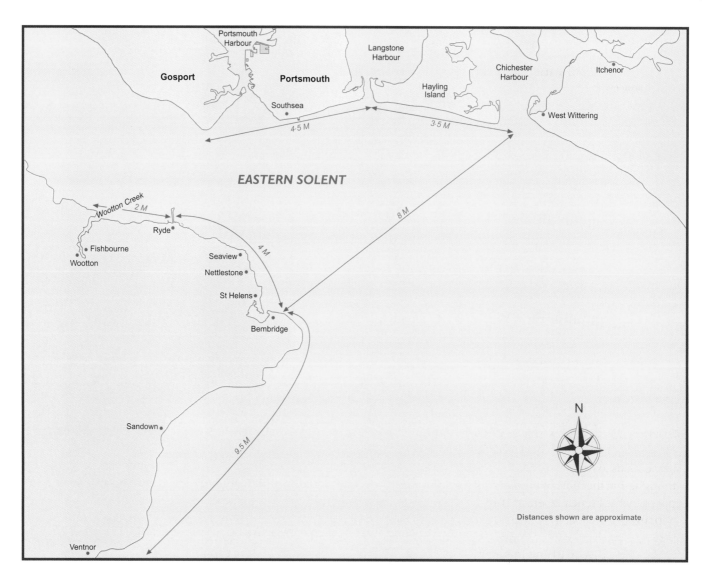

Point exists at High Water, it is best not to use this without local knowledge. To be on the safe side, keep north of the Royal Victoria Yacht Club's conspicuous starting platform. The man-made submarine barrier between Southsea and Horse Sand Fort is also a potential hazard and can only really be safely crossed through the well-marked Main Passage with a favourable tide. However, with local knowledge, smaller yachts do use the Boat Passage further inshore when sailing between Langstone and Portsmouth.

As is the case in the central Solent, the main hazards are the ferries and large commercial ships entering and leaving the Solent in the shipping lanes between Horse Sand Fort and No Man's Land Fort. Listen out on VHF Ch12 or VHF Ch11 for the Portsmouth area (see p47 for more details) for regular updates of shipping movements.

The submarine barrier runs south from Southsea to Horse Sand Fort. A dolphin marks the Main Passage, but small boats can use the inshore Boat Passage

In more recent years, No Man's Land Fort has been converted into luxurious accommodation

The Solent forts

Standing guard over the Eastern Solent are the four impressive granite, armour-plated Solent forts, built in the 1860s to protect Portsmouth from attack. It was thought that the most likely threat of invasion was posed by the French when, in 1848, Louis Napoleon, nephew of Bonaparte, became President of the French Second Republic. Four years later he declared himself Emperor Napoleon III and this ambition for complete power, along with a huge army at his disposal and the launch of the first fully iron-clad warship, *La Gloire*, led to widespread fear among the English that they would once again come under French attack. Responding to public outcry, the Prime Minister, Lord Palmerston, and his Government set up a Royal Commission, which in 1859 reviewed the defence of Britain's naval harbours. This led to the construction of the Solent forts: St Helen's, situated off the entrance to Bembridge harbour, Horse Sand and No Man's Land, the two largest forts flanking the main shipping channel through the Solent, and to the west, Spitbank, about a mile south of Portsmouth's harbour entrance. A fifth fort, on Ryde Sand, was planned, but this project was soon abandoned when the shifting sands proved unsuitable as foundations.

It took around 15 years to complete all four forts, at a cost of over a million pounds – three times as much as it would have cost to build land forts due to the problems involved in digging foundations 6 to 9m (20-30ft) beneath the surface of the water.

By the time all four forts were completed, the threat of invasion had subsided and the forts became known as 'Palmerston's Follies'. Although not a single shot was fired in anger from any of the forts, they remained armed as a deterrent to invasion right up until the end of the Second World War, after which they were used for coastal artillery until 1956. In the 1960s they were deemed surplus to military requirements, but weren't actually sold until the 1980s.

Having withstood the ravages of the sea for over 130 years, the Solent forts bear testament to the brilliance of Victorian engineering. Designed by Captain EH Steward, with civil engineer Sir John Hawkshaw as advisor, the forts are solidly constructed, with 4.5m (14ft 8in)-thick walls and 2.5m (8ft 2in)-deep floors.

Today two of the forts, Spitbank and No Man's Land, have been turned into commercial enterprises. Spitbank attracts around 25,000 tourists a year and incorporates a restaurant, bar and museum (see p118). It is also available for hire for private functions and has limited accommodation. No Man's Land was converted into luxury private accommodation in the 1990s and was later used for corporate events and weddings. However, it was put up for sale again in 2007.

North of No Man's Land, Horse Sand Fort has lain derelict for over 40 years, but plans are said to be underway to convert it into luxury apartments.

St Helen's Fort is privately owned and not open to the public. However, every August, on one of the lowest tides of the year, hundreds of people take part in a walk from St Helen's beach out to the fort and back. Although this is not an organised event, more details can be provided by the Isle of Wight Tourist Board (Tel: 01983 813813). Note, however, that the fort is only accessible on certain Spring tides and walking out to it should not be attempted without first seeking local advice.

Wootton Creek offers excellent shelter
in all but strong north to easterly winds,
but does dry at Low Water

Wootton Creek & Fishbourne

Wootton Creek entrance: 50°44'.42N 01°12'.25W

Despite being the Isle of Wight's main ferry terminal from
Portsmouth, Wootton Creek is in fact a charming little
harbour. Unfortunately, it has no deep-water moorings
but offers excellent shelter for shoal-draught yachts in all
but strong north to easterly winds.

NAVIGATION

Charts: Admiralty Charts: SC5600, 2022, 2036; Imray: C3,
C15, 2200; Stanfords: 11, chartpack 24, chartpack 25, L11
Tides: Use Ryde differences (see p98).

Watch out for the hazardous Wootton Rocks to the west of the entrance

Approaches: From the west, stay north of the Royal
Victoria Yacht Club's (RVYC) starting platform (position
50°44'.58N 01°12'.69W), as this will keep you well clear of
the Wootton Rocks. From the east, with a good offing, there
are no hazards to look out for apart from Ryde Sand and
the regular Portsmouth to Fishbourne ferries, which often
heave-to just outside the entrance.

Pilotage: Situated approximately 2 miles west of Ryde pier,
the entrance to Wootton Creek, with the regular Wightlink
ferries and the RVYC starting platform just to the west
of it, is not that difficult to make out against the wooded
shoreline. Entry to the harbour is straightforward – make
for the waypoint 50°44'.57N 01°12'.01W, just north-east of
the Wootton north cardinal mark (Q 1M), at the seaward
end of the fairway (dredged to 3m). Steering 226° from this
waypoint will take you into the straight channel, which
is well marked by four starboard-hand marks and two
port-hand marks, all of which are lit (beacons No 1 SHM Fl
(2) G5s; No 3 SHM Fl G 3s; No 5 SHM Fl G 2.5s; No 7 SHM
Q G; No 2 PHM Fl R 5s; No 4 PHM Fl R 2.5s). The ferry
pier is also lit (2 FR [vert]) and has a fog light (FY) and bell.
Beyond the pier is a leading sectored directional light

(Oc WRG 10s, G221° – 224°, W224° – 225.5°, R225.5° – 230.5°), which at night shows the narrow white sector if you are on course. As manoeuvring in the channel can be restricted by the ferries, which run every 30 minutes on the hour and half hour, it is better to time your arrival to avoid them. Once you have passed the No 7 beacon and are abeam of the outer ferry terminal, turn to starboard leaving the RVYC pontoon to port; this should bring the two triangular leading marks on the western bank into line. If you want to continue further into the creek, stick to the row of mooring buoys to stay in the deepest water and look out for a small green buoy, which you need to keep just to starboard in order to avoid the gravel spit that protrudes out on the port-hand side. Following on from this, a small red buoy and a line of old piles, both of which must be left to port, bring you to Fishbourne Quay.

BERTHING
Visiting yachts may tie up alongside the Royal Victoria Yacht Club (RVYC)'s 100m (300ft) pontoon, although bear in mind that this can dry out to soft mud.

If you want to explore the creek further, keep close to the moorings

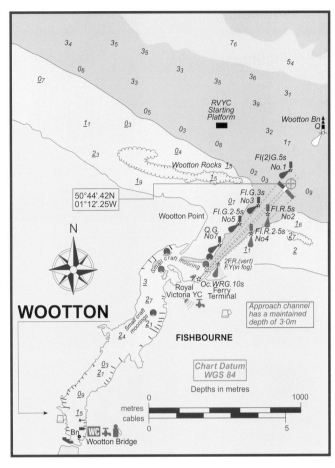

Berthing charges: Overnight: £1.50 per metre per night. Short stay (up to four hours): £5.

ANCHORAGES
Anchoring is forbidden in the fairway, but you may anchor, free of charge, directly opposite the RVYC on the northern side of the channel, where you will dry out at half-tide on soft mud. Note, however, that locals advise buoying your anchor as the ground is foul with old chains.

Manoeuvring in the channel can be difficult and restricted, especially when the Wightlink ferries are arriving from or departing to Portsmouth

Useful information – Wootton Creek & Fishbourne

Visiting yachts can berth alongside the Royal Victoria Yacht Club's pontoon. Overnight and short-stay charges apply

FACILITIES

The Royal Victoria Yacht Club (RVYC), which was originally set up in Ryde in 1845 by Prince Albert to enable Queen Victoria, as a female, to enter a yacht club, welcomes visiting yachtsmen. The club's facilities include water and electricity on the pontoon, showers and toilets ashore, and a very pleasant bar that offers basic bar meals throughout the week (closed on Mondays). All the facilities are available to members of other yacht clubs.

PROVISIONING

Wootton Bridge is the nearest shopping area and is about a mile's walk from RVYC. Depending on the state of the tide, it is also accessible by dinghy. Here you will find two supermarkets, a chemist and a post office.

EATING OUT

If it's an exciting night-life or haute cuisine that you are after, then Wootton Creek is not for you. However, for those who enjoy more peaceful surroundings, there are two delightful pubs nearby. The nearest is the Fishbourne Inn (Tel: 01983 882823), reached by turning left immediately after the ferry car park. Alternatively, it is well worth making the effort to walk (or go by dinghy with the right tide) to the Sloop Inn (Tel: 01983 882544) at Wootton Bridge. Located right on the edge of the creek, its extensive menu comes with daily specials. With a friendly atmosphere, it also has a large garden at the back.

ASHORE

As an area of outstanding natural beauty, a walk

along Wootton Creek from Fishbourne to Wootton Bridge is well worth while, especially as you can be rewarded for your efforts at the Sloop Inn (see above). Next to this pub, at the head of the creek, there once stood a tide mill and indeed the mill dam is now the causeway carrying the road. As one of six or seven tide mills on the Isle of Wight, barges from Southampton used to come here with corn, which would then be ground

into flour and transported around the island. The mill ceased to work in 1945 and was demolished in 1962.

The village of Wootton itself, although less frequented by visiting yachtsmen, certainly has historic interest, with references to it in the Domesday Book. Saint Edmund's Church, at the north end of Church Road, was originally the chapel of Wootton Manor, and

The Fishbourne Inn, near the ferry terminal, and the Sloop Inn at Wootton Bridge are both recommended as good places to find quality food and drink

dates back to Saxon times. Immediately before the Norman invasion the Manor was owned by Queen Edith, the wife of Edward the Confessor. This small church, like many Saxon churches throughout East Anglia and Wessex, is dedicated to Edmund, King of East Anglia. When the Danes invaded his kingdom in 870, they were so struck by Edmund's courage in defending his land that they proposed he should continue to rule his kingdom, but under their jurisdiction.

Equally, they wanted him to worship Odin rather than Christ. As Edmund defiantly refused their offer, the Danes tied him to a tree and shot him dead with arrows. It is alleged that miracles took place at the site of his burial, which resulted in his canonisation.

With the church having been rebuilt and restored several times throughout its history, the oldest part still standing today is the Norman nave, which can be traced back to 1087.

TRANSPORT
Ferries: Wightlink ferries (Tel: 0870 582 7744) runs a car ferry service to Portsmouth every 30 minutes, on the hour and half hour, depending on the time of year. The crossing takes about 35 minutes. There is also a hovercraft service that operates out of Ryde, see p102.
Taxis: Amber Cars (Tel: 01983 812222); Ralph Taxis (Tel: 01983 811666).
Buses: Southern Vectis (Tel: 01983 292082) operates a number of bus services from Wootton Bridge to Ryde, Newport and East Cowes.

OTHER INFORMATION
Royal Victoria Yacht Club: Tel: 01983 882325.
Police: Tel: 0845 0454545.
Coastguard: Lee on Solent: Tel: 023 9255 2100.
Hospital: St Mary's, Newport: Tel: 01983 524081.
Doctor: Tel: 01983 562955.
NHS Direct: Tel: 0845 4647.
Dental helpline: Tel: 01983 537424.
Tourist Information Office: Ryde: Tel: 01983 813813.

Wootton Creek is an area of outstanding natural beauty, and there are some good walks nearby if you want to stretch your legs for an hour or two

Ryde

Entrance to Ryde Harbour: 50°43'.99N 01°09'.31W

Known as 'the gateway to the Island', Ryde, with its elegant houses and abundant shops, is one of the Isle of Wight's most popular resorts. The well-protected harbour, although drying to about 2.5m, is conveniently close to the exceptional beaches and peaceful walks to the east and west as well as to the town's restaurants, amusements and 'candy-floss' atmosphere, which makes it an ideal cruising destination for families.

NAVIGATION

Charts: Admiralty Charts: SC5600, 2036, 2045; Imray: C3, C15, 2200; Stanfords: 11, chartpack 24

Tides: HW Springs are 10 minutes before and Neaps 10 minutes after HW Portsmouth. LW Neaps are 10 minutes before and Springs 5 minutes before LW Portsmouth. MHWS: 4.5m; MHWN: 3.7m; MLWN: 1.9m; MLWS: 0.9m.

Approaches: From the east, Ryde Sand is waiting to snare those who take short cuts, so first-timers to the Solent should stay north of No Man's Land Fort to avoid running aground. From the west, Ryde Pier, with its three sets of 2FR (vert) and FY fog lights, needs to be kept well to starboard to avoid hindering the high-speed ferry operating from the pierhead. East of the pier,

the Ryde/Portsmouth hovercraft has absolute right of way, with the buoyed marina channel being your only safe water.

Pilotage: Although the harbour is difficult to recognise, the town and pier are very obvious. The harbour is about ¼-mile to the east of the pier and immediately east of a large modern building, which incorporates the ice rink. Make for waypoint 50°44'.70N 01°09'.00W. From here use the spire of the Holy Trinity church, bearing 196°, as an initial approach across Ryde Sand until you reach waypoint 50°44'.28N 01°09'.17W, which puts you in the

Ryde Marina can be difficult to identify, but the conspicuous spire of the Holy Trinity church bearing 196° is used as a transit when making an approach

Ryde's harbour, which lies to the east of the pier, can accommodate up to 75 visiting yachts. It does dry, however, and is more suited to smaller boats

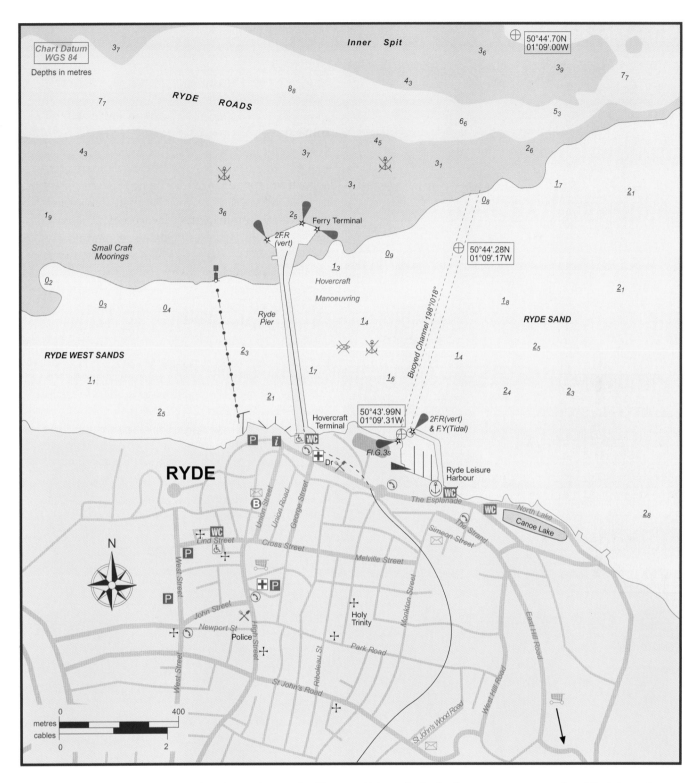

straight drying channel (1.5m). This channel is marked by three starboard-hand and three port-hand unlit buoys. The marina breakwaters, both of which are lit (starboard: Fl G 3s 7m 1M; port: 2 FR [vert] 7m 1M), are less than half a mile directly ahead. On entering the harbour, turn to port as soon as the port-hand breakwater is abeam of you. A tide gauge is situated on the starboard-hand breakwater.

BERTHING

Before making your initial approach over the sands you are advised to contact the harbourmaster (VHF Ch80; Tel: 01983 613879) for berthing availability and location.

Although the harbour can accommodate 75 visitors, its popularity with families often makes it crowded in the summer. Bilge-keelers and other boats that are able to take the ground can berth on the pontoons, while the eastern inner breakwater is well equipped with fender-boards and mooring cleats to deal with deep-draughted yachts willing to take the sandy bottom. Being a small, drying harbour, pumping out of any description is rightly forbidden.

Berthing fees: The harbour is ideally suited to smaller craft. Berthing fees vary, but an 8m (26ft) yacht would be charged £10 per night or £5 for a short stay.

Useful information – Ryde

The marina's entrance is clearly marked and the breakwaters are lit at night

Ryde's joint harbourmaster Colin Merrifield is on hand to offer advice

Bilge-keelers and other shallow-draught craft berth alongside the pontoons

Deeper draught yachts can berth alongside the eastern inner breakwater

FACILITIES

Showers, toilets, fresh water and rubbish disposal are available within the harbour, but obtaining fuel and gas involves a trip to the local garage. The harbour offers no boatyard or engineering facilities, but visiting engineers can be contacted.

PROVISIONING

Within about 50m of the harbour you will find a launderette, newsagent and corner shop that stays open until 2200. There are a couple of supermarkets scattered around Ryde, one of the nearest being Somerfield on Anglesea Street. To get there, make your way up the High Street and turn left at Boots the chemist. Alternatively, Tesco is located further out of the town on Brading Road and is open 24 hours, Monday to Saturday, and from 1000–1600 on Sunday.

Banks and cashpoints certainly don't come in short supply and most of the major banks and building societies are situated in either Union Street, High Street or St Thomas Square, many of which have cash dispensers. Besides the banks, High Street and Union Street are also packed full of interesting shops ranging from book shops and bakeries to hairdressers and stationers.

For medical needs, the nearest chemist to the marina is Lloyds Pharmacy on the Esplanade, otherwise you can find several more in the centre of Ryde.

Both the post office and the tourist information centre are situated in Union Street, which is opposite the pier. Market day is Thursday.

EATING OUT

When it comes to eating out, you are spoilt for choice in Ryde, which has always been awash with traditional seaside pubs, cafés and restaurants. In the past few years many of these have been modernised and upgraded to cater for a new, younger clientele.

Close to the marina on the Esplanade, the recently renovated Ryde Castle Hotel (Tel: 01983 503755) offers excellent bar meals and snacks, or you can choose from an extensive à la carte menu at its Brasserie.

Union Street is home to the majority of Ryde's eateries – Joe Daflos Café-bar (Tel: 01983 567047), Room 4 (Tel: 01983 611973), Liberty's Café Bar (Tel: 01983 811007), Bar 53 (Tel: 01983 811006) and Smithfields (Tel: 01983 611118) are modern café/bars with menus to match, while the Crown Hotel (Tel: 01983 562080), S Fowlers and Company (Tel: 01983 812112) and Yelf's Hotel (Tel: 01983 564062) provide more traditional food. Alternatively, try Simeon Arms (Tel: 01983 614954) or the Solent Inn (01243 563546). Popular with the locals, both these pubs serve real beer and bar meals.

A cosmopolitan flavour is added with the Dos Amigos Tex Mex (Tel: 01983 568866), Yan-Woo Malaysian restaurant (Tel: 01983 568818), the Moroccan Kasbah (Tel: 01983 810088) and the

The Ryde beaches are quite exceptional

Ryde Tandori (Tel: 01983 563165), all of which are on Union Street, as well as the popular Michelangelo restaurant and pizzeria (Tel: 01983 811966), situated on St Thomas Street with views across the Solent. A short walk east along the beach to the marina brings you to the Seashore Restaurant (Tel: 01983 811212). This restaurant also overlooks the Solent, and has a good reputation for fine seafood.

ASHORE

Ryde is renowned for its miles of sandy beaches, which extend from West Beach on the western side of the pier to Appley, Puckpool and Springvale to the east. The Esplanade runs the complete length of the seafront and offers great views across the Eastern Solent towards Portsmouth Harbour.

As an alternative to swimming in the sea, a large indoor heated swimming pool with a retractable roof is situated at the eastern end of the Esplanade and is open all year round, while the small open-air heated junior pool can be used from May to September. You will also find a tenpin bowling alley, an indoor children's play area, an ice rink and a small fun fair along the Esplanade. Other activities include a canoe lake and the challenging Appley nine-hole pitch and putt golf course. Most of the seafront tourist attractions are linked by a Dotto Train, comprising three carriages that run on tyres.

The sea wall promenade provides a popular walk, passing Appley Tower, the Victorian watchtower, and continuing on to Puckpool Park where refreshments, tennis, bowling and crazy golf can be enjoyed in the gardens adjacent to the remains of a 19th century battery. If you fancy doing something less

Union Street is packed full of interesting and diverse shops, including book shops, bakeries, cafés and bars. The Orrery (above), one of the UK's largest working planetariums, can also be found here

Useful information – Ryde

The canoe lake – where real swans meet their larger, fake siblings!

The Ryde Castle hotel serves excellent bar meals and an à la carte menu

An electric train runs from the pierhead to Shanklin via Sandown

A hovercraft service operates between Ryde and Southsea

The Crown Hotel in St Thomas Square, Ryde, serves traditional cuisine

strenuous, a visit to the Royal Victoria Arcade, enclosing boutiques, antique shops and an intriguing cellar market, is well worth while.

A fairly recent addition to Ryde's attractions is the Orrery (Tel: 01983 568555) in Union Street. One of the country's largest working planetariums, it also incorporates a themed café and is open during high season from 1000–1700, Monday to Saturday.

TRANSPORT

Ferries: Wightlink ferries (Tel: 0870 582 7744) run from Portsmouth Harbour to Ryde generally twice every hour at 15 minutes and 45 minutes past the hour. The crossing takes around 15 minutes.
Hovercraft: Hovertravel (Tel: 01983 811000) runs a half-hourly service between Ryde and Southsea. It is the only commercial passenger-carrying hovercraft service left in operation in the UK.
Trains: Island Line's electric train (Tel: 0845 7484950), which consists of refurbished 1930s London Underground carriages, runs from the pierhead to Shanklin, with stops at Ryde Esplanade, Ryde St John's, Brading, Sandown and Lake. It also connects up with the Isle of Wight steam railway at Smallbrook Junction.
Taxis: Diamond Taxis (Tel: 01983 811593); Ryde Taxis (Tel: 01983 811111).
Buses: Regular services run from Ryde to Newport and Cowes, as well as to all the island's major tourist attractions. Contact Southern Vectis on Tel: 01983 827000 or the Traveline on 0871 2002230.

OTHER INFORMATION
Harbourmaster: Tel: 01983 613879.
Police: Tel: 999; Tel: 0845 0454545.
Coastguard: Lee on Solent: Tel: 02392 552100.
Hospital: St Mary's, Newport: Tel: 01983 524081.
Doctor: Tel: 01983 562955.
NHS Direct: Tel: 0845 4647.
Dental helpline: Tel: 01983 537424.
Tourist Information Office: Tel: 01983 813813.

Seaview lies on the north coast of the Isle of Wight, two miles north-west of Bembridge

Seaview

Seaview moorings: 50°43'.49N 01°05'.98W

Approximately two miles north-west of the entrance to Bembridge, Seaview, with its attractive and friendly yacht club, is well worth a visit, especially for a lunch or evening stopover during the summer.

NAVIGATION

Charts: Admiralty Charts: SC5600, 2036, 2037; Imray: C3, C15, 2200; Stanfords: 11, chartpack 24
Tides: HW Springs are 20 minutes after and Neaps the same time as HW Portsmouth. LW Neaps are 20 minutes and Springs are 1 hour after LW Portsmouth. MHWS: 3.2m; MHWN 2.4m; MLWN: 0.6m; MLWS 0.2m.

Approach: From the west, keep north of No Man's Land Fort. From the east, keep in soundings and make for the waypoint 50°43'.82N 01°05'.36W. The moorings bear 230° and are approximately half a mile away. They have depths of around 2m at Mean Low Water Springs.

BERTHING

The club very generously and conveniently lays two trots of visitors' moorings about half a mile offshore. The outer trots are for vessels up to 5 tons, while the inner trot of moorings is suitable for 14 10-ton boats and five large vessels of around 20 tons. The moorings are protected from the south-east round to the north-west, although like any offshore moorings or anchorage in the Solent are susceptible to wash from commercial traffic.

You should contact the club on VHF ChM10 before picking up a mooring. The club also maintains a ferry service for getting ashore, which runs up until 1700. At other times, even in settled conditions, take great care when using a small tender, as the moorings are quite exposed and there is a strong current in this area.

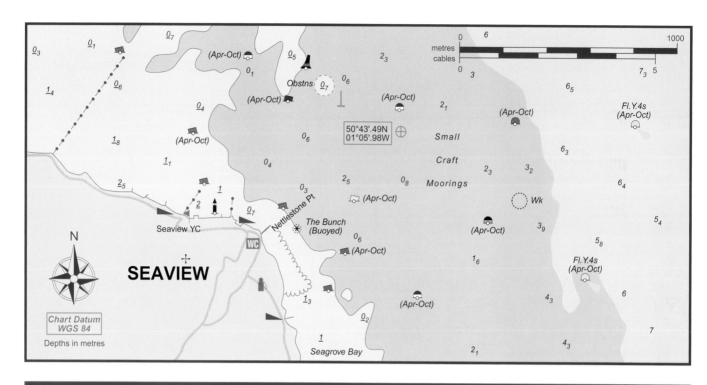

Useful information – Seaview

FACILITIES
The club is a popular destination for visiting clubs and offers good facilities, including showers, toilets and a bar and restaurant.

PROVISIONING
Seaview has a post office, a shop that sells sailing clothing, and a small grocery store, the Galley Provisions, useful for basic items.

The Seaview Hotel and Restaurant is a highly regarded place to eat

EATING OUT
For such a small village you are spoilt for choice – with its glorious spithead views, the Seaview Yacht Club (Tel: 01983 613268) welcomes affiliated yacht club members and is most visitors' choice, especially for its excellent value Sunday lunch. Booking ahead is advised, particularly at weekends during the summer, when the club is packed with Sea View One-Design and Mermaid sailors.

Next door to the club is the popular Old Fort Bar Café (Tel: 01983 612363), with crab sandwiches being a speciality. Fifty yards up the road is the world-famous Seaview Hotel and Restaurant (Tel: 01983 612711), which offers specialities such as lobster, crab and sea bass, while a little further along is the Khrua Thai Orchid (Tel: 01983 568899) restaurant, which has a takeaway service, too. Opposite, the Copper Kettle (Tel: 01983 612230) tea shop has a well-deserved reputation for delicious homemade snacks and cakes.

The pebble beach at Seaview has magnificent views across the Solent

Seaview Yacht Club welcomes visiting yachtsmen from affiliated clubs

Bembridge Harbour is well protected from most directions. There is also a good marina in the harbour, with excellent facilities for visiting yachtsmen

Bembridge

Entrance to Bembridge Harbour: 50°42'.34N 01°05'.36W

Bembridge is a compact, pretty harbour whose entrance, although limited by the tides, is well sheltered in all but north to northeasterly gales. Offering excellent sailing clubs, beautiful beaches and fine restaurants, this Isle of Wight port is a first class haven with plenty of charm.

NAVIGATION

Charts: Admiralty Charts: SC5600, 2022, 2037, 2045; Imray: C3, C9, C15, 2200; Stanfords: chartpack 10, chartpack 24, chartpack 25, L11

Tides: HW Springs are 20 minutes after and Neaps the same time as HW Portsmouth. LW Neaps are 20 minutes and Springs 1 hour after LW Portsmouth. MHWS: 3.2m; MHWN: 2.4m; MLWN: 0.6m; MLW S: 0.2m.

The tide gauge lies 400m east of the meandering but well-marked channel, from where the Duver shore white landmark is prominent

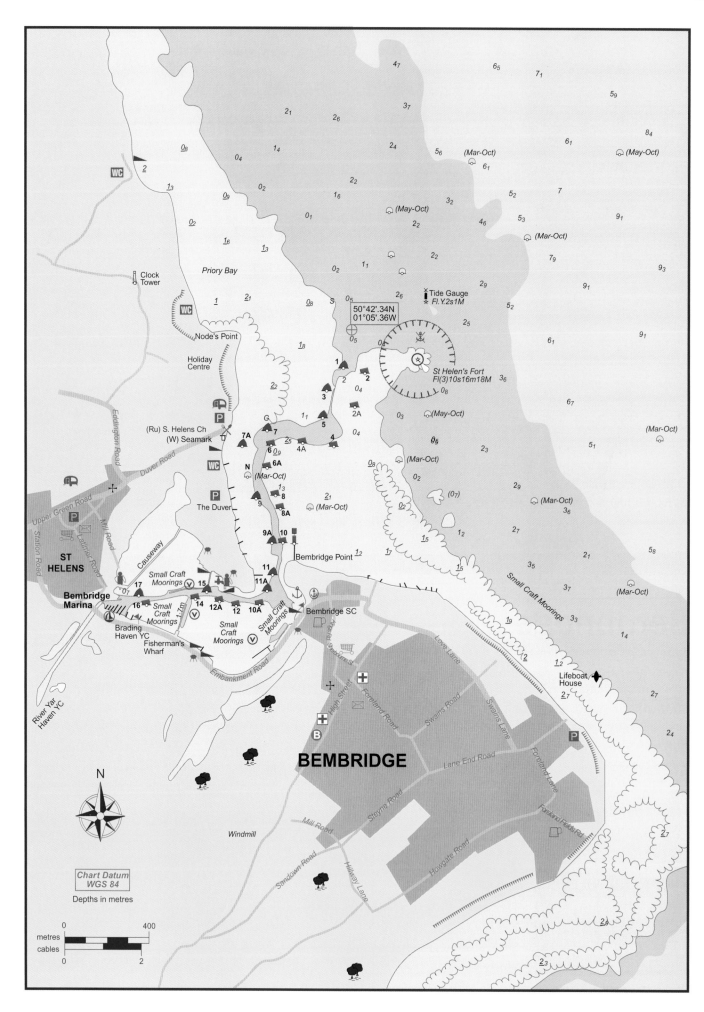

Priory Bay

Clock
Tower

WC

Node's Point

Holiday
Centre

(Ru) S. Helens Ch
(W) Seamark

P

WC

N

The Duver

P

Causeway

ST
HELENS

Bembridge
Marina

Brading
Haven YC

Fisherman's
Wharf

River Yar
Haven YC

G

7A   7
6   0.9
6A

8
9

8A

9A   10

11

11A

15
17
16   12A 12 10A
14

Small Craft
Moorings

Small
Craft
Moorings

Small
Craft
Moorings

Small Craft
Moorings

Bembridge Point

Bembridge SC

Embankment Road

1

3

5

2A

4
4A

Tide Gauge
Fl.Y.2s1M

50°42'.34N
01°05'.36W

St Helen's Fort
Fl(3)10s16m18M

(May-Oct)

(Mar-Oct)

(May-Oct)

(Mar-Oct)

(May-Oct)

(Mar-Oct)

(Mar-Oct)

(Mar-Oct)

(Mar-Oct)

Small Craft Moorings

Lifeboat
House

P

B

BEMBRIDGE

High Street

Foreland Road

Love Lane

Swains Road

Swains Lane

Lane End Road

Foreland Lane

Steyne Road

Howgate Road

Hillway Lane

Mill Road

Sandown Road

Foreland Fields Rd

Windmill

N

Chart Datum
WGS 84

Depths in metres

metres
0   400

cables
0   2

Bembridge can accommodate around 100 visiting yachts, but it can get very busy peak season, so it pays to arrive early if you want to guarantee a berth

Approaches: From the north-west, the rocks and shoals off Nettlestone and Nodes Point should be given a good offing. Coming from the south-east, Bembridge Ledge (BYB Q [3] 10s) and St Helen's Fort (Fl 3 10s 16m 8M) are the port-hand marks. During March to October there are numerous unlit, yellow racing buoys around Bembridge and Seaview. The entrance can be difficult in north to northeasterly gales.

Pilotage: Thanks to the conspicuous St Helen's Fort and the Duver shore white seamark, identifying the entrance to Bembridge is straightforward. Make a course for the Bembridge tide gauge (Fl Y 2s top mark 'X'; position 50°42'.46N 01°05'.02W), which is 400m east of the unlit but well buoyed channel. Keep at least 200m off St Helen's Fort (position 50°42'.30N 01°05'.05W). The tide gauge, which is marked in metres, indicates the minimum depth of water in the approach channel. When the Portsmouth High Water is less than 4m, the depth in the channel sometimes does not exceed 1.6m, so on those days in particular do not ignore the tide gauge.

A course of 240° from the tide gauge beacon brings you to the start of the channel and the first of the numbered buoys (even numbers are to port, odd to starboard). From sea level, the twisting channel looks confusing but by carefully checking off the buoys' numbers and with a rising tide (recommended entry for a 1.5m [4ft 9in] draught boat is three hours before High Water), you should encounter no difficulty. With its unlit, meandering buoys a night-time approach into Bembridge is inadvisable. Once through the entrance, past 11A, turn west. About 200m further on, the Duver visitors' marina, which is equipped with electricity and water, lies to starboard. The speed limit in the harbour is six knots.

BERTHING

Bembridge can accommodate approximately 100 visiting yachts but during the summer, especially on weekends, it often gets completely full, and unfortunately it is not possible to book a berth in advance. Although the

St Helen's Fort stands guard to the east of Bembridge's entrance

Bembridge's inner harbour is well marked and anyone visiting should follow the numbered buoys that identify the channel

channel becomes too shallow for most yachts at mid-tide, Duver Marina is dredged to about 2m. The marina is the main place to berth for visiting yachts, and currently has 80 berths although there are plans to install another 40. Bembridge Marina, at the western end of the harbour, has no specific visitors' berths, although if there is space available, the harbour staff may be able to squeeze you in. There are also some small craft drying visitors' moorings south-west of Bembridge Sailing Club.

Anchoring is forbidden in the harbour, but multihulls and bilge-keeled vessels are allowed to run up the beach to port, just inside the entrance, for a flat fee (see below). Fisherman's Wharf, or Embankment Marina as it is now known, on the southern shore has a few visitors' berths but the numbers are very restricted.

For berthing instructions and availability, contact Bembridge Harbour on VHF Ch 80; Tel: 01983 872828. **Berthing fees:** Duver Marina pontoon: March to October: £2.20 per metre per night, November to February: £1.50 per metre. Short stay (one tide): up to 7.5m (24ft 6in): £6 (mid-week and weekends); over 7.5m: £10 (weekends and Bank Holidays), £6 (mid-week). Seven nights for a 10m (32ft 8in) yacht: £132. If you are planning to stay any longer than a week, contact the harbourmaster in advance. Beach moorings: boats under 7.5m: £6, over 7.5m: £10. All prices may be subject to a small increase.

Bembridge Sailing Club lies in the eastern corner of the harbour. Permanent moorings are laid in front of the club, the majority of which dry at Low Water

Visiting yachts berth alongside the pontoons at Duver Marina

Useful information – Bembridge

FACILITIES

Showers, toilets and laundry facilities are located ashore at Duver Marina, while water and electricity are available on its pontoons. Diesel can be obtained from the H Attril & Sons (Tel: 01983 872319) pontoon or Ken Stratton's Boatyard, north of Bembridge Marina, but there are plans for a floating fuel pontoon to be installed next to the water-taxi berth at Duver Marina during winter 2007. Petrol in cans is available from the Hodge & Childs Peugeot garage (Tel: 01983 872121) in Church Row, Bembridge. None of the above are open on Sundays, so you should call them in advance.

A water taxi ferries people around the harbour and, with its callsign as 'Bembridge Water Taxi', can be contacted on VHF Ch 80; Tel: 01983 872828. During April, May, June and September it operates three hours either side of High Water, while in July and August it runs throughout the day and evening. Price: adult single: £1; child single: 50p.

Brading Haven Yacht Club (Tel: 01983 872289), east of the marina, and Bembridge Sailing Club (Tel: 01983 872237), in the eastern

Both Brading Haven Yacht Club and Bembridge Sailing Club have active dinghy fleets

corner of the harbour, have their own private jetties for tenders. The former welcomes visitors to its bar and restaurant. If you need any repairs, the slipway can be used for boats up to 25 tons and there are several boatyards in the vicinity (see p111 for contact details).

PROVISIONING

Conveniently situated in Duver Marina, the Galley is a licensed deli selling, among other things, excellent homemade fish pies, quiches and lobsters and, for

breakfast, barbecued bacon sandwiches. It is open seven days a week from 0830.

Although a good 30-minute walk from the marina, Bembridge village, east of the harbour, has a comprehensive range of shops. Davids supermarket in Sherbourne Street is closest to the harbour but, a few steps further on, the High Street is home to the more conventional shopping outlets – Food for Thought Delicatessen, the Bembridge Bakery and the butchers Woodford & Son. There is

also a Lloyds TSB bank in the High Street, although without a cashpoint. There is one, however, at Davids supermarket. Other facilities include a post office in Forelands Road and a chemist in the High Street.

St Helens, on the western side, is closer to the marina and can be reached via a wooden footbridge after which you walk up Latimer Road to the village green. Here you will find a post office, incorporating a cashpoint, and the local store, which conveniently

Bembridge is a lovely place to spend a day or two, even in peak season

Bembridge's traditional butchers is a 30-minute walk from the marina

Useful information – Bembridge

stays open from 0800–2000 all year round. It is good for vital provisions, but if you need to stock up seriously you would be better off going to Davids in Bembridge or catching the bus to Ryde, on the way to which is a Tesco.

EATING OUT

With five pubs, two hotels and two restaurants in Bembridge alone, there is certainly no shortage of places to eat in this area. The nearest pub, the Pilot Boat Inn (Tel: 01983 872077), is just a water taxi-ride from the marina and has a good restaurant serving local seafood. A bit further afield, the Crab & Lobster Inn (Tel: 01983 872244), offers superb views of the eastern approaches to the Solent and enjoys a reputation for its bar meals and evening à la carte menu. Not surprisingly, its speciality is seafood.

Serving bar food of an equally high standard is the Windmill Hotel & Restaurant (Tel: 01983 872875). Its Garden Room Restaurant also comes highly recommended and has an excellent wine list. For a convivial atmosphere, go to

Fox's Restaurant (Tel: 01983 872626) in the High Street which, besides evening meals, offers morning coffees and light lunches. For fish and chips try the Bay Tree (Tel: 01983 873334), which is on Foreland Road .

On the St Helens' side you are equally spoilt for choice. In St Helens alone there are two restaurants, the Ganders (Tel: 01983 872014) and St Helens Restaurant and Bar (Tel: 01983 872303), both of which serve high quality, bistro-type food. Alternatively, try the Vine Inn (Tel: 01983 872337) for good pub grub.

One restaurant that shouldn't be overlooked is Baywatch on the Beach (Tel: 01983 873259). Located in a superb position in St Helens Bay, it serves outstanding seafood as well as steaks, pastas, vegetarian dishes and light snacks. It opens from March to November and, as with all restaurants in this area, booking in advance peak season is necessary.

If you really want to spoil your crew then you would be hard pushed to beat the Priory Bay Hotel (Tel: 01983

613146). Set in spectacular surroundings with magnificent views across the bay, it is not too far away to walk to from the marina. With ingredients sourced locally whenever possible, the menu, although fairly expensive, is very special. Book in advance.

ASHORE

Surrounded on three sides by the sea, Bembridge is renowned for its beautiful, quiet sandy beaches, many of which are covered at High Water. The tide drops, however, to reveal some fascinating rock pools, and Forelands beach in particular is strewn with interesting

shells. It is well worth going on one of the spectacular walks around Bembridge; the route over Culver Down to Sandown, for example, provides some of the best views on the island. If you are a keen walker, the Bembridge Trail takes you from the harbour along the old sea wall to Brading. Alternatively, if pushed for time, there are several shorter walks. For details, contact the Tourist Office (Tel: 01983 813813).

Bembridge is justly recognised for its abundance of water birds. To observe them at close quarters, the best place is the mill wall, which separates the harbour from the old mill

The windmill is now owned by the National Trust and open to the public

Although in completely different surroundings, both Baywatch on the Beach (left) and the Crab and Lobster Inn (right) offer spectacular sea views

The lifeboat station is open to the public several days a week during the summer. There are also some excellent walks nearby, along the beach

pond. Kingfishers, lapwings, curlews and little egrets are just some of the inhabitants you are likely to see.

The town of Bembridge itself has several attractions, including an art gallery that displays the work of local artists and, a little inland, the Bembridge Windmill (Tel: 01983 873945). Built in 1700, this was a working mill until the First World War. During the Great War it sheltered the Volunteer Reserves while in the Second World War it served as the headquarters to the local Home Guard and was used as an army lookout post. Complete with sails, the windmill is now owned by the National Trust and is open to the public daily between March and October.

The Bembridge Lifeboat Station (Tel: 01983 872201) is open to the public, too, but only during the summer on three afternoons a week and on Bank Holidays.

Despite the age of mobile phones, it is worth taking the trouble to use the public phone box in Bembridge. Made in 1921 and therefore older than British Telecom itself, this is the only

remaining Post Office kiosk 1 phone box in southern England. With its metal spike and distinctive shape, it is hard to miss.

If you have time to explore further afield there are plenty of other attractions in nearby towns and villages. The ancient port of Brading, for example, is steeped in history and incorporates one of the oldest parish churches on the island, believed to date back to the 12th century. Brading is also home to the popular Wax Works (Tel: 01983 407286, open daily from 1000–1700, from Easter to October) and a Roman villa, whose fine mosaic floors can still be seen today (Tel: 01983 406223, open daily from 0930–1700).

Not far from Brading are the beautiful mansions of Nunwell House and Gardens (Tel: 01983 407240) and

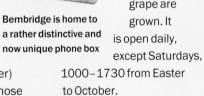

Bembridge is home to a rather distinctive and now unique phone box

Morton Manor (Tel: 01983 406168). The former, which has a history extending over five centuries, was visited by King Henry VIII and was where King Charles I spent his last night of freedom. It is open from the beginning of July to the early part of September, 1300–1700, Mondays, Tuesdays and Wednesdays.

Morton Manor is set in delightful gardens with a vineyard in which seven varieties of grape are grown. It is open daily, except Saturdays, 1000–1730 from Easter to October.

TRANSPORT

Buses: Southern Vectis (Tel: 01983 827000) runs hourly bus services in the summer between Bembridge and the harbour, Ryde, Sandown and Newport, from where you

will find connections to other parts of the island.

Taxis: Bembridge & Harbour Taxis (Tel: 01983 874132); Diamond Taxis, Ryde (Tel: 01983 811593).

OTHER INFORMATION

Bembridge Harbour (includes information on Duver Marina): VHF Ch80; Tel: 01983 872828.
Brading Haven Yacht Club: Tel: 01983 872289.
Bembridge Sailing Club: Tel: 01983 872686; Tel: 01983 872237.
Bembridge Water Taxi: VHF Ch 80; Tel: 01983 872828.
Boatyard/engineers: Bembridge Boatyard Marine Works: Tel: 01983 872911; Bembridge Outboards: Tel: 01983 872817; H Attrill & Sons: Tel: 01983 872319.
Police: Tel: 999; Tel: 0845 0454545.
Coastguard: Lee on Solent: Tel: 023 9255 2100.
Hospital: St Mary's Newport: Tel: 01983 524081.
Doctor: St Helens Health Centre: Tel: 01983 872772.
NHS Direct: Tel: 0845 4647.
Dental helpline: Tel: 01983 537424.
Tourist Information Office: Tel: 01983 813813.

Ventnor

Harbour entrance: 50°35'.54N 01°12'.23W
Deep-water moorings: 50°35'.44N 01°12'.24W
to 50°35'.41N 01°12'.44W

Ventnor, a traditional seaside town, is the only harbour on the south side of the Isle of Wight. It lies about four miles east of St Catherine's Point, making it a convenient place to stop off if circumnavigating the island, crossing the Channel, or day sailing from the Solent. However, this drying haven, primarily built for local fishing boats, does have its limitations and is really only suitable for small craft up to 9m (30ft) in length that are able to take the sandy bottom. Larger yachts may be able to pick up one of the eight deep-water moorings just off the harbour entrance, but only in settled weather (Force 3 or under).

NAVIGATION

Charts: Admiralty Charts: SC5600, 2045; Imray: C3;
Stanfords: S11
Tides: HW Springs are 30 minutes before and
Neaps 25 minutes before HW Portsmouth. LW Neaps

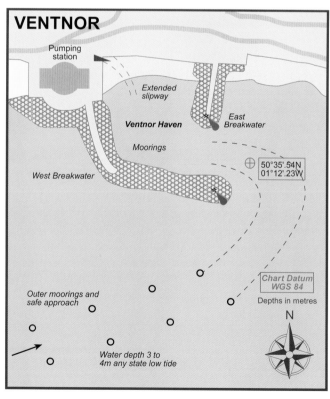

VENTNOR

Pumping station

Extended slipway

Ventnor Haven

East Breakwater

Moorings

West Breakwater

50°35'.54N
01°12'.23W

Outer moorings and safe approach

Chart Datum WGS 84

Depths in metres

N

Water depth 3 to
4m any state low tide

are 25 minutes and Springs 30 minutes before LW Portsmouth. MHWS: 3.9m; MHWN: 3.2m; MLWN: 1.7m; MLWS: 1m.

Pilotage: Keep well offshore in soundings until the haven bears approximately north, at which point make a course for the outer deep-water moorings. The mooring buoys are laid east to west in two rows of four, with the end ones being flagged. The waypoint for the western end of these moorings is 50°35′.41N 01°12′.44W and the eastern end is 50°35′.44N 01°12′.24W. Depths here are around 4m at Low Water Springs.

Yachts heading for the haven should make their approach through the middle of the line of mooring buoys, using them as a back transit until the entrance opens up to port. This approach is essential to avoid the many lobster pots laid by the Ventnor fishermen. The haven is a drying harbour, although there is about 0.6m of water at Low Water Neaps. The best time for yachts drawing 1.5m (5ft) to enter the harbour is about 1½ hours either side of High Water, but it is probably best to contact the harbourmaster on Tel: 07976 009260 or VHF Ch 80 (callsign Ventnor harbourmaster) before approaching to find out tidal height information.

BERTHING

Contact the harbourmaster for berthing availability.
Berthing fees: Berths in the haven cost £1 per metre for up to three hours, £1.50 per metre for the day or £2 per metre for an overnight stay. The deep-water moorings cost £1 per metre per day or £2 per metre for an overnight stay.

A water taxi service runs from 1000 to 2200 in the summer and from 1000 to 1700 in the winter. This service is free inside the haven, but there is a charge of £1 per person to the outer moorings. To use the water taxi, call the harbourmaster on Tel: 07976 009260 or VHF Ch 80.

Useful information – Ventnor

Ventnor's harbour dries, so check with the harbourmaster before entering

The Spyglass Inn sits right on the water's edge

FACILITIES

The haven is due to have its own showers and toilets as well as a bistro and fish restaurant by Summer 2008. Also part of the haven development currently underway is an on site chandlery and yacht repair service. There are no convenient gas or fuel supplies nearby, so make sure they are not needed when planning a visit.

PROVISIONING

The main part of Ventnor is a rigorous three-minute walk up the hill from the haven. Here you will find reasonable amenities, including a Somerfield supermarket.

EATING OUT

The Esplanade adjacent to the haven has various cafés and restaurants, including two pubs, the Mill Bay Inn (Tel: 01983 852892) and the Spy Glass Inn (Tel: 01983 855338), both of which serve locally caught fish and seafood. The Spy Glass, at the western end of the bay, is full of nautical artefacts that create an atmosphere reminiscent of the days of smuggling and piracy. Locally recommended is the wine bar The Met (Tel: 01983 855441). Situated next to the Mill Bay Inn, the Mediterranean-style bar serves a variety of tapas in the evenings.

ASHORE

Protected by St Boniface Down, the highest point on the Isle of Wight, Ventnor has a microclimate that encourages varied wildlife and lush vegetation. Believing this climate was ideal for respiratory diseases, the Victorians developed Ventnor as a health resort and referred to it as 'England's Madeira'. Among the attractions is Ventnor Botanic Garden, built on the 22-acre site of the former Royal National Hospital for Diseases of the Chest. Located just to the west of Ventnor, the garden's visitor centre (Tel: 01983 855397) is open daily 1000 to 1800.

From the gardens you can walk down to Steephill Cove, a traditional fishing bay that is, as yet, unspoilt by tourism and is thought by some people to be the prettiest place on the island.

Alternatively, you could walk east of Ventnor, along the sea wall, to Bonchurch, a quaint village that has an 11th-century church.

The town's centre for entertainment and arts is the Ventnor Winter Gardens (Tel: 01983 855215). Situated on Pier Street, at the top of the Esplanade, it hosts a Jazz festival in April and a Blues and Folk festival in September. A carnival is held in Ventnor in mid-August.

Portsmouth Harbour

Entrance to Portsmouth Harbour: 50°47'.38N 01°06'.67W

One of the world's great naval bases, Portsmouth is inextricably linked with maritime history. Among Britain's premier waterfront destinations, it is a naturally formed and well-protected harbour offering yachtsmen a choice of marinas with comprehensive facilities as well as a wealth of visitors' attractions.

The war memorial and block of flats are the Swashway's leading marks

NAVIGATION

Charts: Admiralty Charts: SC5600, 2036, 2037, 2045, 2628, 2629, 2631; Imray: C3, C9, C15, 2200; Stanfords: 11, chartpack 10, chartpack 24, L1
Tides: Portsmouth is a standard port. MHWS: 4.7m; MHWN: 3.8m; MLWN: 1.9m; MLWS: 0.8m.
Strong winds from the north-east to south-east combined with high pressure may lower tide levels by 1m and delay High Water and Low Water times by an hour. The opposite may occur in strong westerlies with a low pressure.

Approaches: From the east, the submerged barrier running from Horse Sand Fort north to Southsea means passing south of the fort unless you take the short cut on a rising tide through the barrier at the Main Passage (waypoint 50°46'.00N 01°04'.10W). The gap in the barrier is marked by a south dolphin (Q R) and a starboard pile.

Approaching from the west, craft can use the Swashway channel north-west of Spitbank Fort, which has a depth of about 2m. Ideally you should cross Spit Sand on approximately 049°, giving you the transit of the

Portsmouth Harbour has a long and distinguished maritime history, and is now thriving as a major yachting destination in the Solent

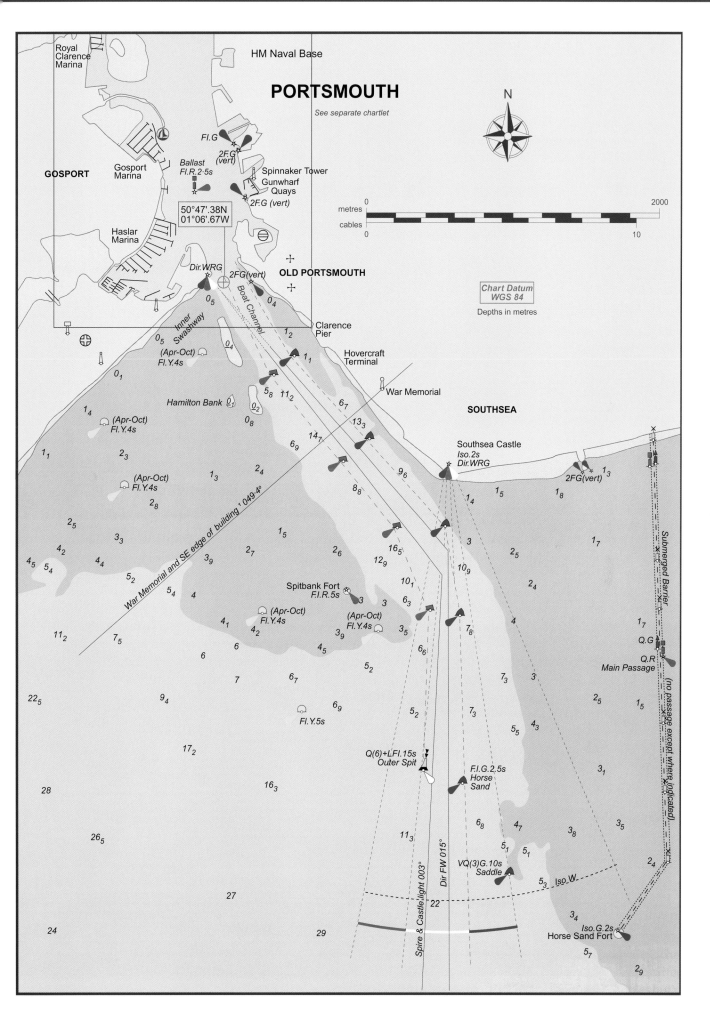

Boats under 20m must use the Small Boat channel in and out of Portsmouth

The PHM Ballast Beacon must be left close to port when entering the harbour

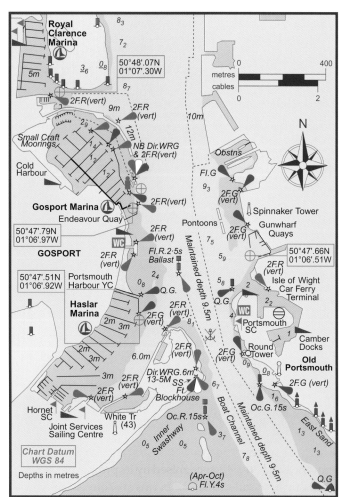

prominent war memorial and the right-hand side of an isolated block of flats on the Southsea shore. Resident boats often use the inner Swashway channel, a short cut along the Haslar shore. However, with numerous obstructions and the unpredictable Hamilton Bank, it needs local knowledge. It should also be noted that vessels over 20m (65ft) are forbidden to use this channel.

Pilotage: The entrance and inner harbour can be extremely congested with commercial and naval shipping. Keep a keen lookout for the Isle of Wight ferries and hovercrafts using the Swashway channel and making 90° turns to or from the main channel. When entering or leaving Portsmouth Harbour craft up to 20m (65ft) LOA must use the Small Boat channel on the western edge of the main channel and all yachts with engines are obliged to motor from abeam the No 4 Bar Buoy (see below), just outside the entrance to the east, to the inner PHM Ballast Beacon.

The Small Boat channel, which is 50m wide, starts from No 4 Bar Buoy QR (Position 50°47'.01N 01°06'.36W), which is about 0.5M from the entrance bearing 332° to waypoint 50°47'.38N 01°06'.67W. It extends about 50m from Fort Blockhouse (keep as close to the red marks as possible) and runs inside the harbour to the Ballast Beacon PHM (Fl R 2.5s). Note that vessels under 20m (65ft) LOA must past the Ballast Beacon close to port when entering the harbour and close to starboard when leaving it. At night the Oc R sector (324°–330°) of the Dir WRG lt (6m 13-5M) on Fort Blockhouse covers the Small Boat Channel until close to the entrance, after which the ISO R 2s sector 337.5°–345° of the Dir WRG lt (2m 1M) to the east of

Gosport Marina takes you through the entrance on 341° to close abeam of the PHM Ballast Beacon. Yachtsmen using the Small Boat channel who wish to cross the harbour from the west to the east side of the main channel must call the QHM on VHF Ch 11 for permission and only cross once they are north of the Ballast Beacon. When crossing from east to west, the same procedure is necessary. Note that all craft must keep 50m clear of MOD facilities, including berthed warships.

The Spinnaker Tower is a distinctive landmark at the entrance to the harbour

Haslar Marina

Haslar Marina entrance: 50°47'.51N 01°06'.92W

This marina lies to port on the western side of the harbour entrance and is easily recognised by its prominent lightship. Dedicated visitors' berths are conveniently located on the pontoons immediately shoreside of the lightship. There are no tidal access restrictions into Haslar and, with 24-hour staffing, lighting and cameras, it is a secure place if you need to leave your boat for some time.

For berthing availability, contact the marina on VHF Channel 80 or call Tel: 023 9260 1201.

Berthing fees: The daily summer rate is £2.80 per metre on a weekend and £2.65 per metre midweek, while a short stay (under four hours) costs between £7 and £10. Winter rates are cheaper, with an overnight stay costing £1.40 per metre and between £4 and £6 for a short stay.

Useful information – Haslar Marina

FACILITIES

Although the marina lacks a fuel pump, the Gosport Marina fuel jetty is only a couple of hundred metres to the north, and the rest of the facilities at Haslar Marina are excellent. Water and electricity are available on the pontoons while shower blocks are located on the lightship, as well as on pontoons A and G.

The lightship also incorporates a restaurant and launderette, while telephone and fax machines can be found in the marina office. Other amenities include rubbish and oil waste disposal units, gas, which can be obtained from the on-site chandlery, and ice (available from the marina office at £1.50 per bag). For repairs there is a comprehensive range of independent marine operators from engineering to yacht rigging (see under 'Other Information' on p119 for contact details).

The marina office is manned 24 hours a day and staff will keep any incoming mail for up to 45 days.

PROVISIONING

For provisioning, eating out and information on things to do ashore, see p118.

Haslar's lightship houses a restaurant, bar, launderette and shower block

Landers Bar & Restaurant, near to the marina office

Gosport Marina

Gosport Marina entrance: 50°47'.84N 01°06'.98W

About 400m north of Haslar Marina (just north of the PHM Ballast Beacon), again on the port-hand side, lies the entrance to Gosport Marina. With 150 visitors' berths available, there is usually plenty of room for visiting yachts, but you should contact the marina in advance on VHF Ch 80 or Tel: 023 9252 4811 to check availability.

Berthing fees: An overnight stay in the marina during the summer season for a 10m (33ft) yacht is £25 while a short stay of up to four hours is £7. These prices may be subject to a slight increase.

Gosport Marina is geared up for visiting yachts, with 150 berths available

Useful information

The fuel barge at Gosport Marina is very conveniently located

FACILITIES

The fuel barge, on the marina's southern entrance breakwater, is manned in the summer from 0900–1745 and in winter from 0900–1445. Other services include showers and a launderette, as well as water and electricity on the pontoons.

As with Haslar Marina, there are numerous boatyard and engineering facilities in and around the premises, including Endeavour Quay (Tel: 023 9258 4200), see p119, which is situated on the site of the former Camper & Nicholsons yard.

PROVISIONING

Gosport High Street is just a few minutes' walk away from both Haslar and Gosport marinas and has everything from chemists and newsagents to banks and post offices. Morrisons supermarket is at the very top of the High Street.

The open-air market in the High Street takes place on Tuesdays and Saturdays and is reputed to be among the largest in Hampshire.

If the shopping facilities at Gosport don't suffice, you could always hop on a ferry to Gunwharf Quays, on the opposite side of the harbour (see p122) where there is a plethora of shops both on the historic waterfront and in Portsmouth city centre.

EATING OUT

With an abundance of restaurants and pubs you won't starve in Gosport. If you like oriental food, then the Great Wall Chinese Restaurant (Tel: 023 9250 3388) on the High Street comes highly recommended and provides superb views of the harbour. As an alternative, the T&J Chinese Restaurant (Tel: 023 9258 2564) can be found a little further away on South Street and offers an excellent takeaway and delivery service. If Indian food appeals to your taste buds more then the New Bengal (Tel: 023 9258 3722) on Stoke Road serves good food in convivial surroundings while, practically next door, is the New Jalalabad Balti House (Tel: 023 9258 2927).

A good view can be had at The Pebble Beach (Tel: 023 9251 0789), situated on the beach at Stokes Bay and well known for its Italian and French cuisine, or, if you don't mind a 15-minute ferry ride, at the historic Spitbank Fort (Tel: 01329 242077). It is a good idea to phone ahead of time, though, to see when they are serving food.

Another original setting can be found in the bar and restaurant on board Portsmouth Harbour Yacht Club's old lightship, *Mary Mouse 2*, in Haslar Marina (Tel: 023 9252 5200). Originally built in 1947, this lightship was on station in several locations off the East Coast of England and the English Channel before being decommissioned in 1993.

There are plenty of pubs in the area, including the Clarence Tavern (Tel: 023 9252 9726) on Clarence Road, established for its good food and efficient service. Alternatively, try the Jolly Roger (Tel: 023 9258 2584) at Priddys Hard, right on the water's edge, or Landers Bar and Restaurant (Tel: 023 9258 8810), which is at the northern end of Haslar Bridge, opposite Haslar Marina.

The High Street has numerous fast food outlets and cafés, including McDonalds, Burger King and Frydays, which is good for fish and chips, and Costa Coffee. You can always take a ferry to the eastern side of Portsmouth Harbour, too, where there is an even greater selection of restaurants to choose from. See p123 for details.

Endeavour Quay

Entrance to Endeavour Quay: **50°47'.79N 01°06'.97W**

Established in Spring 2006, Endeavour Quay is situated on the site of the former legendary Camper & Nicholsons boatyard, whose famous builds included four of the 10 J-Class yachts and Sir Francis Chichester's ketch *Gipsy Moth IV*. Today run by Marina Projects, which also operates the nearby Royal Clarence Marina (see p120), the yard offers a range of services and welcomes all types of craft, ranging from small 5m (16ft) sailing yachts to Grand Prix race boats.

Endeavour Quay has deep-water access at all states of the tide

FACILITIES

The site provides around 4,250m² of secure undercover space for vessels of up to 40m (131ft) in length and has a 37-tonne crane and a 180-tonne boat hoist, as well as a dock area with deep-water access at all states of the tide. Yachts come to the yard for a variety of services, from new builds and major refits to maintenance, storage or even a simple scrub off. Skilled marine specialists also based on site include: Boatshed.com (yacht brokers): Tel: 023 9258 5546; Hillyards (traditional yacht repairs and maintenance): Tel: 023 9250 3218; Kiwi Marine Ltd (rigging services): Tel: 023 9251 0900; Marine Composites (UK) Ltd (yacht repairs and maintenance): Tel: 023 9252 4553; MarineTech Engineering (marine engineers): Tel: 023 9252 5858 and Tyne Slipway (boat repairs): Tel: 023 9251 3749.

Endeavour Quay can be contacted on Tel: 023 9258 4200.

Useful information – Gosport

The Castle Tavern on Mumby Road is one of several pubs in Gosport

The retro Sweet Talk café is a refreshing new addition to Gosport

USEFUL CONTACTS

Marinas: Haslar Marina: VHF Ch 80; Tel: 023 9260 1201. Gosport Marina: Tel: 023 9252 4811. Hardway Marine: Tel: 023 9258 0420.

Portsmouth Harbour Yacht Club: Tel: 023 9222 2228

Chandleries: Peculiars Chandler (Haslar): Tel: 023 9258 8815; Solent Marine, Mumby Road: Tel: 023 9258 4622; Arthurs Chandlery: Tel: 023 9252 6522.

Marine engineers/repairs: Motortech Marine Engineering: Tel: 023 9251 3200; Marine Maintenance: Tel: 023 9260 2344; Endeavour Quay: Tel: 023 92584200; Hillyards: Tel: 023 92503218; Marine Composites: 023 9252 4553; MarineTech Engineering: Tel: 023 9252 5858; Tyne Slipway: 023 9251 3749; Gosport Boat Yard: Tel: 023 9258 6216; XW Rigging at Haslar Marina: Tel: 023 9251 3553; Hardway Marine Tel: 023 9258 0420.

Electronic repairs: AW Marine: Tel: 023 9260 2344.

Sail repairs: A & V Leisure: Tel: 023 9251 0204; Hood Sails: Tel: 01590 675011; North Sails: Tel: 01329 231525; Ratsey & Lapthorne Sails: Tel: 01983 294051 (a sail collection and delivery point is based at Gosport Marina).

Police: Tel: 999; Tel: 023 9258 4666.

Hospitals: Royal Hospital Haslar: Tel: 023 9258 4255; (Minor Accident Unit) Tel: 023 9276 2414; Queen Alexandra Tel: 023 9228 6000.

Coastguard: Lee on Solent: Tel: 023 9255 2100.

NHS Direct: Tel: 0845 4647.

Doctor: (Gunwharf Quays): Tel: 023 9282 1371.

Dentist: Tel: 023 9273 6078.

Tourist information office: Gosport Tel: 023 9252 2944.

TRANSPORT

For information on transport in the area, see p133.

Royal Clarence Marina

Marina entrance: 50°48'.07N 01°07'.30W

Immediately to the north of Gosport Marina is the Royal Clarence Marina, set in a deep-water basin in front of the Royal Navy's former victualling yard. It was here in the 1700s that beer was brewed for the fleet, before the site was converted in the 1830s to the Royal Clarence Victualling Yard. A slaughterhouse, granary and a couple of mills all formed part of this facility. Today, it's a marina owned by Marina Projects, which also operates Endeavour Quay (see p119), and enjoys a lovely setting that is conveniently close to Gosport town centre. It is also the headquarters of Clipper Ventures which, set up by Sir Robin Knox-Johnston in 1995, owns the rights to the Clipper Round the World yacht race and the Velux 5 Oceans (former BOC Challenge/Around Alone).

BERTHING

The berths are well sheltered and, with depths of 5m below chart datum, are accessible at all states of the tide. As well as accommodating yachts of up to 18m (59ft) LOA on its finger berths, the marina also has several heavy duty pontoons suitable for superyachts of up to 65m (213ft) LOA. To find out about berthing availability, Tel: 023 9252 3810 or VHF Ch 80, callsign Royal Clarence Marina.
Berthing fees: Overnight in season (April to Sept), 9.1-12m (30-39ft): £24 per night; 12-15m (39-49ft): £32 per night. Overnight out of season (Oct to March), 9.1-12m (30-39ft): £18 per night; 12-15m (39-49ft): £29 per night. Short stay (up to four hours): up to 12m (39ft): £12 (summer), £10 (winter); 12-18m (39-59ft): £17 (summer), £14 (winter).

Royal Clarence Marina is a relatively new addition to the harbour. Although still in the development stage, it has good potential

Useful information – Royal Clarence Marina

FACILITIES
All pontoons are equipped with electricity and water, but overnight visitors are charged an additional £3 for the use of electricity. Showers, toilets and a launderette are housed in the facilities block, which is situated next to the marina office in Cooperage Green. Containers for disposing rubbish can be found next to the bridgehead.

The marina also offers wireless internet access and, with further development currently underway, more facilities should be available in 2008.

PROVISIONING AND EATING OUT
An on-site convenience store is part of the marina

The Pump House coffee shop

Useful information – Royal Clarence Marina

development and is due to open by mid-summer 2008. The nearest supermarket is Morrisons on Walpole Road, Gosport, which is about 10 minutes away on foot.

Already established on the site is one of Gosport's finest coffee shops, the Pump House (Tel: 023 9252 5522), which serves a selection of hot meals, sandwiches, paninis and baguettes. Now fully licensed, it also hosts a tapas night every Friday and is happy to provide catering for yachts, particularly for rallies using the marina.

For further information on provisioning and eating out in Gosport, see p118-19.

Former Naval buildings surround the marina

The marina has plenty of room for visitors and is also the base for several sea schools and Sir Robin Knox-Johnston's round-the-world Clipper Race

Hardway Marine   Hardway visitors' moorings: 50°48'.87N 01°07'.89W

North of Royal Clarence Marina, still on your port-hand side, is Hardway Marine, which offers deep-water swinging moorings to visitors. For more information on availability, Tel: 01329 825861.
Berthing fees: Contact Hardway Marine for more details.

FACILITIES

Toilets and showers can be found ashore and gas, diesel and water is also available here. Other facilities include a drying berth for fin-keelers (Tel: 023 9258 0420 for booking details) and a full repair service and well-stocked on-site chandlery.

PROVISIONING

The nearest shop at which you can buy basic provisions is about a five-minute walk away. Otherwise go to Gosport town centre, which takes about 20 minutes to get to on foot.

See p118-119 for more information on provisioning and where to eat out and p130-3 for things to do ashore.

Gunwharf Quays Marina stands in the shadow of the Spinnaker Tower

Gunwharf Quays Marina

Marina entrance: 50°47'.66N 01°06'.51W

The closest berths to the Portsmouth waterside attractions can be found at Gunwharf Quays Marina on the eastern side of the harbour. In the season, however, it caters mainly for the likes of major waterborne events, leaving little room for your average cruising yacht.

Before attempting to cross the main channel to get to the eastern shore, remember to clear the PHM Ballast Beacon and contact the QHM on VHF Ch 11, who will expect you to have a confirmed berth at the marina before contacting him. Great care should be taken around the entrance to Gunwharf Quays Marina to keep clear of the frequent car ferries manoeuvring in and around their dock just to the south. It is always necessary to book a berth at Gunwharf Quays Marina in advance so that the QHM can be informed. Yachts failing to do so may be refused permission by the QHM to cross the deep-water channel (see p116). To contact the marina office, call 'Gunwharf Berths' on VHF Ch 80 or Tel: 023 9283 6732.

Berthing fees: During the season (1 April to 31 October), an overnight berth costs £3.30 per metre, while a short stay (up to four hours) costs a minimum of £8. Off season (1 November to 31 March), you need to contact the berthing office to check the overnight rates, but a short stay costs a minimum of £8. Note that short stay bookings are only available after midday.

The Spinnaker Tower can be seen many miles out at sea

Useful information – Gunwharf Quays Marina

FACILITIES
Facilities include water and electricity on the pontoons and a facilities block ashore incorporating showers, toilets and a launderette.

PROVISIONING
If any of your crew are shopaholics then Gunwharf Quays is a shopper's paradise, boasting over 95 designer outlets from Oakley and Calvin Klein to Timberland, White Stuff and Fat Face. Amid this abundance of clothes shops you will find the Gunwharf Express convenience store (Tel: 023 9287 6875), a speciality food shop, Julian Graves (Tel: 023 9286 1257), a newsagent, Gunwharf News (Tel: 023 9275 0223) and several cash machines.

The nearest large supermarkets can be found in the city centre – Sainsburys on Commercial Road can be reached by walking down Queen Street, which then becomes Edinburgh Road. You will need to make your way into the city centre to find your post offices and banks. Commercial Road and Palmerston Road are the two main locations for high street banks and cashpoints.

EATING OUT
You will be spoilt for choice when it comes to restaurants at Gunwharf Quays, let alone throughout the whole of Portsmouth. In a truly cosmopolitan style it offers a selection of eating places, from American diners and

Local fishermen's own tower

The Old Customs House, built in 1790, is now a stylish bar/restaurant

Useful information – Gunwharf Quays Marina

traditional English menus through to Spanish tapas bars and Italian cuisine. Perhaps if you are hungry after a day's sail you could try Tootsies (Tel: 023 9283 3787) or Sante Fe (Tel: 023 9289 0070) for those big American portions. On the other hand, you may want to fill up on pizza or pasta at Azzurro (Tel: 023 9283 2111) or Pizza Express (Tel: 023 9283 2989), with the latter also offering a takeaway service. Alternatively the Old Customs House (Tel: 023 9283 2333), now a listed ancient monument, is the ultimate traditional English pub. Other pubs in the area include the Still and West (Tel: 023 9282 1567) in Bath Square and the Bridge Tavern (Tel: 023 9275 2992)

in Old Portsmouth .

For bistros, go to the American Bar (Tel: 023 9281 1585) on the north side of Camber Dock, or to Old Portsmouth's High Street, which has numerous interesting restaurants, including Monks Wine Bar and Brasserie (Tel: 023 9281 2040) and the Good Fortune (Tel: 023 9286 3293), a Chinese restaurant. Alternatively, if you like fish, try Lemon Sole (Tel: 023 9281 1303), which is also on the High Street.

ASHORE

Gunwharf Quays is a major entertainment centre and incorporates a 14-screen cinema (Tel: 08712 240240), a casino (Tel: 023 9273 2277), a comedy club

(Tel: 023 9229 8563) and a 26-lane bowling complex (Tel: 023 9229 1234).

OTHER INFORMATION
Gunwharf Marina: VHF Ch 80; Tel: 023 9283 6732.

For all other useful information, see under Gosport Marina on p118-19 or Port Solent on p129 and p133 for transport.

A regular ferry runs from Gosport to Gunwharf Quays

Warships from three different eras are just one of the spectacular views from the Spinnaker Tower

Fareham

Fareham Channel approach: 50°49'.48N 01°08'.42W

Pilotage: Fareham is situated about 4½ miles north of the entrance to Portsmouth Harbour at the head of Fareham Lake. Leave the entrance to Portchester Lake to starboard, following the main channel to the north-north-west. Keep to the line of mooring buoys until you reach a south cardinal mark (VQ [6] + LFl 10s) to starboard and a port-hand mark (Fl [2] R), which lead you into the Fareham Lake channel. The channel is clearly marked by piles but is only partially lit up until Bedenham Pier. Note that craft should not come within 12m (39ft) of this pier without permission. The final mile, although still well marked, is unlit except at Foxbury Point (2 FR [hor]). Here the channel starts to shallow, with the final half mile to the Town Quay drying to 0.9m. Yachts drawing 1.5m (4ft 9in) should only attempt to get up this fairway 2½ to 3 hours either side of High Water.

The berths at Fareham Yacht Harbour dry out and are therefore suitable only for yachts that can take the bottom.

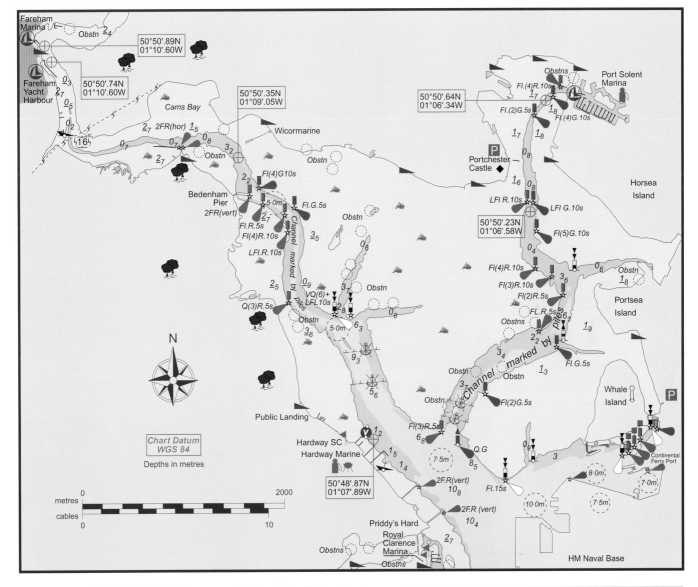

Fareham Yacht Harbour (Portsmouth Marine Engineering)

Yacht Harbour pontoons: 50°50'.74N 01°10'.60W

Although there are no allocated visitors' berths here, Fareham Yacht Harbour will accommodate visiting yachts when resident berth-holders are away. To find out about berthing availability and information contact the Yacht Harbour on Tel: 01329 232854. Note, it cannot be contacted by VHF.

Berthing fees: A flat rate of £10 per night.

FACILITIES

Facilities here are limited but consist of water, showers and a crane-out service. Local independent engineers can be arranged on request.

For the nearest fuel station, head for Wicormarine (see below) or, further down towards Portsmouth, Hardway Marine (p121) or Gosport Marina (p118).

PROVISIONING

There is a One Stop about 400m away, which also has a cash machine. See below for more information on provisioning in the area.

Useful information – Fareham

PROVISIONING

Fareham town centre has a large shopping centre incorporating almost 100 shops, including a Marks and Spencer and Boots the chemist. Besides the shopping mall, West Street and High Street are two key areas where you are likely to find everything you need.

The major banks, most of which have cashpoints, are predominantly situated in West Street, as is the chemist, the post office and Somerfield supermarket. A traditional market is held every Monday and a farmers' market every first Saturday in the month.

EATING OUT

Fareham is cosmopolitan when it comes to eating places, with menus ranging from Chinese and Indian to French and Italian. At the more expensive end of the scale are Edwinns (Tel: 01329 221338), serving international cuisine, and the two French restaurants Truffles Restaurant Français (Tel: 01329 231265) and Lauro's Brasserie (Tel: 01329 234179). All three are on the High Street.

If you like Italian, then you will be spoilt for choice. L'Ancora (Tel: 01329 829445) and ASK (Tel: 01329 239210), both on West Street, come highly recommended. Another good Italian restaurant is Villa Romano (Tel: 01329 825316) in the Old Coach House on the High Street, although this is slightly more expensive than the other two restaurants mentioned.

For those preferring Oriental or Indian food, go to LJ Chinese Cuisine (Tel: 01329 236262) or the Indian restaurant New Spice (Tel: 01329 828807), both of which are in West Street.

The pub Castle in the Air (Tel: 01329 280320) is right by Fareham Marina and serves good bar food (only until 1530 and not at all on Saturdays) and ales. It also has a garden to sit out in during the summer and welcomes children.

OTHER INFORMATION

Portsmouth Marine Engineering: Tel: 01329 232854.
Wicormarine: Tel: 01329 237112.
Repairs: Gordon Vasey Marine Engineering: Tel: 07798 638625;

Wicormarine: Tel: 01329 237112.
Chandlery: Trafalgar Yacht Services: Tel: 01329 823577.
Fareham Sailing & Motor Boat Club: Tel: 01329 280738.
Police: Tel: 999; Tel: 0845 045 4545.
Hospitals: Royal Hospital Haslar: Tel: 023 9258 4255; (Minor Accident Unit): Tel: 023 9276 2414; Queen Alexandra Hospital (Portsmouth): Tel: 023 9228 6000.
HM Customs Portsmouth: Tel: 0845 300 0628.
HM Coastguard: Lee on Solent: Tel: 023 9255 2100.
Doctor: Tel: 01329 823456.
Dentist: Tel: 01329 233502.
NHS Direct: Tel: 0845 4647.
Tourist Information Office: Tel: 01329 221342.

Wicormarine

Approach to Wicormarine: 50°50'.35N 01°09'.05W

Situated to the north of Bedenham Pier on the east side of the channel, Wicormarine has several deep-water moorings and is happy to accommodate visiting yachtsmen. However, you should call in advance to check on berthing availability. Tel: 01329 237112.

Berthing fees: From £15 per night.

FACILITIES

These include water, shoreside fuel and gas as well as a 10-ton boat hoist, slip, chandlery and repairs.

The nearby village of Wicor takes only 10 minutes to get to by foot and includes several grocery shops, a bakery and a post office.

Port Solent Marina lies in the north-east corner of Portsmouth Harbour, but is self-contained with a comprehensive range of shops, bars and restaurants

Port Solent Marina

Port Solent approach channel: 50°50'.23N 01°06'.58W
Port Solent waiting pontoon: 50°50'.64N 01°06'.34W

This marina is located to the north-east of Portsmouth harbour, not far from the historic Portchester Castle. The approach channel is well marked with port and starboard-numbered piles – the first SHM (about 1 mile north of Portsmouth entrance) being No 95 and the first PHM, which is also lit (Fl [3] R 5s), being No 57.

Two unlit yellow buoys marking foul ground lie immediately north of pile 94. Leaving these to starboard, the best water in this fairly wide section of the channel is to starboard of the large craft moorings. Once past the moorings, the channel narrows and starts a long, sweeping

There is a military range nearby, so take note of any signs and regulations

The final approach to the marina is straightforward and well marked

Before entering the lock to the marina, contact the lockmaster for details

Port Solent Marina has room for 500 boats, and can usually take visitors. Facilities are comprehensive and there is also a very good chandlery based here

left-hand turn. At pile 86, where the bend tightens, the safest water lies close to the three lit port-hand piles Nos 66, 67 and 68. As soon as you pass No 68 (Fl [4] R 10s) and the starboard pile No 80 (Fl [4] G 10s), the channel turns north and is well marked by moorings on either side. At and around Low Water, keep to the port side of the channel until reaching the PHM 72a, when you should then cross to the starboard pile 76 (Fl G 5s). The final approach to the marina is between the rows of piled moorings where the piles A (Fl [4] R 10s) and B (Fl [3] G 10s) eventually lead you to the lock with waiting pontoons to starboard. The marina staff recommend contacting Port Solent on VHF Ch 80 or Tel: 023 9221 0765 when passing starboard pile 78 just below Portchester Castle to request a 'lock in' (see sign on pile). If the lock is available you will be told to continue up the channel and enter it on a green light. Once in the lock a crewmember needs to contact the lockmaster for berthing instructions.

Berthing fees: Overnight (throughout the year): £2.55 per metre. Short stay (up to four hours): £1.05 per metre.

Sir Alec Rose's famous yawl *Lively Lady*, in which he circumnavigated the world in 1967, is one of several historic craft based at Port Solent Marina

Useful information – Port Solent

FACILITIES

Port Solent offers extensive facilities, from a 24-hour fuel service to round-the-clock security. The fuel pump sells diesel and unleaded petrol. If you have to fill up with fuel you should contact Port Solent Marina on VHF Ch 80 ahead of time.

Water and electricity are on the pontoons, and ice can be bought from the marina office. It is easy to get rid of rubbish here, too, with waste disposal areas situated near each bridgehead and at the marina reception.

With an array of local marine services (for contact details see below under 'Other Information') as well as an 18-ton mobile crane and a 40-ton travel hoist, Port Solent Marina is a convenient place to be if you need to have repairs carried out.

The marina staff are helpful, too, providing a daily weather forecast and a post collection service. Superb ablution facilities can be found ashore along with a launderette and there's even a David Lloyd Health and Fitness Club nearby for the more energetic.

PROVISIONING

A large, 24-hour Tesco supermarket (with cash machine), is about a 10-minute walk from the marina. Retail shops, situated along the Boardwalk, are not in short supply and you will also come across a cash machine.

EATING OUT

Several eating places along the Boardwalk mean that you don't have to go too far from your boat to enjoy a good meal. Among those recommended are Caffé Uno (Tel: 023 9237 5223) and Gordons Restaurant and Bar (Tel: 023 9278 0777), whose menu comprises mainly Cajun food and seafood. Caffé Uno serves bistro-type food with an emphasis on Italian dishes, while Chiquito (Tel: 023 9220

1181) offers Mexican cuisine at reasonable prices. There are also other international choices to be had, such as Indian and Chinese. As the Boardwalk is literally adjacent to the marina pontoons your best bet is probably to wander around and decide what type of restaurant appeals to you, although they can all get fairly busy in the summer.

OTHER INFORMATION

Port Solent Marina: VHF Ch 80; Tel: 023 9221 0765.
Port Solent Yacht Club: Tel: 023 9271 8196.
Chandlery: Marine Super Store: Tel: 023 9221 9433.
Marine engineers/repairs: Goodacre Yacht Services: Tel: 023 9221 0220; Motortech Marine Engineering: Tel: 023 9220 1171; JWS Marine Services Ltd: Tel: 023 9220 0670.
Electronics: Euronav: Tel: 023 9237 3855; Marine Electronic Installation: Tel: 023 9232 6366; Mobile Marine Electrical Services: Tel: 023 9220 1668.
Police: Tel: 023 9289 1622.
Coastguard: Lee on Solent: Tel: 023 9255 2100.
Hospital: Queen Alexandra: Tel: 023 9228 6000.
Doctor: Tel: 08444 778708.
Dentist: Tel: 023 9237 9695.
Tourist information centre: Tel: 023 9282 6722.

Portchester Castle is within easy reach of Port Solent and, now owned by English Heritage, is an interesting place to visit if you have an hour to spare

Useful information – Portsmouth Harbour

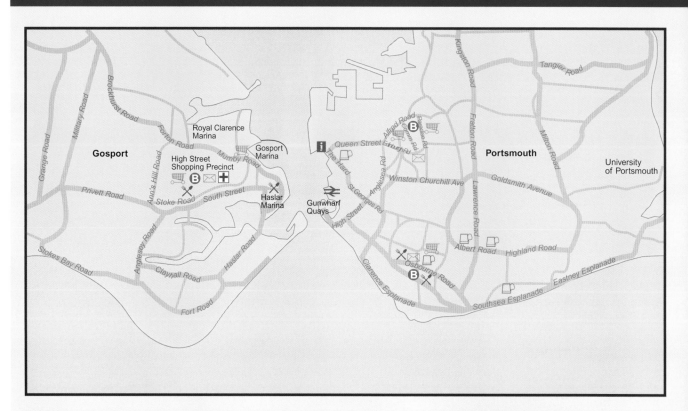

ASHORE

Portsmouth Harbour has played a significant role in British history for over 800 years and its rich maritime heritage is reflected in its many tourist attractions. No visit to Portsmouth is complete without a trip to the Historic Dockyard (Tel: 023 9283 9766), home to King Henry VIII's *Mary Rose*, Nelson's HMS *Victory* and the first iron battleship, HMS *Warrior*, built in 1860. You can also take a Harbour Tour to see the modern naval fleet as well as look at the impressive Georgian buildings and magnificently restored boathouses that now enclose the Royal Naval Museum (Tel: 023 9272 7562) and the Dockyard Apprentice Exhibition.

One thing you shouldn't miss is Action Stations (Tel: 023 9289 3316), an interactive attraction that immerses you in the challenges faced by the Royal Navy. Opening times

HMS *Warrior*, the first iron battleship to be built, is now at Portsmouth

HMS *Victory*, our most famous ship

The Royal Navy Submarine Museum at Gosport is a fascinating place to visit

are 1000–1730 from April to October and 1000–1700 from November until March.

The D-Day Museum (Tel: 023 9282 7261) in Southsea vividly depicts the Allied landings in Normandy on 6 June 1944, which marked the beginning of the end of the Second World War. Its centrepiece is the Overlord Embroidery, named after Operation Overlord, the codename given to the four-year preparation for the invasion. Measuring 83m in length, the embroidery was conceived by Lord Dulverton as a contemporary counterpart to the Bayeux Tapestry. The museum opens daily from 1000–1730 in the summer and from 1000–1630 in the winter.

Also in Southsea is the Royal Marines Museum (Tel: 023 9281 9385), portraying the colourful and exciting history of the Royal Marines and housing one of the most extensive collections of medals in the world. It is open daily from 1000–1700 in June, July and August and 1000–1630 from September through to May .

Staying on maritime attractions, over on the Gosport side of the harbour you will find the Royal Navy Submarine Museum (Tel: 023 9252 9217) and the Museum of Naval Firepower 'Explosion' (Tel: 023 9250 5600). The former exhibits the Royal Navy's first submarine, *Holland I*, and offers a guided tour of Britain's only walk-through submarine, HMS *Alliance*. It is open daily, 1000–1730, from April to October and until 1630 from November to March. 'Explosion', based at the Royal Navy's former armaments depot at Priddy's Hard, is also a great day out. You are given a fascinating insight into the lives of the men and women who stored and filled these explosives as well as coming face to face with the atom bomb, the Gatling Gun and the Exocet missile. Highly recommended, this museum opens on weekends only from 1000–1600 .

As Portsmouth became King Henry VII's Royal Dockyard in 1495, reinforcement of the harbour and its surrounding areas has continually played a crucial role in history. Today several of these fortifications are

Camber Dock is mainly used by local fishing boats

The D-Day Museum in Southsea

Useful information – Portsmouth Harbour

A view from the top of the Spinnaker Tower across the entrance to Portsmouth Harbour and the Isle of Wight beyond

The Portsmouth pilot boat is a familiar sight in the Solent, guiding commercial ships into the harbour

open to the public, including Fort Brockhurst (Tel: 023 9258 1059), which was built in the middle of the 19th century as a result of the introduction of gunpowder. The Fort is now open on the second Friday of every month between February and October, 1200-1500.

Southsea Castle (Tel: 023 9282 7261), built by King Henry VIII in 1544 to protect Portsmouth Harbour, is open 1000-1730 from 1 April to 30 September, while going much further back in time, Portchester Castle (Tel: 023 9237 8291), situated not far from Port Solent Marina, towards the north of the harbour, originally dates back to Roman times and was occupied by the Saxons between the 5th and 10th centuries, allegedly as a defence against the Vikings. The castle is open from 1000–1600 in the winter and from 1000–1800 throughout the summer.

Portsmouth Harbour's attractions do not stop there and to absorb the full history of the area would take days. However, other places of interest include the Gosport Museum (Tel: 023 9258 8035), which houses local collections of photographs and paintings, as well as life-sized costume figures, and the City Museum (Tel: 023 9282 7261), which tells the story of Portsmouth from Stone Age man.

If you feel that after visiting all these museums you are suffering from information overload then you may well want to do something less taxing, such as relaxing in front of a film at the Odeon cinema (Tel: 08712 244007) in Port Solent or visiting the bowling alley at

There are plenty of pubs and bars to choose from in old Portsmouth

Gunwharf Quays (Tel: 023 9229 1234). There are also several interesting walks in the area, in particular the two-mile Millennium Promenade, which starts at the Submarine Museum and runs along Haslar Marina's shoreside boundary right up to Priddy's Hard. For more information about walks in the area, contact the tourist offices on Tel: 023 9282 6722; Tel: 023 9252 2944.

TRANSPORT

As you would expect for a major city on the South Coast, Portsmouth's public transport services are good.
Ferries: Ferries run regularly not just across the harbour and to the Isle of Wight but also to the north coast of France, the Channel Islands and Spain. Contact: P&O: Tel: 08716 646464; Brittany Ferries: Tel: 0870 536 0360; Wightlink: Tel: 0870 582

7744; Hovertravel Tel: 023 9281 1000; Gosport Ferry Tel: 023 9252 4551.
Buses: There are good bus connections linking Portsmouth with all the nearby towns and villages. Contact: Traveline: Tel: 0871 200 2233; National Express: Tel: 0870 580 8080.
Rail: Portsmouth has two stations, Portsmouth City Centre and Portsmouth Harbour, with frequent direct services to London (80 minutes) and Southampton (45 minutes) Tel: 0845 748 4950 for details.
Airports: There are two airports in the vicinity, the closest being Southampton (22 miles/Tel: 0870 040 0009) and the other Bournemouth (54 miles/ Tel: 01202 364000). It is also worth noting that the major UK airports, Heathrow (Tel: 0870 000 0123) and Gatwick (Tel: 0870 000

2468), are not that far away (approximately 60 miles).
Taxis: Amber Cars (Tel: 023 9235 3535); Bridge Cars (Tel: 023 9252 2333); Cols

Cars (Tel: 023 9255 2233); Ferry Taxis (Tel: 023 9255 1166); Sky Cars (Tel: 023 9252 2522); Streamline (Tel: 0800 3281808).

Langstone Harbour

Langstone harbour entrance: 50°47'.20N 01°01'.51W

An expansive tidal bay situated between Hayling Island and Portsmouth, Langstone Harbour is a rather muddy, slightly desolate but charming haven. Incorporating a few deep-water moorings as well as a modern marina on the western shore, it is regarded as a Special Area of Conservation and is therefore home to a wealth of wildlife.

NAVIGATION

Charts: Admiralty Charts: SC5600, 2045, 3418; Imray: C9, Y33, 2200; Stanfords: 11, chartpack 10, L2
Tides: HW Springs and Neaps are the same as HW Portsmouth. LW Neaps and Springs are 10 minutes after LW Portsmouth. MHWS: 4.8m; MHWN: 3.9m; MLWN: 1.9m; MLWS: 0.8m.

Approaches: From the east you need to stay well clear of the East Winner bank, which protrudes about 1¼ miles offshore. Leave the unlit SCM to starboard, making for the waypoint 50°45'.00N 01°01'.00W. From the west, sailing due east from south of Horse Sand Fort to the above waypoint leaves plenty of sea room from the West Winner bank and its shoals. With the right tide underneath you, especially if you are coming from Portsmouth, using the Main Passage (waypoint 50°46'.00N 01°04'.10W), which

The Langstone Fairway beacon

The chimney to the west of the entrance is a good landmark

A view north through the entrance to Langstone Harbour. The harbour has been designated a Special Area of Conservation due to its wildlife

cuts through the Horse Sand Fort to Southsea submarine barrier (the gap is marked by a south dolphin (QR) and a green pile), saves a good deal of time. From the gap a course of approximately 120° and a distance of about two miles brings you to the waypoint transit. Inbound sea dredgers drawing up to 5.2m (17ft) may be encountered in the Langstone fairway between the pilot boarding station (50°44'.80N 01°01'.30W) and the Langstone Fairway pile.

These vessels have limited room to manoeuvre and should not be impeded by small craft.

Pilotage: The prominent chimney on its western bank identifies the entrance to Langstone Harbour, which lies about 3½ miles east of Portsmouth. From waypoint 50°45'.00N 01°01'.00W the chimney should bear 348°. Once abeam of the Langstone Fairway beacon (LFl 10s/

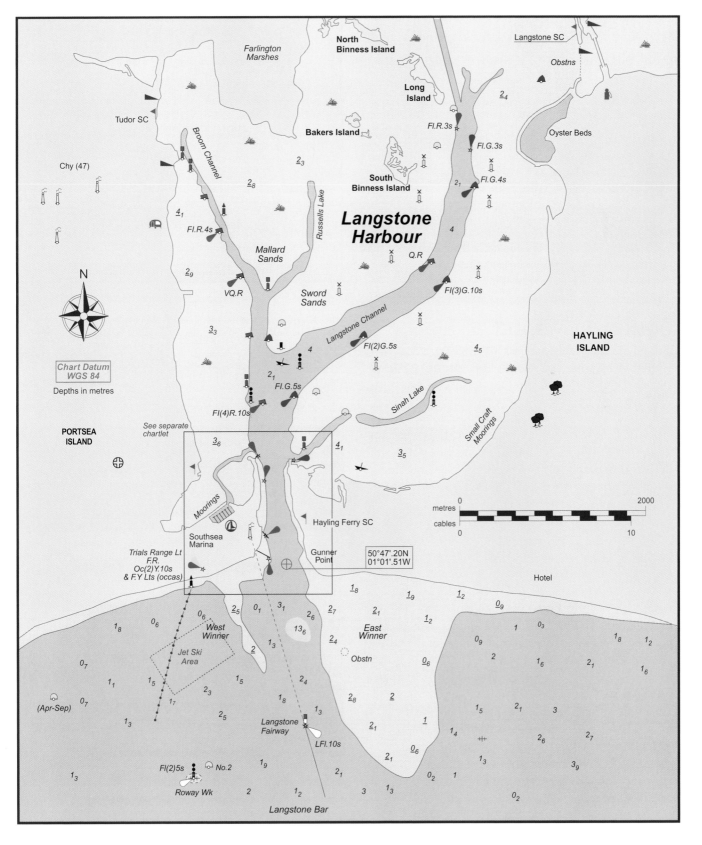

position 50°46'.31N 01°01'.36W), which must not be confused with the R and B Isolated Danger beacon (Fl [2] 5s/position 50°46'.11N 01°02'.25W), a course of 352° takes you into the entrance, although you will need to make allowance for any cross tides. At night there is a transit of 348° from the fairway beacon to the QR dolphin light on the western side of the entrance. In moderate weather entry presents no problems, although it is best attempted from HW –3 to +1. Try to avoid going in on an ebb tide, especially at Springs if a strong offshore wind is blowing. The entrance should not be negotiated in southerly to southeasterly gales. Note that there is a jet ski area marked by six yellow buoys to the west of the main channel.

Don't confuse the Isolated Danger beacon with the Langstone fairway beacon, which is situated to the north-east

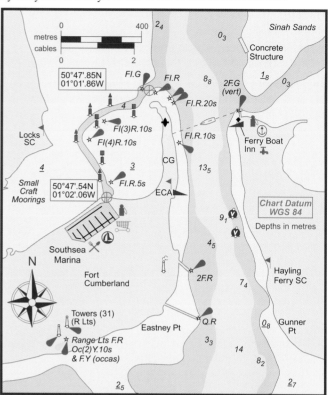

Southsea Marina

Entrance to marina channel: 50°47'.85N 01°01'.86W
Entrance to Southsea marina: 50°47'.54N 01°02'.06W

The start of the Southsea Marina approach channel lies to the north-west of the Hayling ferry pontoon, with its twisting channel clearly marked by five starboard-hand marks (only the first of which is lit), and nine port-hand marks, some of which are lit. A tidal gate operates the marina entrance, which closes around half tide when the depth is about 1.6m. With a tide gauge giving you the depths over the sill, a red light indicates that the gate is closed and a green means it is open. There is a waiting pontoon with shore access on the port-hand side of the entrance and you are advised to contact the marina for berthing availability on VHF Ch 80 or Tel: 023 9282 2719 while approaching the marina channel.

Berthing fees: To berth in Southsea Marina costs £1.80 per metre per day with a minimum charge of £14.40. At present there are no short stay fees.

FACILITIES

The marina's facilities include showers and toilets, diesel, petrol, gas, water and electricity as well as a 20-ton travel hoist and an 18-ton crane. The nearest chandlery is a 10-minute walk away in Milton (Chris Hornsey, Tel: 023 9273 4278), and marina staff can organise a range of marine services for you.

The approach channel to Southsea Marina is clearly marked with beacons

A green light indicates the marina entrance's tidal gate is open

Anchoring and harbour moorings

You can only anchor with the permission of the harbourmaster, with the favoured spots being either in the Langstone Fairway or in Russells Lake.

There are two deep-water visitors' mooring buoys on the starboard side of the inner entrance, which come under the jurisdiction of Langstone harbourmaster (Tel: 023 9246 3419/VHF Ch 12). On the port side of the inner entrance are six mooring buoys maintained by the Eastney Cruising Association (Tel: 023 9273 4103). Though strictly private, the association does allow visitors to use them if they are available. Vessels over 7.6m (25ft) LOA, however, are not permitted to use them.

Berthing fees: Moorings cost £10.50 per day. Harbour dues of £5.25 per day apply to all visiting yachts. Prices on arrival for the Eastney Cruising Association buoys.

FACILITIES
No real facilities come with the harbour moorings although the ferry pontoon to starboard provides water and diesel, and fuel is available from the nearby Southsea Marina. Both shores are serviced by Hayling Island Ferry (VHF Ch 10). Eastney Cruising Association (Tel: 023 9273 4103) offers the usual sailing club amenities such as a bar, showers and toilets.

Useful information – Langstone Harbour

The Eastney Cruising Association's slip, with its deep-water moorings beyond, are on the opposite side of the inner entrance to the harbour moorings

PROVISIONING
Within a 10-minute walk of Southsea Marina is a convenience store (with cashpoint) that sells basic provisions and is open daily, 0600-1900.

Besides this and a few other convenience stores nearby, the nearest supermarkets in Southsea are Tesco and Somerfield on Albert Road and Waitrose on Marmion Road. As these are a fair distance from the marina you are advised to catch the bus or take a taxi.

Several banks can be found on Albert Road and Palmerston Road, all of which have cash machines.

The post office is also in Palmerston Road, as is Boots the chemist and Rowlands pharmacy is on Albert Road.

EATING OUT
On the eastern shore of Langstone harbour is the Ferry Boat Inn (Tel: 023 9246 3459), which has a good reputation for its bar meals. However, as you are more likely to be berthed in Southsea Marina, you would be better off going into Southsea itself. If you don't want to go too far afield, try the Bombay Bay Indian restaurant (Tel: 023 9281 6066), which is open daily and within the marina.

A short taxi or bus ride away will get you to the heart of Southsea. Fatty Arbuckles (Tel: 023 9273 9179) on Osborne Road is great if you're really hungry as it serves American food in good-sized portions.

For something a little more sophisticated, Sur-La-Mer (Tel: 023 9287 6678) on Palmerston Road fits the bill as does Truffles (Tel: 023 9273 0796) on Castle Street, which offers French cuisine in a quaint and cosy atmosphere.

If you are after value for money go to Staffords (Tel: 023 9275 5291) on Clarendon Road.

For those who like Indian food, Southsea is definitely the place to come to as it boasts at least 14 Indian restaurants. One recommended is Spice Merchants (Tel: 023 9282 8900) on Osborne Road. Pizza Hut (Tel: 023 9286 2323) on Palmerston Road is good for a cheap and cheerful pizza either on the premises or takeaway, whereas Sopranos (Tel: 023 9281 1139), located in the same road, has an impressive Italian menu that is reflected in its prices.

Several pubs in Southsea reputed for their bar meals include the Jolly Sailor (Tel: 023 9282 6139) on Clarence Parade. Alternatively, there's the Slug and Lettuce (Tel: 023 9286 3981) on Palmerston Road.

ASHORE
With Hayling Island on one side and Southsea on the other, there is plenty to do and see in the Langstone Harbour area. If moored in the marina your first port of call should be Southsea Castle (Tel: 023 9282 7261). Located on Clarence

Useful information – Langstone Harbour

Esplanade, this fortification was built by King Henry VIII in 1545. It is open daily, 1000–1730, from April to October. Also on Clarence Parade is the D-Day Museum & Overlord Embroidery (Tel: 023 9282 7261), see p131 for details. The Royal Marines Museum (Tel: 023 9281 9385) is situated along the seafront towards the Eastney end of Southsea. Open daily 1000–1700 from June to August and 1000–1630 September to May, it gives a fascinating insight into these soldiers' lives.

Southsea Model Village (Tel: 023 9229 4706) is a fun day out for children. Incorporating a miniature model village, garden railway and toy museum, it is open seven days a week from Easter through to October, 1030–1800.

For more information about things to do in Portsmouth, see p130-131.

Hayling Island is renowned for its long, sandy beaches, which have been awarded for their cleanliness and outstanding facilities. Bear in mind, however, that it is a popular holiday destination and can get very crowded in the summer.

The Ferry Boat Inn on the eastern side of Langstone Harbour has a good reputation for bar meals

TRANSPORT

Trains: The nearest railway station to the marina is Portsmouth and Southsea, which is actually in Fratton, about 40 minutes' walk from the marina. You would therefore probably rather catch the bus or go by taxi to the station. Havant is the nearest station to Hayling Island, which takes about 20 minutes to get to by bus and slightly less by taxi. Here a direct service to London gets you there in just over an hour. For all train enquiries, Tel: 08457 48 49 50.

Buses: Buses run between the marina and Southsea Central – call the Traveline on Tel: 0871 200 2233 or the Travel shop on Tel: 023 9263 0352. To find out about bus times in the Hayling Island area, call Stagecoach South

on Tel: 0845 121 0170 or Traveline: 0871 200 2233.

Hovercraft: A frequent hovercraft service (Tel: 023 9281 1000) runs between Southsea and Ryde. For ferry information, see p133.

Taxis: Southsea: Aqua (Tel: 023 9265 4321); Streamline Taxis (Tel: 023 9281 1111). Hayling Island: C Cars (Tel: 023 9246 8888); Island Cars (Tel: 023 9242 2828).

Car hire: Southsea: Enterprise: Tel: 023 9275 5566; Hayling Island: Hayden Garages: Tel: 023 9246 8800.

OTHER INFORMATION

Langstone Harbourmaster: VHF Channel 12; Tel: 023 9246 3419.

Southsea Marina: VHF Ch 80; Tel: 023 9282 2719.

Eastney Cruising

Association: Tel: 023 9273 4103.

Langstone Sailing Club: Tel: 023 9248 4577.

Locks Sailing Club: Tel: 023 9282 9833.

Tudor Sailing Club: Tel: 023 9266 2002.

Chandleries: Chris Hornsey (Southsea): Tel: 023 9273 4728; Sparkes Marina (Hayling Island): Tel: 023 9246 3572.

Marine Services: Southsea Marina: Tel: 023 9282 2719; JWS Marine Services: Tel: 023 9275 5155; 1st Degree West (marine engineering and rigging): Tel: 023 9283 8335; Halsey Lidgard Sailmakers (Southsea): Tel: 023 9229 4700; Evolution Sails & Henderson Covers: Tel: 023 9229 4700.

Police: Tel: 0845 0454545.

Hospital: Queen Alexandra: Tel: 023 9228 6000.

HM Coastguard: Lee on Solent: Tel: 023 9255 2100.

Doctor: Southsea: Tel: 023 9283 9937.

Hayling Health Centre: Tel: 023 9246 6225.

Dentist: Southsea: Tel: 023 9273 2047; Hayling Island: Tel: 023 9246 2003.

Tourist Information: Portsmouth/Southsea: Tel: 023 9282 6722; Hayling Island: Tel: 023 9246 7111.

This large concrete structure is part of Mulberry harbour, a floating harbour built on Hayling for use during the D-Day landings. It later sank on Sinah Sands, opposite the entrance to the marina's approach channel

Chichester Harbour offers 17 miles of navigable deep-water channels and is home to over 10,000 boats and a wide variety of marinas and boatyards

Chichester Harbour

Chichester harbour entrance: 50°46'.69N 00°56'.07W

Although technically not in the Solent, Chichester Harbour is still considered by most locals to be part of the Solent scene. Set against the backdrop of the Sussex Downs, it boasts 17 miles of wide, deep-water channels flanked by picturesque historic towns and villages. Well served with moorings and anchorages, it is a must for visiting yachtsmen. On summer weekends you will have to share the channels with the local dinghy and keelboat racing community but by Sunday evening the place empties, becoming one of the most beautiful rural ports on the South Coast.

NAVIGATION

Charts: Admiralty Charts: SC5600, 2045, 3418; Imray: C9, Y33, 2200; Stanfords: 11, chartpack 10, chartpack 24, L3
Tides: HW Springs are 5 minutes after and Neaps 10 minutes before HW Portsmouth. LW Neaps are 15 minutes after and Springs 20 minutes after LW

Portsmouth. MHWS; 4.9m; MHWN: 4.0m; MLWN: 1.9m; MLWS: 0.9m.

Approaches: With its low-lying entrance set against the backdrop of the South Downs, Chichester Harbour is not easy to identify from seaward until you get close to the beacons. Approaching from the east or south-east, via the Looe Channel, you should give the Bracklesham shoals and East Pole sands a wide berth, keeping due west for at least two miles before altering course to the north-west until the Nab Tower (position 50°40'.07N 00°57'.15W) bears 184° astern of waypoint 50°44'.80N 00°56'.70W (about a mile south of the West Pole beacon). From the west a course of 090° from Horse Sand Fort keeps you well clear of the East Winner and West Pole shoals.

The bar across the entrance is periodically dredged to 1.5m, but this depth can decrease considerably in severe weather conditions. Strong winds from the south-east through to the south-west, coinciding with a strong Spring ebb, which can run up to 6 knots at the entrance, create dangerous seas over the bar. In this situation it is advisable

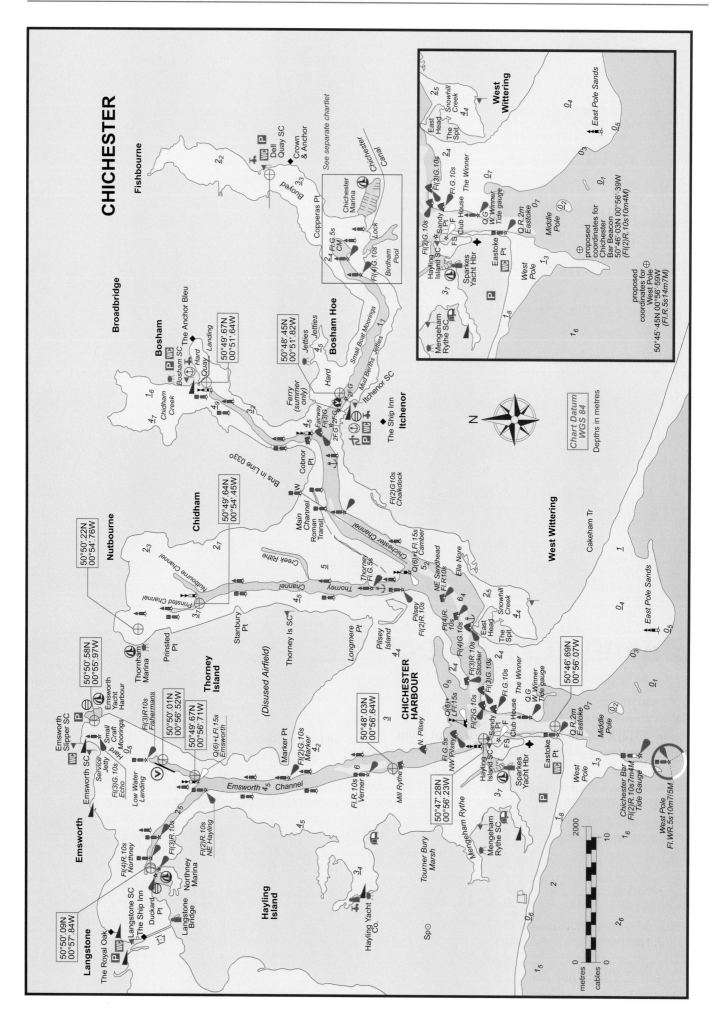

CHICHESTER

Fishbourne

Broadbridge

Bosham

Chidham

Nutbourne

Thorney Island

(Disused Airfield)

West Wittering

Emsworth

Hayling Island

Langstone

West Wittering

CHICHESTER HARBOUR

Chart Datum WGS 84
Depths in metres

Looking north up the Emsworth Channel. Sweare Deep forks off to port and leads to Northney Marina, while the starboard-hand channel leads to Emsworth

to be cautious and enter between three hours before and one hour after High Water.

Pilotage: From the waypoint 50°44'.80N 00°56'.70W steer 013° in order to pass the West Pole Beacon (Fl WR 5s 10m 7/5M) close to port. A little further on the Chichester Bar beacon (Fl [2] R 10s 7m 4M) should be left about 100m to port. Continue to steer 013° towards the gap between Eastoke beacon (Q R 2m) and the West Winner beacon QG (tide gauge), leaving Eastoke at least 50m to port. Once past Eastoke the Winner shoal to starboard is marked by three starboard-hand buoys – NW Winner (Fl G 10s), N Winner (Fl [2] G 10s) and the Mid Winner (Fl [3] G 10s). These are right on the edge of the shingle bank so do not attempt to cut inside them.

The channel divide is indicated by the Fishery SCM (Q [6] + L Fl 15s). Leaving this to starboard, the Emsworth Channel continues northwards and is clearly marked by day and partially lit by night. Heading east-north-east from this cardinal buoy takes you towards Chichester, with Stocker sand to port marked by four port-hand buoys – Stocker (Fl [3] R 10s), the unlit Copyhold, Sandhead

NEW PROPOSED POSITIONS FOR WEST POLE AND CHICHESTER BAR BEACON

The Chichester Harbour Conservancy has decided that the present West Pole and Chichester Bar Beacon need replacing and repositioning to take account of the changes to the West Pole Bank and the Bar. Some time in early 2008 the West Pole Beacon will be moved further south to a proposed position of 50°45'.45N 00°56'.59W and rebuilt as a large tripod tower. It will lose the sectored light and instead will have an all-round flashing red light (Fl R 5s 14m 7M). The Chichester Bar Beacon will be moved north-east to the proposed position of 50°46'.03N 00°56'.39W and changed to a single pole structure. Its light characteristics will change to Fl (2) R 10s 10m 4M. The existing given approach waypoint, 50°44'.80N 00°56'.70W, will stay the same, with the new beacons acting as a transit. Once abeam the West Pole Beacon, the pilotage into the harbour will be as before.

(Fl [4] R 10s) and NE Sandhead (Fl R 10s). The East Head starboard-hand mark (Fl [4] G 10s) signifies the beginning of the East Head anchorage.

A night-time entry should only be attempted in favourable conditions and you need to stay in the white sector of the West Pole Beacon (Fl WR 5s, 10m, 7/5M, vis W 321°–081°, R 081°–321°).

The Emsworth Channel, which is well marked and lit, runs for about 2½ miles to the Emsworth south cardinal mark (Q [6] + L Fl 15s), where Sweare Deep forks north-west to Northney Marina.

The entrance to the Thorney Channel is at the Camber SCM (Q [6] + L Fl 15s). From here, head due north to pass between the Pilsey port-hand beacon (Fl [2] R 10s) and the Thorney starboard-hand beacon (Fl G 5s). The channel divides above Stanbury Point, with the Prinsted branch, full of moorings and ultimately leading to Thornham Marina, to port and the Nutbourne Channel to starboard. Both channels dry out towards their northern ends.

The Chichester Channel runs north-east to the Bosham Channel and then to the Itchenor Reach and on to Birdham Pool, Chichester Marina and Dell Quay. From the north-east Sandhead port-hand mark (Fl R 10s), a transit of 033° on the port-hand Roman beacon and the Main Channel beacon, which is on the shore north-west of Cobnor Point, brings you to Chaldock Beacon (Fl [2] G 10s). From Chaldock the Itchenor Fairway buoy (Fl [3] G 10s) bears approximately 080°. Just beyond the Fairway buoy the Deepend south cardinal mark signals the divide into the north-bound Bosham Channel or the east-south-east-running Itchenor Reach.

The Bosham Channel has a depth of about 1.8m at Low Water on a moderate Spring tide until about 400m from the quay. Although the channel is marked with red and green withies, the best water is between the port and starboard swinging moorings. The approach to the quay is

The Mid Winner buoy is virtually on the shingle bank

made when the quay and the old wooden pilings open up. Keep the south cardinal mark at the end of the dinghy slip about 4m to port, taking care on a Spring flood not to be carried onto the steep-to slip between the end of the quay and the south cardinal mark.

In Itchenor Reach you should keep between the swinging moorings until you get to the Birdham starboard-hand mark (Fl [4] G 10s), which marks the beginning of the approach to Birdham Pool. About 100m further north-east is the CM starboard-hand pile (Fl G 5s), identifying the start of the Chichester Marina channel. Beyond this marina the Fishbourne channel leads to Dell Quay, which shallows very quickly and is not suitable for deep-draughted yachts.

With this number of channels in Chichester Harbour finding a sheltered berth or an anchorage for the night is not a problem.

Anchorages

There are three recognised anchorages in Chichester Harbour. East Head (pictured), the most popular one, is conveniently close to the harbour entrance, just to the east of the East Head Spit Buoy (Fl [4] G) and north of the beach outside the main channel. Three quarters of a mile further north-east along the Chichester Channel, just inside the Thorney Channel, lies the quieter though slightly more exposed Pilsey Island anchorage. You can also anchor half a mile west of Itchenor, north of Chaldock Point along the southern edge of the channel, which is convenient if waiting for the tide. The harbour authorities require all anchored craft to display day or night-time anchorage signals and do not like vessels left unattended for more than four hours.

Sparkes Marina is situated just round the corner from Hayling Island Sailing Club, a distinctive building close to the water on Sandy Point

Sparkes Marina   (Hayling Island)

Entrance to marina channel: 50°47'.28N 00°56'.23W

Just inside the entrance to Chichester Harbour, on the eastern shores of Hayling Island, lies Sparkes Marina and Boatyard. Its approach channel has been dredged to 2m Mean Low Water and can be identified by an unlit east cardinal mark with tide gauge. Accessible at all states of the tide, Sparkes has several berths designated to visitors. Contact the marina on VHF Ch 80 or Tel: 023 9246 3572.
Berthing fees: £2.60 per metre per day or £15.75 per metre per week. A short stay is a flat rate of £5 for yachts up to 10m (33ft) and £10 for those over 10m (33ft).

Useful information – Sparkes Marina

FACILITIES
Amenities include electricity and water on the pontoons and 24-hour access to showers and toilets. There is also a launderette at the marina, as well as a rubbish and recycling centre and waste oil facility.

The fuel pontoon sells diesel and petrol seven days a week while an on-site chandlery supplies gas cylinders as well as most essential nautical items.

Among the services offered are craning out and hard standing, as well as maintenance and repairs, which range from electronics and engineering to painting and carpentry. For more details, see under 'Useful Information' on p144).

PROVISIONING
The on-site chandlery sells essential basic items, including ice. Otherwise there is a newsagents with a cashpoint in Creek Road, which is within easy walking distance of a farm shop in Sandy Point Road. For more serious provisioning catch a bus or taxi to Mengham where you will find a Somerfield supermarket and most of the high street banks.

EATING OUT
The marina has its own bar and restaurant – Marina Jaks (Tel: 023 9246 9459), which has a good reputation for seafood. It can get very busy during the summer, so you may need to book in advance. Alternatively,

The approach to Sparkes Marina is straightforward and clearly marked

about a 10 or 15-minute walk away you come to Southwood Road where you will find several takeaways comprising Indian, Chinese and traditional English fish and chips. Situated along the seafront is the Olive Leaf pub (Tel: 023 9246 4149), reputed for its bar menu.

Further afield in Station Road – a good 30-minutes away on foot – Jaspers (Tel: 023 9246 3226) is renowned for its international cuisine, although its high standards are reflected in its high prices. During the summer you need to reserve a table in advance.

Hayling Yacht Company (Hayling Island)

Hayling Yacht Company channel entrance: 50°48'.03N 00°56'.64W

Hayling Yacht Company is a family-run boatyard at the end of Mill Rythe Creek, about a mile from the southern end of the Emsworth Channel. Within its complex is a half-tide marina accommodating 116 boats of up to 18m (59ft) in length. As a full working boatyard, its services include boat repairs and general maintenance. Also on the premises are toilets, showers, water and electricity.

To find out about berthing information, contact the yard on Tel: 023 9246 3592.
Berthing fees: £1.20 per metre per day.

PROVISIONING

Hayling Yacht Company is not the most convenient place to come to if you run out of milk or bread. The nearest shop is the Co-op in Church Road, which is about a 15-20 minute walk away. If you need to replenish your stores, however, catch a bus or take a taxi to the Somerfield supermarket in Mengham.

EATING OUT

Although there are no shops in close proximity to Hayling Yacht Company, there are two pubs, both of which are situated on Havant Road – the Maypole (Tel: 023 9246 3670) and the Yew Tree (Tel: 023 9246 5258).

Hayling Yacht Company offers some berths to visitors but it does dry out

Useful information – Hayling Island

The Royal Oak pub is at Langstone – the other side of the Hayling bridge from Northney Marina

Sparkes Marina: VHF Ch 80; Tel: 023 9246 3572.
Hayling Yacht Company: Tel: 023 9246 3592.
Hayling Island Sailing Club: Tel: 023 9246 3768.
Mengeham Rythe Sailing Club: Tel: 023 9246 3337.
Langstone Sailing Club:

Tel: 023 9248 4577.
Chandleries: Ship'N Shore, Sparkes Marina, Hayling Island: Tel: 023 9263 7373 Mengham Marine, Mengham Road, Hayling Island: Tel: 023 9246 4333.
Marine services: Sparkes

Marina: VHF Ch 80; Tel: 023 9246 3572; Hayling Yacht Company: Tel: 023 9246 3592; Wilsons Boatyard: Tel: 023 9246 4869.
Police: Tel: 999; Tel: 0845 0454545.
Hospital: Queen Alexandra Hospital (Portsmouth):

Tel: 023 9228 6000.
HM Coastguard: Lee on Solent: Tel: 023 9255 2100.
Doctor: Hayling Island: Tel: 023 9246 8413.
Dentist: Tel: 023 9246 2003.
Tourist Information Office: Hayling Island: Tel: 023 9246 7111.

Northney Marina is accessible at all states of the tide, and is in a good position at the top of Sweare Deep Channel, off the Emsworth Channel

Northney Marina (Hayling Island)

Northney Marina entrance: 50°50'.09N 00°57'.84W

Accessible at all states of the tide, Northney Marina is on the northern shore of Hayling Island in the well-marked Sweare Deep Channel, which branches off to port almost at the end of the Emsworth Channel. Providing good shelter, it welcomes visitors, although there are no designated visitors' berths and availability is subject to whether resident berth-holders are away or not. To contact the marina for more information on berthing availability, call VHF Ch 80 or Tel: 023 9246 6321.

Berthing fees: All fees are subject to a slight increase, but currently stand at £3 per metre per night or a flat rate of £8 for a short stay of up to four hours.

Useful information

FACILITIES

Water and electricity are on the pontoons, with gas available 24 hours a day from the marina office. Also on tap 24 hours a day is diesel, which can be obtained from the fuel berth on the end of G pontoon. Contact the duty dock officer for assistance.

The showers and toilets are located in the facilities building, access to which is gained with a push-button code. Coin-operated laundry facilities are nearby, while refuse containers are positioned at the head of each pontoon.

The marina offers good security, with a code-functioning gate leading on to the pontoons. The marina office is manned day and night, although in an emergency you can call Mobile: 07774 458886 if you need assistance. Other services include hard standing and a 35-ton boat hoist. Ask at the marina office for yacht repair and maintenance services or tidal and weather information. There is a chandlery – Monkey's Fist (Tel: 02392 461610) – on site.

PROVISIONING

The nearest shops are about two miles away in Havant town centre. However, basic items are sold at a petrol station at the end of Northney Road, about half a mile from the marina, and the on-site facilities building houses a small provisions shop.

EATING OUT

Within the marina complex is the Langstone Hotel (Tel: 023 9246 5011) with a restaurant that serves lunch and evening meals. Popular with yachtsmen are the Ship Inn (Tel: 023 9247 1719) and Royal Oak (Tel: 023 9248 3125), both situated at the head of Langstone Harbour just a short walk away on the other side of the Hayling Island bridge.

See p147 for more information on them.

Emsworth
Start of the Emsworth Channel: 50°49'.67N 00°56'.71W

Emsworth lies at the top of Chichester Harbour's most western inlet. Believed to have started out as a small Saxon settlement, by the Middle Ages it was a prosperous little port, where large quantities of wine were imported from Europe. Famous in the 18th and 19th centuries for, among other things, its corn trade and oyster fishing industry, today it has a lively town centre, full of independent shops, pubs and restaurants. This, combined with a marina, a traditional boatyard and a visitors' pontoon, makes it a popular destination for visiting yachtsmen.

Emsworth visitors' pontoon
Alongside pontoon: 50°50'.01N 00°56'.52W

The floating pontoon in Emsworth harbour can be used by visitors. For instructions or availability, contact the Chichester Harbour office on Tel: 01243 512301; VHF Ch 14 (callsign 'Chichester Harbour Radio' or 'Chichester Harbour Patrol').
Berthing fees: £6.50 per night or £40 per week for a maximum of two weeks, and harbour dues of £3.50 per night or £5 for the weekend.

FACILITIES
There are no real facilities for yachtsmen on the pontoons, although further north up the channel you will come to the Emsworth jetty, where you can obtain fresh water. This jetty should only be approached about two hours either side of High Water Neaps if you draw 1.5m (4ft 9in), as the channel dries out.

Emsworth has two sailing clubs, the Emsworth Slipper SC (Tel: 01243 372523) in South Street and Emsworth SC (Tel: 01243 372850/373065) in Bath Road, both of which welcome visitors and allow them to use their bars, restaurants and washing amenities. You would need to check with the clubs as to when they are serving food as times vary from season to season.

A ferry servicing the moorings and the visitors' pontoon runs on weekends and bank holidays from Easter to late September, 2½ hours either side of High Water from 0800-2000 or sunset, whichever is earlier. Call 'Emsworth Mobile' on VHF Ch 14. To use the scrubbing piles at Emsworth, contact the harbour office.

Emsworth Yacht Harbour

Start of the channel to Emsworth Yacht Harbour: 50°50'.19N 00°56'.40W   Marina Entrance: 50°50'.58N 00°55'.97W

The final approach channel to Emsworth Yacht Harbour

The marina is within a 10-minute walk of the delightful town of Emsworth

Accessible for about one and a half to two hours either side of High Water, Emsworth Yacht Harbour is a sheltered, friendly haven offering good facilities to yachtsmen. Created in 1964 from a pond used to soak timber for Foster's Boatyard, it is within easy walking distance of the pretty town of Emsworth. For more information, contact the Yacht Harbour on VHF Ch 80 or Tel: 01243 377727.

Berthing fees: Subject to a slight increase, the current fees are £2.50 per metre per day or £12 per metre per week.

FACILITIES

It has all the usual facilities, including diesel, gas, water and electricity as well as showers and toilets. There is also a 40-ton mobile crane, chandlery and hard-standing area.

Useful information – Emsworth

PROVISIONING

There are a couple of newsagents and grocery shops in the centre of Emsworth, as well as a bakery, two butchers, a fishmongers and a Co-op supermarket, in South Street, which incorporates the post office. In North Street you'll find a Tesco Metro. There are also several banks with cash machines and a hardware store in the centre of Emsworth.

EATING OUT

Emsworth has at least 10 pubs, so a pint of ale and a good bar meal are easy to come by. On South Street are the Blue Bell Inn (Tel: 01243 373394) and the Coal Exchange (Tel: 01243 375866), while on Havant Street is the King's Arms (Tel: 01243 374941) which is well known for its organic food.

A close walk from Emsworth Yacht Harbour

Emsworth dries at Low Water

The Coal Exchange pub

Emsworth is good for victualling

Spoil yourself at 36 on the Quay

is the Sussex Brewery (Tel: 01243 371533), renowned for its numerous types of sausages and the Lord Raglan (Tel: 01243 372587), whose garden overlooks Dolphin Quay Boatyard.

The Ship Inn (Tel: 023 9247 1719) and the Royal Oak (Tel: 023 9248 3125) are tucked away on the harbour front at Langstone, about two miles away by public footpath. Reputed to have once been smugglers' haunts, they both serve good pub food and are popular with visitors and locals alike.

Among the restaurants in Emsworth are Fat Olives (Tel: 01243 377914) in South Street, providing high quality Mediterranean food at reasonable prices, and 36 on the Quay (Tel: 01243 375592) – a good choice if you want to really spoil yourself. Serving à la carte menus, it is one of the most expensive restaurants in

the area, so be prepared to burn a hole in your pocket. Spencers (Tel: 01243 372744) on North Street is recommended for its French and English cuisine, while the nearby Italian restaurant Nicolinos (Tel: 01243 379809) is also very popular with the locals.

In addition, there are several cafés in the centre of Emsworth serving breakfasts and lunches.

ASHORE

If moored in the area with a couple of hours to spare one weekend, go to the Emsworth Museum (Tel: 01243 378091) on North Street. Full of maritime history, it also explains the town's literary connections with the novels of PG Wodehouse. Situated next to the Fire Station, it only opens during the Spring and Summer months on Saturday 1000–1300; 1400–1600 and Sunday 1400–1600.

The marina has a pool in which you can stay afloat 24 hours a day

Thornham is a popular destination for multihulls, which can take the ground

Thornham Marina

Start of Thornham channel: 50°49'.64N 00°54'.45W
Thornham Marina final approach: 50°50'.22N 00°54'.76W

At the head of Prinsted Bay on the east side of Thorney Island, about two miles along the Thorney Channel, lies Thornham Marina. Only really accessible to 1.5m (4ft 9in) draught yachts about one hour either side of High Water Springs, it has a charmingly rustic atmosphere. The marina does not tend to get that many visitors and has no dedicated berths for visiting yachtsmen, although it will accommodate them if it has space. There are 78 drying berths here as well as a small number of pontoon berths within a gated basin, catering for vessels with a draught of up to 1.75m (5ft 7in). For berthing information and navigational advice, Tel: 01243 375335.
Berthing fees: A flat rate of £20 per night.

FACILITIES

The pontoons are equipped with electricity and water, with showers and toilets ashore. A 12-ton hoist can lift and launch vessels of up to 12m (39ft) in length and a pressure wash facility is also available. On site services include John Cutler Marine Engineering, Nick Gates & Co wooden boat repair and restoration, Cover Care, JBT Marine and the brokers Multihull World.

PROVISIONING

Both Southbourne and Emsworth are approximately a mile from the marina, the former of which has a post office, a chemist, two farm shops and a Co-op supermarket. See p147 for details of Emsworth.

EATING OUT

Boaters Bar and Restaurant (Tel: 01243 377465), situated on the premises, opens at 0900 and serves breakfast and lunch each day and evening meals in the summer.

Useful information– Thorney Channel

Northney Marina: VHF Ch 80; Tel: 023 9246 6321.
Emsworth Yacht Harbour: VHF Channel 80; Tel: 01243 377727.
Chichester Harbour Conservancy (harbour office): VHF Ch 14; Tel: 01243 512301.
Thornham Marina: Tel: 01243 375335.
Emsworth Sailing Club: Tel: 01243 373065.
Emsworth Slipper Sailing Club: Tel: 01243 372523.

Thorney Sailing Club: Tel: 01243 371731.
Emsworth Ferry: VHF Ch 14.
Chandleries: Sea Teach, Emsworth: Tel: 01243 375774; Harbour Chandlers (Emsworth Yacht Harbour): Tel: 01243 375500.
Marine services: Emsworth Yacht Harbour: Tel: 01243 377727; Northney Marina: Tel: 023 9246 6321; Dolphin Quay Boatyard (specialists in wooden boats): Tel: 01243 373234; Nick Gates & Co

(specialists in wooden boats): Tel: 07957 422941; John Cutler Marine Engineering: Tel: 01243 375014; Cover Care: Tel: 01243 372759.
Sailmakers: Arun & Rockall Sails, Bosham: Tel: 01243 573185; Halsey Lidgard Sailmakers, Chichester: Tel: 01243 545410.
Police: Tel: 999; Tel: 0845 045 4545.
Coastguard: Lee on Solent Tel: 023 9255 2100.
Hospital: St Richard's

Hospital, Chichester: Tel: 01243 788122.
Doctor: Southbourne Surgery: Tel: 01243 372623.
NHS Direct: Tel: 0845 4647.
Dentist: Emsworth: Tel: 01243 372666; Mobile: 07770 772488.
Tourist Information Office: Chichester: Tel: 01243 775888; Hayling Island: Tel: 023 9246 7111; Havant: Tel: 023 9248 0024.
Emsworth Museum: Tel: 01243 378091.

Bosham Quay Bosham Quay: 50°49'.67N 00°51'.64W

Craft drawing up to 2m (6ft 6in) can dry out against Bosham Quay (access is two hours either side of HW) in soft mud. At the eastern end there is room for up to four boats to sit on the purpose-built grid. Swinging moorings are occasionally available with the permission of the quaymaster, who can be contacted on Tel: 01243 573336.

Berthing fees: Short stay (up to six hours): 6.4-7.6m (21-25ft): £6; 9m (30ft): £7; 10.6m (35ft): £8; 12m (39ft): £9. If moored at the scrubbing area, charges are £1.30 per foot per day, inclusive of the pressure hose, which works out at £45.50 for a 10.7m (35ft) yacht. If you want to stay for a longer period of time, contact the quaymaster.

Useful information – Bosham

FACILITIES
Fender boards can be obtained on the quay as can pressure washers for scrubbing off. Fresh water, limited electricity and a small 2-ton crane for lifting masts and engines are also available. Bosham SC (Tel: 01243 572341), right on the quay, allows visiting yachtsmen to use its shower and toilet facilities.

PROVISIONING
The nearest shop for essentials is the Bosham

Farm Shop in Delling Lane, about a 15 to 20-minute walk away from the quay. Open until 2100 seven days a week, it incorporates a post office, cash machine and delicatessen.

A little further away, on Station Road, north of the roundabout, is a Co-op which, like the farm shop, stays open until 2100.

For more serious provisioning, catch a bus or taxi to the large Tesco supermarket on the Fishbourne roundabout.

EATING OUT
Bosham Sailing Club (Tel: 01243 572341) has a bar that opens seven days a week and a restaurant serving evening meals from Thursday to Saturday as well as lunches on weekends.

A stone's throw from the quay, with wonderful views across the harbour, is the 300-year Anchor Bleu (Tel: 01243 573956). The pub serves excellent food at reasonable prices, and on big Spring tides has been known to flood, so be prepared to roll up your trousers.

Other pubs in the vicinity include the Berkeley Arms (Tel: 01243 573167), situated on the left-hand corner just before you turn into Delling Lane, and the White Swan (Tel: 01243 576086) on Station Road, on the opposite side of the roundabout to Delling Lane. Facing the White Swan pub,

on Main Road, is the Indian restaurant Memories of India (Tel: 01243 572234), while not far from here, on Station Road, is Butler's fish and chip shop (Tel: 01243 576388), open seven days a week.

To treat your crew, go to the Millstream Hotel (Tel: 01243 573234) in Bosham Lane, about a five-minute walk from the quay. With a garden to sit out in, it serves lunches, teas and dinners.

Popular with daytrippers, it is not surprising that Bosham incorporates two tea shops: the Mariners (Tel: 01243 572960) in the High Street, offering a pretty vista across the creek, and the Captain's Table Tea Room (Tel: 01243 572475) in Bosham Walk.

OTHER INFORMATION
Bosham Quaymaster: Tel: 01243 573336.
Bosham Sailing Club: Tel: 01243 572341.

Itchenor moorings

Visitors' moorings: 50°48'.45N 00°51'.82W

Visitors can normally pick up one of the swinging moorings off the pretty village of Itchenor which, for a tidal area, have the added advantage of being accessible by dinghy from the hard at all states of the tide. For berthing information, contact the harbour office on VHF Ch 14 or Tel: 01243 512301.

Berthing fees: £6.50 per night or £40 per week for a maximum of two weeks. Harbour dues are charged at £3.50 per night or £5 for the weekend.

Useful information

The jetty at Itchenor can be accessed at all states of the tide. The village pub is a minute's walk away

FACILITIES

Itchenor jetty can be accessed at all states of the tide (the depth is about 2m at Low Water Springs). To avoid congestion, mooring is restricted to 20 minutes for loading and taking on water, which is available on the pontoon. Showers are installed in the Harbour Office building and are token-operated. Tokens cost £1 and can be obtained from the on-the-water patrol staff, the Itchenor ferry or from the Harbour Office. Electrical, electronic and marine engineering repair services are also on site. The ferry (Tel: 07970 378350; VHF Ch 8), which only operates during the summer, will take you to and from your mooring as well as drop you off on the ferry path at Smugglers Lane in Bosham, which is about a half-hour walk from Bosham village. To use the scrubbing piles at Itchenor, book with the office in advance.

PROVISIONING

There are no shops in the immediate vicinity of Itchenor, the nearest one being Birdham Stores (incorporating a post office) on the main Birdham to Chichester road, which is about a 15 to 20-minute walk away. For more information, see under Chichester Marina on page 152.

EATING OUT

The Ship Inn (Tel: 01243 512284) is the village pub, and is just a minute's walk from the jetty. Its excellent restaurant is popular with both locals and visitors and needs to be booked in advance at weekends. Besides this, there are no other restaurants within walking distance. Itchenor Sailing Club (Tel: 01243 512400), opposite the pub, welcomes visiting yachtsmen and offers lunchtime and evening meals.

Birdham Pool

Birdham Pool approach: 50°48'.33N 00°50'.20W

This must be one of the most rustic and charming marinas in the UK. Although it is only accessible three hours either side of High Water via a lock, if you do get the chance to berth here you won't be disappointed with its unique and picturesque setting. To get to Birdham Pool, enter the channel at the Birdham SHM beacon (Fl [4] G 10s) with its tide gauge. The channel to the lock is marked by green piles that should be left no more than 3m to starboard. For further advice on the approach and berthing facilities, call VHF Ch 80 or Tel: 07831 466815.

Berthing fees: These may be subject to a slight increase but are currently £2.10 per metre per night.

Birdham Pool was built in the 1930s and is thought to be the oldest marina in the UK. It certainly has rustic charm and is well placed for exploring ashore

Useful information

FACILITIES
Amenities include water, electricity, diesel, petrol and ablution facilities. On hand are comprehensive repair facilities with a 20-ton slip and a 10-ton crane.

A small chandlery is open weekdays and Saturday mornings, although it is not as well stocked as the one at Chichester Marina, which is also open on Sundays.

PROVISIONING
The closest shop for essential provisions is at Chichester Marina, which is only a five-minute walk away from Birdham Pool, so long as you take the short cut across the lock at the end of the canal. There is also a Spar (Birdham Stores) on the Birdham to Chichester road as you head towards the Witterings, which also incorporates a Spar supermarket. This is however, a good 20-minutes walk away, so taking a taxi might be a better idea.

For more information on provisioning, where to eat and things to do ashore, see p152-156.

Birdham Pool is accessed via a lock that opens three hours either side of High Water

Chichester Marina

Marina channel entrance: 50°48'.44N 00°49'.87W

Chichester Marina, nestling in an enormous natural harbour, has more than 1,000 berths and welcomes yachtsmen from all parts of the globe. Situated a little further upstream from Birdham Pool, still on the starboard hand side, its channel is identified by the CM starboard-hand pile (Fl G 5s). This well-marked channel dries to 0.5m and access is therefore restricted to around 1½ hours either side of Low Water Springs if you have a draught over 1m (3ft). Two tide gauges (one on pile No 6 and one in the lock) indicates the depth of water underneath you. Watch out for a flashing red light on the roof of the lock control, which signifies that the depth has dropped to less than a metre. The lock is manned 24 hours a day, but if you have any queries, call VHF Ch 80 or Tel: 01243 512731.

Berthing fees: Up to 12.5m (41ft) LOA: £2.85 per metre per day; over 12.5m (41ft): £2.95 per metre per day.

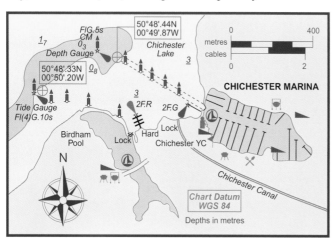

The well-marked channel to the marina is restricted at Low Water Springs

The lock gate is manned 24 hours a day and its staff are very helpful

Useful information

FACILITIES

Besides the travel hoist and full boat-repair services, there is winter storage, should you require it, and 24-hour security. Good shower, toilet and laundry amenities are ashore while recycling and rubbish bins are strategically placed around the site. There is also an outboard engine flush tank near M pontoon. Gas, petrol and diesel are all easily obtained and water and electricity are available on the pontoons. The on-site chandlery, Peters Chandlery (Tel: 01243 511033), is well stocked and has friendly staff who are always willing to help. Wireless internet access is also available at the marina free of charge.

PROVISIONING

The small shop on the marina complex, the Galley Stores, in the same building as the bar/restaurant and chandlery, stocks basic provisions. However, for more serious provisioning, get a bus or taxi into Chichester (buses run from the marina entrance every half hour), which is only about five minutes away by car. In the centre of Chichester is a Marks & Spencers in East Street and an Iceland and Tesco Metro in South Street. Alternatively, go to the large Tesco supermarket on the Fishbourne roundabout, which again is a car ride away, or Waitrose, situated opposite the leisure centre on Cathedral Way.

A market takes place every Wednesday and Saturday in the Cattle Market car park to the east of the city, which is good for cheap fruit and veg. Chichester is well stocked with other shops ranging from clothing outlets and stationers to bookshops and hardware stores.

EATING OUT

The Spinnaker Bar (Tel: 01243 511032) at Chichester Marina is convenient if you don't fancy going too far afield. It serves excellent breakfasts every day from 0900 to 1200 as well as lunchtime and evening meals throughout the summer. In the marina complex, Chichester YC (Tel: 01243 512918) welcomes visitors to its bar and restaurant, while a 15-20 minute walk along the Birdham Road will take you to the Crouchers Country Hotel (Tel: 01243 784995) and the Black Horse pub (Tel: 01243 784068). Often quite crowded in summer, the pub welcomes children and has converted part of its garden into a play area. A 15-minute stroll along the footpath will get you to Dell Quay, where the Crown and Anchor (Tel: 01243 781712) pub is superbly located right on the waterfront.

Dell Quay   Dell Quay: 50°49'.15N 00°49'.02W

Dell Quay lies about a mile north-east of Chichester Marina and is only really accessible to shallow-draught yachts that are able to take the ground. The narrow, snake-like channel starts at Copperas buoy, after which the port and starboard-hand buoys are numbered in sequence, 1 to 4. The moorings then lead you to the quay, which will provide a secure berth if you are prepared to dry out. The quay is accessible two to three hours either side of High Water for draughts of about 1.5m (4ft 9in), but you should contact the harbourmaster (Tel: 01243 512301; VHF Ch 14, callsign Chichester Harbour Radio) before going alongside. If used for just a few hours, you will not normally be charged a fee. The harbourmaster also controls a lifting pontoon just north of the quay, which can be used free of charge up to a maximum of one hour. A fine may be imposed, though, if you stay longer than an hour.

The Dell Quay SC (Tel: 01243 785080) is situated on the quay and its jetty, adjoined to the south side of the

quay, is a secure place to leave your dinghy if going ashore to either the clubhouse or the popular Crown and Anchor pub (Tel: 01243 781712). The club welcomes visiting yachtsmen to its clubhouse, and refreshments are normally available on racing weekends. It also has a visitors' mooring close to the quay, but this dries out onto mud approximately three hours either side of High Water. The club doesn't charge for the use of this mooring, but it doesn't encourage visitors to stay beyond 24 hours, and anyone wishing to use it must get permission from the club's moorings officer first. Fuel is not available at Dell Quay, the nearest fuel pontoon being at Chichester or Birdham Pool marinas, but fresh water is available at the main entrance to the quay or on the sailing club's jetty.

Two boatyards located at Dell Quay are Wyche Marine (Tel: 01243 782768) and Dell Quay Marine (Tel: 01243 785954), both of which offer storage as well as a variety of repair and maintenance services.

Useful information – Chichester and the surrounding area

Chichester is an attractive town and offers a good selection of shops

EATING OUT

Woodies Wine Bar & Brasserie (Tel: 01243 779895) in St Pancras Street, on the east side of Chichester, has a congenial atmosphere and serves good quality food at reasonable prices. Practically the whole of St Pancras Street is devoted to restaurants on the one side, so if you find Woodies is full you won't need to look too far for a suitable alternative. Pizza Express (Tel: 01243 786648) on South Street and ASK (Tel: 01243 775040) on East Street are great if you are after cheap and cheerful Italian food. The Old Cottage (Tel: 01243 780859) on West Street is reputed to be good for quality Indian cuisine, while Confucius (Tel: 01243 783712) on Cooper Street is considered one of the best Chinese restaurants in the area without being extortionately expensive.

St Martins Tea Rooms (Tel: 01243 786715) on St Martins Street, tucked away down the side of Marks & Spencer, is ideal for a light lunch and its homemade organic food takes some beating, although be warned, it is rather expensive.

ASHORE

Chichester offers a wide range of interesting places to visit, the most obvious one being the cathedral (Tel: 01243 782595). Of Norman origin with Gothic additions, it includes an impressive

Useful information –Chichester Harbour

The tower mill at Langstone was built in the 18th century and was used to mill cereal. There was also a tide mill next to it, which was in use until 1968

piece of Roman mosaic flooring and a selection of 20th century art, including Marc Chagall's stained glass window and Graham Sutherland's painting entitled *Noli Me Tangere*. The cathedral is open daily from 0715–1900 in the summer and from 0715–1800 in the winter. Admission is free.

Pallant House Gallery (01243 536038) in North Pallant Street, Chichester, is also worth visiting. It houses one of the finest permanent collections of British Modern Art in the country, including works by Henry Moore, Pablo Picasso and Graham Sutherland. The gallery is open from Tuesday to Saturday 1000–1700.

For evening entertainment, the Chichester Festival Theatre (Tel: 01243 781312; 01243 784437) is justly renowned for its performances, with many of its productions transferring to the West End in London. The Chichester Cinema at the New Park (Tel: 01243

786650) is also good for interesting, non-mainstream films, while if it's a Hollywood blockbuster you are after, try Cineworld (Tel: 0871 200 2000) near the train station.

Among other places of historic importance in the area is the Fishbourne Roman Palace (Tel: 01243 785859). Built in 75AD, it is allegedly the largest Roman domestic architecture discovered north of the Alps. The remains of the north wing of the palace, enclosing an outstanding collection of mosaic floors, is now covered by a protective building and is open to the public daily from 22 January to 15 December. From 16 December to 21 January it is open on weekends only from 1000–1600.

A train or bus ride away to the east is the picturesque hilltop town of Arundel whose prime attraction is the castle (Tel: 01903 882173), the seat of the Dukes of Norfolk for more than 400 years. With a chequered history,

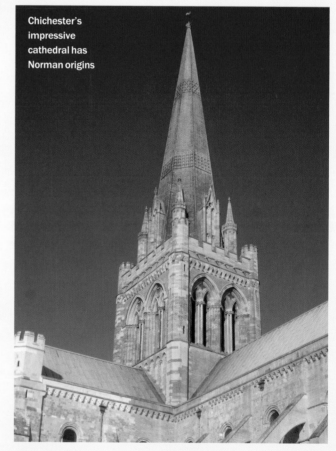

Chichester's impressive cathedral has Norman origins

parts of the castle date back to the 11th century when it was built by Roger de Montgomery, Earl of Arundel. Its treasured possessions comprise tapestries, portraits by artists such as Van Dyck,

Reynolds and Gainsborough, and exquisite furniture from the 16th century. The castle is open Tuesday to Sunday.

Goodwood House (Tel: 01243 755048), situated not far north of Chichester

Bosham Quay is a lovely place to visit, but it gets very busy in the summer

Terror, built c1880, was originally used for ferrying oysters to Emsworth

on the South Downs, is also open to the public from March to September. The house still encapsulates the flamboyant style of the Richmond family, displaying the magnificent French furniture that the 3rd Duke of Richmond collected while he was British Ambassador to Paris. It was this same duke who, 200 years ago, laid out a race course on the estate to accommodate the Sussex Militia Officers' annual horse racing. The duke was so pleased with the success of the event that in 1802 he arranged a three-day public

meeting and horse racing has continued here ever since.

Today, set high on the Sussex Downs, providing impressive views of the Solent, it has come to be regarded by some as the most beautiful race course in the world. To find out more, Tel: 01243 755022.

If you sail to Chichester Harbour in June, don't miss the Goodwood Festival of Speed (Tel: 01243 755055), reputedly one of the most impressive meetings of racing cars in the world.

Many of Chichester's surrounding areas are worth

a visit in their own right. West Wittering, with its long sandy beach, is great for children. You can anchor off East Head and row ashore, although it can get very congested during the summer months.

Bosham, perhaps the prettiest of the harbour villages, is popular with tourists and is best avoided at weekends. It was the home village of King Harold and it was from here that he sailed to Normandy in 1064.

The church, although thought to pre-date Harold by about 300 years, making it one of the oldest in

England, is depicted on the Bayeux Tapestry along with the history of the Battle of Hastings. A trip to this ancient church can be followed by a tour around Bosham Walk, the arts and crafts centre consisting of 19 little shops spread out over two floors.

As an area of outstanding natural beauty, there are plenty of charming walks and cycle paths to choose from. For more details, contact the Chichester Tourist Information Centre (Tel: 01243 775888) or the Chichester Harbour Conservancy (Tel: 01243

Chichester Harbour is an area of outstanding natural beauty, and there are some lovely walks and cycle paths to choose from

Useful information – Chichester Harbour

512301) which organises guided walks around the harbour throughout the year.

TRANSPORT

Buses: Good bus services link Chichester to the surrounding villages and towns. Tel: 0871 200 2233.
Trains: Many of the smaller towns and villages have stations with frequent connections to Chichester, Portsmouth and London. Tel: 0845 748 4950.
Taxis: Chichester: Donaways Taxis (Tel: 01243 782403); Central Cars (Tel: 01243 789432); Star Line Minicabs (Tel: 01243 531666); Chichester Cab Co (Tel: 01243 785765). Hayling Island: C Cars (Tel: 023 9246 8888).
Car hire: Hendy Hire: Tel: 01243 536100; Panther Cars: Tel: 01243 778109; Enterprise Rentacar Ltd: Tel: 01243 779500.
Cycle hire: Barreg Cycles: Tel: 01243 786104.
Ferries: The Itchenor ferry runs from the Itchenor jetty to Smugglers Lane in Bosham, or to and from moorings from Deep End to Birdham. Call 'Ferry' on VHF Ch 8 or Tel: 07970 378350. It operates daily from 0900–1800 during May to September and on weekends and bank holidays only during March to May and the month of October.
Air: Britain's major airports are within easy reach of Chichester: Heathrow (Tel: 0870 000 0123) is 57 miles away, Gatwick (Tel: 0870 000 2468) is 40 miles away and Southampton (Tel: 0870 040 0009) is about 35 minutes away by car.

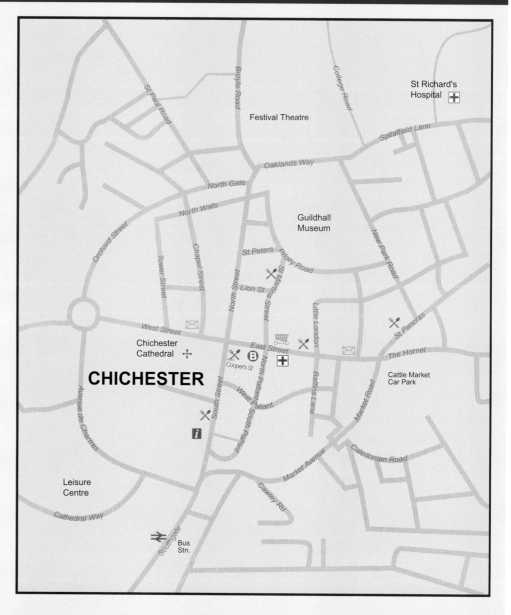

USEFUL INFORMATION

Harbour Office: VHF Ch 14; Tel: 01243 512301.
Chichester Cruiser Racing Club: Tel: 01235 535148.
Chichester Yacht Club: Tel: 01243 512918.
Itchenor Sailing Club: Tel: 01243 512400.
Dell Quay Sailing Club: Tel: 01243 785080.
West Wittering Sailing Club: Tel: 01243 514153.
Chandleries: Force 4 Chandlery (Birdham Road): Tel: 01243 773788; Harbour Chandlers (Emsworth): Tel: 01243 375500; Peters Chandlery: Tel: 01243 511033; Seateach: Tel: 01243 375774.
Marine services: Holman Rigging (Chichester Marina): Tel: 01243 514000; Lansdale Marine Ltd, (Itchenor): Tel: 01243 512374 (repairs outboard engines); Brian Strickland Harbour Engineering (Itchenor): Tel: 01243 513454; Roger Upham Marine Electronics: Tel: 01243 528299; WB Marine (engine and outdrive repair services): Tel: 07860 446199; Haines Boatyard (Itchenor); Tel: 01243 512228; Northshore Yachts: Tel: 01243 512611.
Sailmakers: Arun & Rockall Sails: Tel: 01243 573185; Halsey Lidgard Sailmakers: Tel: 01243 545410.
Police: Tel: 0845 0454545.
Coastguard: Lee on Solent: Tel: 023 9255 2100.
St Richard's Hospital: Tel: 01243 788122.
Doctor: Chichester: Tel: 01243 781833.
Dentist: Chichester: Tel: 01243 532992.
Tourist Information Office: Tel: 01243 775888.

Chapter four
The history of the Solent

Today, we regard the Solent as a single strait of water separating the Isle of Wight from the mainland coast of Hampshire, West Sussex and Dorset. With an eastern and western approach, it stretches approximately 25 miles from the Needles, a notorious group of rocks west of the Isle of Wight, to the Foreland, the easternmost tip of the island.

Although the Solent is now generally thought of as one specific area, historical evidence indicates there to have been a Western and Eastern Solent, with the latter often referred to as Spithead.

THE SOLENT'S ORIGINS

The Solent is basically the flooded valley of a river that once flowed eastwards when the present River Frome was its headstream and the rivers Itchen and Test were its tributaries. It is thought that during the last Ice Age the sea level was so low that not even the English Channel existed. About 10,000 years ago the enormous ice-sheets that had predominantly covered the northern continents started

to melt, causing the sea level to rise. In so doing, the valley of this Solent river and the lower parts of its tributaries and their flood plains were all submerged, resulting in the many estuaries and harbours that we see today. Despite the sea swamping the Solent, the Isle of Wight originally remained joined to the mainland by a ridge of chalk downs stretching westwards to the Dorset coast. Although there have been several theories on the subject, recent evidence suggests that this was not a continuous ridge, as once thought, but was in fact interrupted by paleovalleys that drained the Dorset and Hampshire coastlines. It was not until 2,000 years later that the last connection with the mainland was severed. However, the island that was created was far bigger than the one there today.

Throughout the centuries shingle spits have built up across the estuary and harbour mouths, occasionally even creating small headlands such as Hurst Spit, which stretches 1½ miles across the western approach of the Solent near Keyhaven.

It is generally thought, though, that by about 500BC, the Solent had more-or-less adopted its present form.

EARLY SETTLERS

Due to the rise in sea level not much evidence remains of the early inhabitants of Hampshire and West Sussex, although it is clear that the Mesolithic man, first drawn to the Solent by its rich natural resources, used flint as his primary material for tool and weapon-making. By about 1800BC Southern England was colonised by the Beaker folk whose name originated from the shape of their pottery. Their disappearance brought about the beginning of the Bronze Age, during which metal tools became more widespread. Their primary port is believed to have been Hengistbury Head, near Bournemouth in Dorset, where findings of ornaments made of bronze and amber imply a possible trade with the Eastern Baltic. The additional discovery of imported French bronze goods hints at the cross-Channel trading that must have existed between the Solent and northern France around this time.

In about 1,000BC the Solent shores were once again colonised by another group. These Celtic-speakers, using weapons and tools of iron, practised new methods of farming. Many archaeological finds, however, suggest that they were certainly not just peasant farmers but were in fact wealthy land-owners able to buy and import high-quality products. The significance of the Solent for foreign trading is clear in the final years of the first millennium BC, when initial batches of Italian wine were shipped to Christchurch harbour in Dorset for consumption at the nearby settlement at Hengistbury Head. It seems evident, too, that the shipping of various items fabricated from Isle of Wight stone began in the Iron Age.

In 43AD, at the command of Emperor Claudius, the Romans invaded Britain. Claudius was motivated out of fear that Southern England had the potential to become a dangerous opponent to Roman rule, besides which the country's independence and wealth made it desirable as part of the Roman Empire. It seems that during the early Roman period the Solent became a frequented anchorage and in fact there are indications that even before the Claudian invasion, Roman ships laden with goods were arriving in these waters.

On the eve of their onslaught, the Roman generals were reliably informed by a local king, Togidubnus and his Regnensian collaborators, that Chichester Harbour would offer a safe landing place for their armies. As a result of the king's cooperation he was rewarded with a spectacular palace at Fishbourne, situated at the head of the Chichester channel (the remains of which you can see today).

Throughout the latter years of Roman rule, Saxon pirates were already active, which meant that the Roman settlements and ports on the South Coast played a crucial role in defending England's shores. The fort at Portchester, built around the late third century, is one of the most impressive, and its stone walls and bastions, enclosing an area of about four acres, can still be seen today. Despite the potential strength of these coastal fortifications, once the Roman army officially withdrew in 410AD, the South

Fishbourne Roman Palace in West Sussex, as it would have looked in 75AD. The remains of the villa were discovered and excavated in the early 1960s

Coast entered a new era – 'the Adventus Saxonum, the coming of the Saxons'.

The initial colonising raids took place around 530AD and were well documented by the English historian Bede, although this was some 200 years later when the facts could by then have become distorted. Bede refers to these invaders as the three great nations of Germany: the Angles, Saxons and Jutes. The Solent territory appears to have been seized by the Saxons and Jutes, with the Saxons acquiring the lands of West Saex (Wessex) and South Saex (Sussex) and the Jutes capturing the Isle of Wight and parts of what is today the New Forest.

The *Anglo Saxon Chronicle* illustrates that one of the major Saxon settlements was Selsey, to the east of Chichester Harbour. This Saxon town, however, was most probably eroded by a rise in sea-levels between the eighth and 11th centuries, which could have contributed to the extensive tidal basins that exist today at Portsmouth, Langstone and Chichester.

There is clear evidence that maritime trade, including the importation of table wares from the Carolingian empire, was taking place in the Solent during the eighth century AD. Coins uncovered at Southampton reveal that the prosperity of the settlement of Hamwic, on the banks of the River Itchen, came about in the middle of the 8th century, although it noticeably declined in the 9th century when the Vikings began to raid the Solent. The issue of Hamwic's vulnerability was resolved in the 10th century when the town was re-established on higher grounds to the west. This new site became the medieval, walled town of Hamptun and subsequently trading was vigorously renewed on the eastern shores of Southampton Water. Crossings to and from the Isle of Wight once again got under way, this time transporting Bembridge limestone to the Saxon kingdoms where, due to their new-found Christian faith, they were building churches by the dozen.

During the reign of Edward the Confessor (1042–1066), the most powerful man of Wessex was Earl Godwin whose daughter Edith married the king while his son Harold, who lived in the small village of Bosham, became the last

The Anglo Saxon village of Bosham in Chichester Harbour, West Sussex. It was from here that Harold set sail for Normandy in 1064 to meet William the Conqueror, and where King Canute is said to have attempted to stop the tide. His daughter is thought to have been buried in the church

Anglo-Saxon king of England, defeated and killed by William the Conqueror at the battle of Hastings in 1066. Twenty years later, William the Conqueror ordered the compilation of the Domesday Book, which has given us a good insight into economic life on the South Coast during Norman times. The book depicts the numerous salterns, mills and fishing villages along the mainland coast and the Isle of Wight. In medieval times, the development of the salt industry became increasingly important and continued to thrive until the mid-19th century. Other main sources of income came from fishing, shellfish collecting, wildfowling and oyster fishing. Barge traffic gradually increased between many small ports carrying, among other items, bricks, coal, timber, salt and chalk, while creeks were modified to form reservoirs for tidemills. During the Middle Ages the development of Portsmouth as a major naval base and Southampton as a significant commercial port, importing spices, perfumes and silk from Italy in return for English wool, made the Solent a prime target for invaders. It is no surprise, therefore, that since the 15th century, the fortification of the Solent has played an important part in its history.

THE MILITARY SIGNIFICANCE OF THE SOLENT

During the Hundred Years War (1337–1453), military and naval activity brought varying degrees of prosperity and hardship to Hampshire towns. Both Portsmouth

Calshot Castle was built by King Henry VIII to protect Southampton Water

and Southampton suffered at the hands of the French who, during this period of intermittent unrest, frequently pillaged and burnt to the ground the towns and villages of the Isle of Wight.

However, in 1495, King Henry VII chose Portsmouth as his Royal Dockyard and ordered the construction of the world's first graving dock. And so, Portsmouth's place in history as the official home of the Navy was soon secured and consequently increased the strategic significance of the Isle of Wight.

King Henry VII was succeeded in 1509 by his ambitious younger son, Henry VIII, who began his reign by marrying his brother's widow, Catherine of Aragon, an association

Drawn & Engraved by Cha.ˢ Tomkins.   Published as the Act Directs, by C. and G. Kearsley Fleet Str: 179.

Yarmouth Castle on the Isle of Wight, constructed in 1547 to defend the island from enemy attack

that was to have radical consequences. Acutely aware that the England he had inherited was a minor influence in a Europe dominated by the French, Spanish and the Holy Roman Empire, King Henry VIII immediately set up a permanent navy, establishing Portsmouth Dockyard as his centre for fleet construction. As a result of animosity between himself and Emperor Charles V of Spain, Henry VIII also declared that the Solent should undergo a major refortification programme. Hostility stemmed from the fact that, in 1533, Henry VIII announced the annulment of his marriage to Catherine of Aragon who, beyond her child-bearing years and unable to give Henry a son, happened to be Charles V's aunt. Five years later, in 1538, the king of France, Francis I, and Charles V signed a peace treaty around the time that Henry VIII, assuming the title of Supreme Head of the Church of England, was excommunicated by Pope Paul III. Consequently the pope encouraged Charles V and Francis I to wage war on England, prompting Henry VIII to react quickly to this impending threat.

Henry VIII ordered a national defence project of an enormous scale along the whole of the South Coast. His theory was that if the invaders were prevented from capturing a harbour, they would be unable to land reinforcements and provisions, hence making it impossible for them to back up an army. Henry VIII accordingly demanded the construction of Calshot Castle, situated on a shingle spit close to the deep water channel at Southampton Water, and Hurst Castle, designed to defend the western arm of the Solent. Coastal artillery forts on the Isle of Wight were strategically positioned at Yarmouth, East and West Cowes, and Sandown. These forts were forerunners to the more comprehensive defences constructed in the middle of the 19th century during Queen Victoria's reign. Additional fortifications included Southsea Castle at Portsmouth as well as Netley Castle and St Andrews Castle, which were intended to protect the entrance to Southampton Water and the River Hamble.

Throughout this period the French were a recurring threat and invaded the Isle of Wight in 1545, only to be successfully beaten back by Sir Richard Worsley, Captain of the Island, who commanded the resistance at the time.

The last notable incident in this series of attacks was the sinking of the warship the *Mary Rose*, which was witnessed by the King himself. Having been built between 1509 and 1511, she was one of the first ships with the ability to fire broadside. A firm favourite of King Henry VIII, she tragically sank off Portsmouth Harbour in 1545 with the loss of around 700 men. The ship was recovered in the 1980s and, now on display in Portsmouth's Historic Dockyard, is the sole surviving 16th century warship.

In Queen Elizabeth I's reign from 1558–1603, the Isle of Wight was once again subject to attacks. The queen's cousin, Sir George Carey, who was now Captain of the Island, resided at Carisbrooke Castle near Newport in 1583 and oversaw repairs of all the island's defences. The queen

Carisbrooke Castle, where Charles I was imprisoned for 14 months prior to his execution in 1649

The sinking of the *Mary Rose*, King Henry VIII's flagship

A watercolour of
Old Portsmouth in 1857
by artist William Smyth

Photograph reproduced with the kind permission of Portsmouth Museums and Records Service

also ordered the ramparts at Portsmouth to be rebuilt, but otherwise, despite the fact that England was more-or-less constantly under threat of invasion by the French, Spanish and Spanish Netherlands, her policy was more to oppose any action at sea (hence the defeat of the Spanish Armada in 1588), rather than try to radically improve her father's defences.

With the onset of Civil War in 1642 Parliament took command of the Isle of Wight, retaining control throughout the entire conflict. Despite this, King Charles I who, encouraged by his French Catholic wife, Henrietta Maria, was set on a collision course with Parliament and the Puritans, fled to the island after escaping imprisonment

at Hampton Court in 1647. He was immediately captured and taken to Carisbrooke Castle, from where his several attempts to escape proved futile. He was subsequently transferred to Newport on the Isle of Wight and Hurst Castle on the mainland before being transported to London for his trial and execution in 1649.

A second extensive fortification programme was not seen until the years following the restoration of King Charles II in 1660. This was brought about not only from maritime conflict with the Dutch but also from the new king's enthusiasm for the Navy, which he renamed the Royal Navy. During his reign, the Royal Dockyard at Portsmouth received new ships, wharfs, storehouses

a labour force comprising Dutch prisoners, de Gomme modernised Portsmouth's Elizabethan town defences and reinforced Southsea Castle. The dockyard to the north of the town was enclosed with a rampart while, on the other side of the harbour, a rampart and moat, referred to as the Gosport Lines, were constructed to defend Gosport. With Fort Charles situated just to the north of Gosport Head and Fort James on Rat Island in the harbour, Portsmouth, by the 1680s, had become England's most impressive fortress.

Meanwhile, the latter half of the 17th century saw West Cowes on the Isle of Wight grow into a thriving port with significant trading links with the American colonies. During this time, a shipbuilding industry also developed, first at East Cowes but later spreading across the River Medina to West Cowes.

Between 1689, when William III became King of England, and 1710, during the reign of Queen Anne, radical improvements were made once again to Portsmouth's Royal Dockyard. This was motivated by the fact that Britain had become heavily involved in a battle with France for commercial and colonial supremacy, a conflict that was not to be finally resolved until 1815. By 1710, the dockyard had expanded by 10½ acres but despite this, a steady increase in the number of employees meant that they could no longer squeeze into the existing town. Consequently, the new settlement of Portsea, which was separated from Portsmouth by a mill pond, grew up around the dockyard.

The fact that Portsmouth and Gosport were the only towns to undergo large scale fortification improvements during the 18th century underlines the national strategic importance of Portsmouth Harbour. In 1745, King George II, fearing that the French would come to the help of the Jacobite Rebellion in Scotland, ordered the precursor to Fort Cumberland to be constructed on the south-east corner of Portsea Island in order to protect the entrance to Langstone Harbour. From 1747 to 1777 even further measures were taken to reinforce Portsmouth Harbour.

In 1779, when King George III was on the throne, the French and Spanish once more attempted to invade England, with 66 of their ships reaching the Solent. With the intention of landing at Stokes Bay in Gosport, they were in fact forced to retreat, but this whole episode led to the installation, a year later, of Fort Monckton at Gilkicker Point in Gosport.

Throughout the period of 1750 to 1850, due to near-continuous war, Portsmouth Dockyard was highly prosperous. It is to this era that the dockyard owes its spectacular brick storehouses which, still standing today, now form part of the Royal Naval Museum.

Other shipyards around the Solent also began to thrive around the late 18th century, notably Thomas Raymond in Southampton, Robert Fabian at Cowes and Eling, John Nowlan and Thomas Calhoun on the River Hamble, George Parsons at Bursledon and in particular Henry Adams at Buckler's Hard on the Beaulieu River. Their prosperity came with the onset of war in 1776, which started as a war of independence by the 13 American colonies but

and the first stone docks. The Great Ship basin and its six surrounding dry docks, two of which are now occupied by HMS *Victory* and the *Mary Rose*, bear testament to this great era. King Charles II was also fully aware that with the standing down of Cromwell's New Model Army at the time of the restoration, the Army was now much smaller, therefore accentuating the need to provide the dockyards and naval stores with more protection.

In 1665, Sir Bernard de Gomme, a Dutch military engineer who a few years earlier had been appointed Engineer-in-Chief of all the king's castles in England and Wales, began major reforms to Portsmouth Harbour's defences that were to last for more than 20 years. With

HMS *Euryalus* was launched in 1803 from Buckler's Hard, where Henry Adams (below) ran a prosperous shipyard

evolved into another struggle with France and Spain. The Royal Dockyard was unable to keep up with the fierce demand for new ships so the merchants' yards were called upon to provide assistance, the most successful of which were Parsons and Adams. Both these master shipwrights built ships for Nelson, with Henry Adams providing three of Nelson's Trafalgar fleet, the most notable of which was *Agamemnon*.

During the 10 years of peace from 1783 to the outbreak of the French Revolutionary and Napoleonic Wars in 1793, Henry Adams kept his business going by building three men-of-war. The 74 gun-ship the *Illustrious* was the first ever to be constructed at Buckler's Hard and, with an overall length of 168ft (51m), she was 8ft (2.4m) longer than the *Agamemnon*.

Throughout the French Revolutionary and Napoleonic Wars (1793–1815), the British had a military presence virtually all over the world, hence putting pressure on Portsmouth's role as a primary naval port. By 1800, the Royal Navy had no fewer than 684 ships and the dockyard was one of the world's largest industrial sites. The year 1797 saw the installation of Portsmouth's first steam engine, which pumped water from the dry docks, and in 1803 innovative machinery designed by Marc Brunel, father of the celebrated Isambard Kingdom Brunel, was introduced that could mass produce ship pulley blocks.

However, the end of the Napoleonic Wars brought the golden era of shipbuilding to a close. After two prosperous decades, master shipwrights of wooden craft, such as the Adams family at Buckler's Hard on the Beaulieu River, suffered a dramatic decline. By 1822 the workforce at Portsmouth Harbour's Royal Dockyard had dwindled to just 2,200 employees, although the yard's fortunes soon picked up with the introduction of steam propulsion, which led to its biggest expansion to date. Within a mere 20 years the number of staff had trebled and as early as 1829 work was being carried out on the world's first steam screw warship, HMS *Fox*.

French invasion scares were renewed during the reign of Queen Victoria from 1851–2 as well as in 1859, proving that Britain's alliance with France against Russia during the Crimean War in 1854 did not last long. The threat of attack in 1852 led to the construction of Fort

Albert and Fort Victoria on the Isle of Wight (see p17) and the building of new batteries on either side of Hurst Castle, while Fort Gomer and Fort Elson were set up in Gosport. This was followed in 1857 by the construction of three new ports between Fort Gomer and Fort Elson, each of which provided fire support at roughly 900-metre intervals. However, these forts, collectively known as the Gosport Line, soon became obsolete with the introduction in 1858 of Sir William Armstrong's new rifled, breech-loading guns. More powerful weapons meant that an invader based on Portsdown Hill could easily fire at the Royal Dockyard without worrying about the Gosport Line.

In 1859, under the recommendation of a Royal Commission, an enormous project got under way to reinforce Portsmouth and the Isle of Wight. This consisted of a ring fortress, the only one ever to be built in Britain. Five land forts were developed along the ridge of Portsdown Hill, while Fort Fareham was designed to protect the outer defences of Gosport. By 1863, further fortifications included five granite and steel sea forts constructed to cover Spithead, four of which still stand today. The defences on the Isle of Wight were also improved by the siting of several batteries, including those at Cliff End and the Needles, and the building of the Golden Hill and Bembridge forts. By 1907, however, with dramatic artillery improvements, most of the forts were declared obsolete and were subsequently disarmed.

By the beginning of the 20th century the Royal Dockyard began to produce the dreadnoughts. Launched in record time, HMS *Dreadnought* was the first major warship to have steam turbines. As these vessels were so large, new basins and locks were created to cope with the demand. The year 1913 saw the arrival of the new super-dreadnought, HMS *Queen Elizabeth*, the first British oil-fired battleship. During the First World War the Dockyard was hard-pushed to construct two battleships and five submarines as well as refit 1,200 vessels. Subsequently, by 1918, approximately 23,000 men and women were employed here, working shifts around the clock.

The period of the First World War wasn't just a busy time for the Portsmouth Dockyard. Thornycroft, originally established in London in 1864, but relocating to Southampton in the early 1900s, was also providing a steady stream of destroyers, including the L-Class ship HMS *Lance*, which fired the first naval shot of the war on 5 August 1914. Meanwhile Vosper, a company based in Portsmouth that would eventually merge with Thornycroft in 1966, was busy manufacturing workboats for the Admiralty along with ships' boats, whalers, dinghies and fenders. The interval between the wars was blighted by depression although during the 1930s Thornycroft launched the new D-Class destroyers, capable of reaching speeds of up to 38 knots, while Vosper made its name as a builder of high-speed craft. It was around this time that Vosper's Cdr Peter Du Cane designed *Bluebird II* for Sir Malcolm Campbell, who set out to achieve the world water speed record.

The Second World War meant another hectic spell for both these yards, with Vosper manufacturing hundreds of Motor Torpedo Boats (MTBs) and Thornycroft launching the mine-layer HMS *Latrona*. These times, of course, were also demanding for the Royal Dockyard, whose workforce had expanded to 25,000 people. Despite Portsmouth being heavily bombed by the Germans, by the end of the war the dockyard had repaired or refitted around 2,550 vessels. Armies and naval fleets assembled in the Solent in preparation for the D-Day invasion of Normandy, and Fort Southwick, one of the forts built along Portsdown Hill, became the operations centre for the landings. The entire strategy for the Allied landings on 6 June 1944, known as Operation Overlord, was masterminded at Portsmouth over a period of four years. During the Second World War, as with the First World War, all the Solent forts were re-equipped with modern weapons and searchlights. However, after the war ended, the shore batteries became obsolete and Coastal Defence was abolished in 1956.

As with the forts, the role of Portsmouth Royal Dockyard also dwindled after the Second World War. Due to defence cuts, the frigate HMS *Andromeda*, which was completed in 1967, was the last of the 286 ships to be built here. By 1984 the dockyard was stripped of its Royal title, but Portsmouth still remains the home port of the Royal Navy. With a registered charity charged with the conservation of the many historic buildings, part of the dockyard is now open to the public and provides one of the biggest attractions on the South Coast.

Unlike the Royal Dockyard, Vosper Thornycroft, which, as previously mentioned, was established as a single entity in 1966, has gone from strength to strength. Since the 1970s the company has secured major orders from the Royal Navy as well as from foreign navies, and in 2003 constructed the largest single-masted yacht in the world – the 75.2m (247ft) *Mirabella V*. She was certainly not the first yacht to be built on the Solent to cause great interest, for throughout history many spectacular vessels launched on this stretch of water have revolutionised world yachting.

HMS *Warrior* is berthed at the Portsmouth Historic Dockyard

THE GOLDEN ERA

During the 18th century, the Solent started to become fashionable with Royalty and the aristocracy. In 1750 Prince Frederick went to Southampton to benefit from the sea air, liking it so much that he returned later on in the same year. By chance he died shortly afterwards, but his sons were regular visitors to the town and soon many of the upper class were following their lead, believing that bathing in the sea was good for your health. By 1762, Southampton was referred to as 'one of the prettiest and healthiest towns in England'.

Cowes, too, became a popular resort with the wealthier sector of society during the late 18th and early 19th century. This was partly due to the fact that the French Revolutionary and Napoleonic Wars prevented their visiting the Continent and conducting their 'Grand Tour'. In 1813 Cowes organised its own regatta and two years later, on 1 June 1815, a group of London-based gentry set up the Yacht Club (later, in 1833, to become known as the Royal Yacht Squadron). The Prince Regent was made a member of this club in 1817 and in 1820, when he was crowned King George IV, the club assumed its 'Royal' title. By 1825 it had firmly installed itself on the Isle of Wight, a year later becoming the first yacht club to organise yacht racing in Britain and soon establishing itself as the world authority for devising racing rules and handicapping.

Its annual regatta, held in early August and subsequently known as Cowes Week, confirmed the Isle of Wight as Britain's sailing headquarters.

The Royal Navy certainly supported their exploits and, as a sign of their approval, issued a warrant authorising members of the Royal Yacht Squadron to fly a plain white ensign with the Union Flag in the corner. As sailing gradually became more widespread several other yacht clubs started to emerge. In 1836 the Royal London Yacht Club was set up, its first venue being the Coal Hole Tavern in the Strand. Nowadays the Royal London, as one of Europe's senior yacht clubs, is situated in the centre of Cowes where it has been since 1882. The year 1840 saw the inauguration of the Royal Southern Yacht Club in Southampton's High Street followed several years later by the Royal Albert Yacht Club in 1875 and the Castle Yacht Club at Calshot in 1887. As all these clubs actively encouraged yacht racing, the demand for skippers and deckhands in the Solent dramatically increased.

From the middle of the 19th century Cowes was attracting high profile residents in the form of the Royals themselves. In 1845, with the encouragement of Sir Robert Peel, Queen Victoria and Prince Albert purchased the Osborne Estate close to East Cowes. From the outset the Queen loved her new premises (which gradually expanded from 800 to 2,000 acres), coming here twice a year during the summer and over the Christmas period. The original house became too small for the Royal couple

The Royal Yacht Squadron, one of the world's most famous yacht clubs, has been housed at Cowes Castle at the entrance to the River Medina since 1858

Osborne House, Queen Victoria's Isle of Wight residence, is today owned by English Heritage and is open to the public

1863 that the public's interest in regatta racing really took off, inspiring a remarkably more competitive spirit on the water. Small racing boats were originally divided into classes by their overall length, but in 1887 this was replaced by the Linear Rating Rule. Although there were two and a half-, five- and 10-raters, the rule and length altered in 1896 to include two further rates – the half- and the one-rater. It was at this time that yacht designers Nathaniel Herreshoff, the American who introduced the fin-keel, and Charles E Nicholson of Gosport, really began to come to the fore. Charles Nicholson's first racing design, the half-rater *Coquette*, built in 1881, was an instant success and by 1889 had won no fewer than 110 prizes.

In 1906, the first International Rule was introduced for the smaller classes and as a result of this the 6-Metre boats came about. Racing round the buoys proved so popular in the Solent that many of the local yacht clubs introduced their own racing weeks. One of the most prominent clubs today is the Island Sailing Club which, set up in Cowes in 1889, specialises in small boat sailing and is official organiser of the Round the Island Race (see p178–179).

Cowes Roads was not only awash with sailing boats during this period but also with large steam vessels that would drop anchor between Osborne Bay to the east and Egypt Point to the west in order to get a good view of the action. In those days the smell of coal smoke and hot oil blended with that of seaweed and saltwater contributed to the overall ambience. Several of these steam yachts were designed by the illustrious GL Watson of Glasgow, one of the most memorable of which was among his later designs, the elegant *Nahlin*. Constructed for Lady Yule in 1930, she was a frequent visitor to the Solent. GL Watson had also masterminded what was perhaps the most celebrated of all the big class racing yachts, the Royal cutter *Britannia*. Built for King George V in 1893, she won 360 prizes and continued to excel right up until the king's death in 1935, at which point she was scuttled off the Isle of Wight.

The yachting scene flourished until the start of the First

who set about building a new one. As the view across the Solent had always reminded Prince Albert of the Bay of Naples, he and his builder, Thomas Cubbit, drew up plans for an Italian-styled villa, which today belongs to English Heritage and is open to the public. Having Royalty so close at hand proved a great inspiration to the yachting fraternity, with most clubs boasting at least one 'Queen's Cup' presented by the monarch.

The appearance of the schooner *America* in 1851 was a turning point in the history of yachting and initiated what was to become the most prestigious racing event in the world, the America's Cup.

America's arrival in the Solent on 31 July was prompted by her owner's desire to take part in what was known as the 100 Guinea Cup, an annual race around the island. It was the first year that a foreign yacht was permitted to take part and, due to her subsequent win, the trophy became known as the America's Cup and was taken back to the New York Yacht Club at Newport, Rhode Island. Yachts were accordingly allowed to challenge to win back the cup, which was undoubtedly the catalyst for the new era of technically advanced yachts.

In 1858 the Royal Yacht Squadron moved its premises to the Castle in West Cowes, which is where it resides today. It wasn't until the Prince of Wales became its patron in

The Nicholson-designed J-Class yachts *Endeavour* (left) and *Velsheda* (right) were built in Gosport in the 1930s to challenge for the America's Cup

World War, which broke out on the Monday of Cowes Week in 1914. The boatyards around the Solent were forced to stop building yachts in order to carry out military work. But after the war, yacht racing quickly revived, with the 12-Metre class developing the yachting skills of one man in particular – the famous designer and builder of aeroplanes Sir Thomas Sopwith, who would later go on to challenge for the America's Cup. The Big Class also made a come-back after the Great War, with close-run races taking place between King George V's *Britannia* and the Herreshoff-designed schooner *Westward*.

The late 1920s and 1930s marked the beginning of an age when yachts from both sides of the Atlantic were being raced under one rule – the American Universal Rule. Up until this time, British yachts, as touched on previously, were racing under the International Rule; a rule that was restrictive for craft longer than 14.6m (48ft), although advantageous to bermudan-rigged yachts. Based on suggestions proposed by designer Nathaniel Herreshoff, the Universal Rule, encompassing yachts of between 22.8m (74ft 8in) and 26.5m (86ft 9in) on the waterline, allowed the length of the waterline to be increased without restricting the sail area. This was compensated for by a bigger displacement and draught limit of 4.6m (15ft). Several existing British yachts, including *Astra*, *Candida*, *White Heather II* and King George V's *Britannia*, were converted to comply with the rule so that they could race alongside the revolutionary J-Class yachts. Of the genuine J-Class, however, only 10 were ever built, four of which were constructed in Britain at Camper and Nicholsons

yard in Gosport and six in America. These splendid yachts raced together for only eight seasons, from 1930-37.

In 1929, Sir Thomas Lipton, the legendary tea and grocery magnate, made his fifth and final challenge for the America's Cup. Lipton had first challenged for the cup in 1898, only really ever coming close to winning it on his fourth attempt, when the gaff-rigged *Shamrock IV*, designed by Charles E Nicholson, was just one race from victory in the best of five series. However, it was not to be and the American yacht *Resolute* made sure that the cup didn't leave the New York Yacht Club.

Lipton's fifth challenge denoted a brand new era for yacht design and racing. He again looked to Charles Nicholson and his family yard to design and build the 36.5m (119ft 6in) J-Class yacht *Shamrock V*, which certainly promised to be a hot contender. However, in true competitive style, the Americans constructed no less than four Js – *Enterprise*, *Weetamoe*, *Yankee* and *Whirlwind*, each representing slightly different interpretations of the J-Class rule. *Enterprise* proved to be the winner of the elimination series and was therefore chosen to go head-to-head with *Shamrock V* later that year off Newport, Rhode Island. Although the yachts were thought to be well matched in terms of design, they differed significantly in rig. *Enterprise*'s Park Avenue boom and lighter rigging enabled her to point higher to windward and tack more easily, resulting in her winning the America's Cup by a comfortable margin. On the death of Sir Thomas Lipton in October 1931, *Shamrock V* was sold to Sir Thomas Sopwith.

The second J-Class to be built on British soil, again at

The William Fife III-designed *Cambria* was built in 1928 to the International 23-Metre rule, but regularly raced against the J-Class yachts

Uffa Fox crewing for the Duke of Edinburgh in the Flying Fifteen *Coweslip*, a keelboat class Fox designed in 1947

the Camper & Nicholsons yard in Gosport, was *Velsheda*. Constructed in steel in 1933, she was commissioned by WL Stephenson, owner of a chain of general stores throughout the UK known as Woolworths. Never intended as an America's Cup challenger, *Velsheda* nonetheless enjoyed racing success, winning the King's Cup at Cowes Week in 1936.

In 1934, Thomas Sopwith laid down the gauntlet for the America's Cup, consequently commissioning Charles Nicholson to design his third J. On this occasion, Nicholson did not try to experiment with the hull form but did produce an innovative rig. The result was the spectacular *Endeavour*, although sadly, despite being the favourite to win the America's Cup, she was beaten convincingly by the American J-Class, *Rainbow*.

Undeterred by his defeat, Thomas Sopwith rechallenged for the Cup in 1937, this time towing *Endeavour* and *Endeavour II*, his latest Nicholson-designed J-Class, across the Atlantic. After some trial races, Sopwith eventually decided to put forward *Endeavour II*, but yet again the American defending boat, *Ranger*, proved the stronger, winning 35 out of 37 starts.

With the onset of the Second World War, 1937 marked the end of the Golden Era, for this was to be the last America's Cup contest for 21 years, drawing the Big Class racing to a close. During the war, the British J-Class yachts were laid up and subsequently left to disintegrate.

However, in recent years, the three remaining Js, *Velsheda*, *Endeavour* and *Shamrock V*, have all undergone extensive restoration and are now in regular commission. As a result, there has been a huge resurgence in interest and a number of new Js are also in build or on the drawing board, which are all based on the original designs. A new version of *Ranger*, the last J to be built, was launched in 2003 and now regularly competes against her older siblings.

It was during the period of peace between the two world wars that the Royal Ocean Racing Club (RORC) was established. Determined to organise an event that would compare to the Bermuda Race, the club committee introduced the 600-mile Fastnet Race. It originally started from Ryde but now sets off from Cowes every two years, rounding the Fastnet Rock before finishing at Plymouth.

With the outbreak of the Second World War, several Solent yachts were obliged to partake in military activity. Sir Thomas Sopwith's *Philante*, which he had used to tow *Endeavour* and *Endeavour II* across the Atlantic, was now being employed to escort conveys in the build-up to the invasion of North Africa.

As soon as peace was restored in 1945, sailing in the Solent began to re-emerge once more. Again Royal support played a significant part, with the Duke of Edinburgh doing much to encourage renewed interest in international yacht racing.

Traditional Tall Ships such as the *Stad Amsterdam* are still frequent visitors to the Solent

Two of Britain's most influential yacht designers: Alfred Mylne and Uffa Fox

An accomplished sailor in his own right, he proffered a cup to be competed for by International Dragon class yachts belonging to any nation. He and Princess Elizabeth were in turn presented with the Dragon *Bluebottle* by the Island Sailing Club as a wedding gift in 1948. Closely associated with the Duke of Edinburgh was the well-established yacht designer Uffa Fox: a regular crewmember in *Bluebottle* as well as in *Coweslip*, the Flying Fifteen that he designed himself. Born on the Isle of Wight in 1898, Uffa Fox had set up his own boatbuilding business by the time he was 21 years of age. His Flying Fifteen keelboat was one of the most successful post-war designs and inspired a range of planing keelboats from the Flying Ten through to the Flying Twenty Five. These classes, however, did not flourish in the way that the Flying Fifteen did, which gained a reputation as an exhilarating and competitive two-man racing dinghy.

Interest in offshore racing and sailing was again regenerated by Sir Francis Chichester's solo round-the-world circumnavigation in 1966–7, resulting in the Whitbread Round the World series (now known as the Volvo Ocean Race), which began in 1973. Since then other world-class sailors such as Sir Robin Knox-Johnston, who 33 years ago won the first around-the-world solo yacht race – the Sunday Times Golden Globe – completing a circumnavigation of the globe in 312 days, and Sir Chay Blyth, who in 1971 was the first person to sail non-stop westwards around the world, have also inspired the conception of other yacht races. The Global Challenge, organised by Sir Chay Blyth, was first held in 1992 and was aimed solely at amateur sailors who could pay to race around the world against the prevailing winds and tides, calling at a series of ports en route. Four editions were held before it folded in 2006. Sir Robin Knox-Johnston's biennial Clipper Race followed in 1996, this time sailing east to west, and is currently on its sixth edition.

Nowadays, the Solent is still very much an important centre for yachting expertise, underlined by the fact that many of the top British sailors such as Dame Ellen MacArthur, Dee Caffari, Ben Ainslie and Mike Golding have chosen to make it their home. Incorporating two major ports and an extensive range of other maritime industries, the Solent without doubt remains one of the busiest coastal areas in Britain.

Under headsail off Norris Castle, built in the late eighteenth century on the site of the original East Cowes Castle, which dates back to King Henry VIII's reign

Chapter five
Racing in the Solent

The Solent has long been an international centre for yachting and, as such, is home to some of Britain's oldest and finest yacht clubs, many of which are situated at Cowes on the Isle of Wight (see p54 and p166-72).

Here, races are held continuously throughout the year, and on most weekends during the summer this stretch of water is awash with sails. Even in the chilly and often damp depths of autumn and winter, you'll rarely find a weekend when there isn't some sort of racing taking place in the Solent, whether it is dinghies, keelboats or yachts. Fixtures range from the highly popular and long-running

Garmin Hamble Winter Series (see p181) to Cowes Week and the Round the Island Race (see p178-9), the Solent's premier events, and local club races for dinghies. For offshore racers there's plenty going on, too, including a regular programme of JOG and RORC races, and some of the world's leading round-the world events also make the Solent a port of call. Several of the events cited on the following pages are internationally renowned so you may wish to time your visit to the Solent to coincide with these festivities. Then again, it could help you to plan your route to ensure that you stay well clear of all this activity!

Cowes Week

Cowes Week is one of the most prestigious and largest regattas in the world. First held on 10 August 1926, the week-long regatta has taken place every year since, interrupted only by the two world wars. Around 8,500 sailors, comprising people of all ages and abilities, now take part each year in over 1,000 boats – just a slight improvement on the first race, which attracted only seven entries! It's an event that appeals to a wide-range of boats, from 104-year-old classic Fife-designed cutters to modern high-performance catamarans and offshore racers capable of speeds in excess of 35 knots and traditional Solent-based keelboats.

Since 1964, the event has been organised by Cowes Combined Clubs (CCC), a limited company representing 10 of the Solent's yacht and sailing clubs that co-ordinates the racing. Around 280 races are held over the duration of the event, with at least 34 starts taking place per day.

Besides the sailing, this world-renowned regatta is also a major social occasion, and an important date in the social diary of the British aristocracy, traditionally sandwiched between Goodwood and the grouse-shooting season. Ten thousand spectators visit Cowes each day to watch the racing, and the town's population increases by another 40,000 people on the event's penultimate night, when three tons of rockets are set off at what has become one of the most impressive fireworks demonstrations in the country. Ashore, there's also a carnival-like atmosphere, with a lively social schedule including yacht club balls, live-band line-ups, beer tents and street entertainment giving crews and spectators alike plenty to get involved with. As a result, an estimated £58 million is injected into the local economy each year, making it an event that Cowes is keen to cultivate and cherish.

Whether you're a racing sailor or not, it's a spectacular event to watch or participate in, and one that looks like it has a very healthy future indeed.

Round the Island Race

One of the world's largest yacht races, this annual event is held one Saturday in the latter half of June. Organised by the Island Sailing Club in Cowes, it attracts almost 2,000 yachts and 14,000 competitors, including many of the country's top sailors. Unlike many events of its league, however, the Round the Island Race is also aimed at weekend sailors and family cruisers, and is seen by many as an opportunity to take part in a good day's racing that isn't just for the die-hard, carbon fibre brigade.

You must be prepared for an early start, though: the first gun of the day is fired at 0500, with another 25 starts following in quick succession. With so many boats on the water, too, you must also be prepared for some close quarters manoeuvring during the 50-mile course, particularly through the Hurst Narrows.

The Round the Island Race was conceived by Major Cyril Windeler of the Island Sailing Club in 1930, who suggested that a race should be introduced for small boats between 5 and 25 tons. The first race was held in 1931 and saw 25 entries, and was won by the 6.7m (22ft) Cornish fishing boat *Merry Conceit*.

Today, over 60 trophies are handed out, and although the majority go to high-performance racers, small boats still get a look in, often carrying off the top prize – the Gold Roman Bowl, a replica of a gold bowl dredged from the River Thames that is thought to have come from a nearby Roman site. Contessa 26 and 32 builder Jeremy Rogers has won the Gold Roman Bowl three times with the Contessa 26 *Rosina of Beaulieu*, and in 2007 it was won by the Nordic Folkboat *Madeleine*. The record for the fastest circumnavigation by a monohull currently stands at 4 hours, 5 minutes and 40 seconds, which was set by Mike Slade's *Skandia Life Leopard* in 2001.

Rolex Fastnet Race

Starting every two years, straight after Cowes Week, the Fastnet Race is regarded by many as one of the world's leading ocean races along with the Sydney–Hobart Race. The race was conceived in 1925 by an Englishman called Weston Martyr who, having competed in the 1924 Bermuda Race on board *Northern Light*, became infatuated with ocean racing. Following his proposal a committee was set up consisting of himself, EG Martin, owner of the pilot cutter *Jolie Brise*, and Malden Heckstall-Smith, the editor of *Yachting Monthly* magazine. The committee members planned a route of over 600 miles from the Isle of Wight to the Fastnet Rock off the south-west coast of Ireland and from there to Plymouth.

The first Fastnet Race attracted a total of seven yachts. Competing for the Fastnet Challenge Cup, they set off from the Royal Victoria Yacht Club's start line at Ryde on 15 August 1925. Having secured a resounding victory in *Jolie Brise*, Martin proposed that the race should take place the following year and subsequently announced the formation of the Ocean Racing Club (now RORC).

Since then, the event has attracted a great deal of interest among thousands of sailors from all nationalities. Many, however, will not forget the disaster in 1979, when the largest fleet ever, comprising 303 yachts, was caught out in a Storm Force 10 with the tragic loss of 17 lives. Special regulations were then introduced whereby trysails and VHF radios became mandatory and the number of entrants was restricted to 300.

Taking place over the best part of a week, this ultimate offshore race continues to be an intense and highly competitive challenge, testing the limits of the crews' teamwork and tactical skills.

Cowes Powerboat Festival

It's not just yachts that have all the racing fun along this stretch of water. Each summer, the waters of the central Solent throb with the sound of 2,000hp engines as some of the fastest racing machines in the world charge around courses at break-neck speeds. First held in 1961, the Cowes Classic Powerboat Festival is the Solent's leading motor boat event, and as well as attracting a number of traditional craft – some of which took part in the famous Cowes–Torbay Race – it also plays host to the king of offshore racing, the P1 Powerboat World Championships. The adrenalin-fuelled, petrol and diesel-guzzling event may not be to everyone's taste, but anyone sailing in the Solent while it's taking place can't fail to miss it.

Red Funnel Easter Challenge

Organised by the Royal Ocean Racing Club (RORC) in conjunction with several of the Cowes' yacht clubs, the Red Funnel Easter Challenge is a warm-up regatta for the IRC and IRM boats. In the words of the RORC, the owner of the IRC and IRM rating systems, the IRC 'is a time-on-time rating system for coastal and offshore yacht racing, created principally to enable all types of monohull yachts to be handicapped for racing at club level on an international basis'. They establish the handicap by assigning each yacht a Time Corrector (TCC), which is derived from the dimensions of the hull and rig as well as from various other characteristics of the yacht.

Whereas the IRC embraces the more conventional family cruiser-racers, the IRM rating rule, introduced in 2000, is aimed at the more serious racing boats for top-level sailors, incorporating the grand prix one-designs such as the Mumm 30, the Farr 40 and the Farr 52.

The Easter Challenge, sponsored by the Solent ferry operator Red Funnel, is becoming an increasingly popular event. The tight courses in the central Solent really enable crews to practise their teamwork and boat handling skills, priming them for the rest of the season. Racing takes place over three days between 1000 and 1800, after which the boats return to Cowes Yacht Haven.

Solent Old Gaffers

The Golden Era of yachting is still alive in the Solent thanks to several organisations that continue to promote traditional boats, running a series of events throughout the year. One of these organisations is the Old Gaffers Association (OGA), a national group set up to promote and celebrate gaff rig. The Solent branch of the OGA is one of the biggest in the UK and its annual programme includes events at Yarmouth on the Isle of Wight, Bursledon, Cowes and Chichester Harbour. Its Annual Race & Rally, held in either August or September in alternate parts of the Solent, usually attracts over 60 gaffers and dates back to the early days of the association in 1958.

Little Britain Cup

Not to be confused with the TV comedy programme of the same name, the Little Britain Challenge Cup takes place each September and is based around a series of four races in the Central Solent. Organised by the Royal Yacht Squadron, the event is a corporate bash, open to anyone with a direct link to the construction industry. It features a range of boats including Sigma 38s, Sunsail 37s, Bénéteau 40.7s, and IRC racers, which are divided into two classes – Racing and Cruising.

The event was first held in 1988, organised by Peter Thompson, Phil Davis and Steve Green of Little Britain Office Development on London Wall, and since then has become England's biggest regatta after Cowes Week, and the largest industry-based event in Europe, with over 200 boats taking part each year. Besides the racing, thousands of pounds are also raised for sailing charities such as the Ellen MacArthur Trust, Jubilee Sailing Trust and Skandia Team GBR Palalympic Sailing Team.

Hamble Winter Series

This popular Solent event is organised by the Hamble River Sailing Club and is now in its 26th year. It's the biggest event in the club's calendar and thought to be the largest winter series in Europe, attracting nearly 300 boats each year. Held between October and December, the eight-race series features a range of boats between 6.1m and 14.6m (20-48ft), including Laser SB3s, Maxis, Bénéteau 34.7s and Hunter 707s.

Traditional Solent classes

Racing on the Solent is proving increasingly popular, with no fewer than 40 affiliated classes. Among the larger fleets you are likely to come across are the Etchells, the Contessa 32s, the Laser SB3s and the Sigma 33s and 38s. However, many of the more traditional fleets you see off the South Coast today have in fact been established for well over 50 years, and have formed a significant part of the Solent's yachting history. With their beautiful classic lines, they will hopefully continue to play an important role in the racing scene for many more years to come. The following is a brief insight into the background of a selection of these historic classes.

Bembridge Redwing

A white number on a red sail

This class of distinctive red-sailed one-designs originated in 1896 when Charles E Nicholson designed the first Bembridge Redwing hull to meet the demands of nine gentleman who were keen to replace their costly half-raters. The new 6.7m (22ft 1in) design, which had an overhanging counter stern typical of that era as well as a long, shallow keel to accommodate the shoal waters of Bembridge Harbour, was an enormous success; within a few months 14 Tradwings had been ordered from Camper & Nicholsons for the 1897 season.

Towards the end of the 1930s the original Redwings were beginning to fall apart so Charles Nicholson was once again commissioned to produce a new hull.

The second Redwing, measuring 8m (27ft 11in) LOA, was 1.8m (5ft 10in) longer than its predecessor and a little narrower in the beam with a slightly deeper draught. Constructed of Lagos mahogany on American rock elm timbers with stem and sternposts of grown oak, 20 of the new design were built between 1938 and 1946.

In 1989, 13 out of the 20 Redwing owners opted to replace their wooden boats with glassfibre versions in order to cut down the maintenance costs. The 13 boats were purchased by a charter company and moved to Poole in Dorset, while the remaining seven Redwings, having undergone degrees of restoration, continue to race competitively in the fleet.

Victory class

The Victory class, today comprising a fleet of around 40 boats, was established in 1934. Based on the Alfred Westmacott-designed Bembridge One-Design, which was introduced in 1904, the distinctive 6.4m (20ft 9in) black clinker hulls make the Victorys easy to spot in their home waters. Slightly longer than their Bembridge counterparts, the Victorys also featured a bermudan sail plan – designed by Charles Nicholson – instead of the traditional gaff, and a shallower draught of 0.8m (2ft 6in). Thanks to early involvement from the Navy, the Victory class was soon well established, and a fleet of 23 boats was also set up at the Gibraltar YC, where they are still sailed today.

Victorys could only be built by approved builders using the official templates. R&A Hamper of Fareham were the principle builders of the class, although Harry Feltham and AW Clemens of Portsmouth and Woodnutts of St Helens were also responsible for a good number. Four Victorys, the first to be launched since 1962, were built in the 1980s by Southsea boatbuilder John Perry, and in 2007 the first glassfibre Victory was launched. Like many of its contemporaries that have gone down the glassfibre route, it is hoped that the new minimal maintenance Victorys will inject fresh blood into the class and continue its popularity.

A note of interest is that each boat has a different coloured boot-top, with the colour indicating which of the six local sailing clubs that it belongs to. Portsmouth SC, for example, is red whereas the Hardway SC is yellow and the Royal Naval Sailing Association white. Allocated the letter 'Z' as its sail mark by the Solent Classes Racing Association, the fleet races from mid-April to mid-October on Tuesday and Thursday evenings as well as on Saturday afternoons and at Cowes Week.

X One-Design

The X One-Design (XOD) was created by Alfred Westmacott in 1909. Westmacott, who was based at Woodnutts Boatyard at St Helens on the Isle of Wight, specialised in the construction of small day racing boats and was also responsible for the design of the Solent Sunbeam (see p184) and Seaview Mermaid (see p187).

By the start of the First World War 10 boats had been built while the era between the wars saw the fleet expand to 81. With an LOA of 6.1m (20ft 8in), the XOD was originally constructed of pitch pine on oak, and has a bermudan rig and a fixed iron keel. Although the hull remains true to the original design, changes have been introduced over the years to the approved types of timber, fastenings and surface treatments used. However, great care has been taken to ensure that the older boats in the class remain competitive. Today there are 170 XODs at five locations in the Solent, comprising the Hamble, Itchenor, Lymington, Parkstone (Poole) and Yarmouth. Each location is known as a Division and besides seasonal racing organised by the local clubs there are also yearly races between the Divisions. The class also has its own start at Cowes Week and in 2007, 71 XODs took part.

Solent Sunbeam One-Design

In October 1922 three members of the Hamble River Sailing Club met up to plan the construction of three boats. Designed by Alfred Westmacott, these vessels were launched a year later, forming the beginnings of the Solent Sunbeam fleet. Shortly afterwards several more were built, followed by the start of a second fleet in Falmouth in 1924. Today the class continues to thrive, with 27 Solent Sunbeams kept at the home port of Itchenor and another 21 in Falmouth. Traditionally all the boats' names have to end in a 'Y', although there are one or two in Falmouth that apparently do not comply with this protocol.

With an LOA of 8m (26ft 5in), the Sunbeam has a one-design hull but its sail configuration can vary provided the maximum size of the foresail is 9.3m² (100 sq ft) and the total sail area comes to no more than 27.9 m² (300 sq ft). The Solent Sunbeams, with their 10.7m (35ft) mast, fly a spinnaker of 47m² (506 sq ft), whereas the Falmouth boats have retained the original system of booming out the luff of the jib. Moving with the times the Solent boats are now also allowed to have aluminium masts and booms, along with carbon-fibre spinnaker poles. Their hulls, however, are still made of pitch pine on oak, which fares so well that the older boats are just as capable of winning races as the newer ones.

Since their conception in 1923 Sunbeams have competed each year at Cowes Week and look set to continue to do so for many years to come. A strong

connection exists between the Solent and Falmouth fleets, both of which have some excellent helmsmen, making for high standards of racing. With a crew of two or three, there are many trophies to compete for in the Solent throughout the year, both at Cowes and Itchenor.

National Swallow

The Swallow is an Olympic thoroughbred that has brought pleasure to many of Britain's finest yachtsmen over six decades. Stewart Morris and David Bond achieved a Gold medal for Britain in the class in 1948 at

the Torbay Olympics and stamped an image on the one-design that modern Swallow sailors cherish with pride.

Designed as a two to three-man keelboat by Tom Thornycroft specifically for the 1948 Olympics, the National Swallow soon established itself in Solent waters and has been a long-standing favourite at Cowes Week. At 7.8m (25ft 5in) LOA, the Swallow is slightly shorter than the International Dragon and carries less sail area. However, with its low freeboard and relatively small cockpit, there are few more exciting keelboats to sail and certainly few that are wetter.

Today, more than 30 Swallows are based at Itchenor Sailing Club in Chichester Harbour, with a small fleet at Aldeburgh in Suffolk. The fleet regularly races with 15 to 20 competitors and many boats are owned by small syndicates, several incorporating sailors who previously excelled in top-flight dinghy racing. Two new boats have been built in recent years and the class is highly competitive, with any of a dozen Swallows sharing the winning guns at Itchenor and the trophies at Cowes.

International Dragon

The International Dragon was conceived by Norwegian Johan Anker for a design competition organised by the Royal Yacht Club of Gothenburg in Sweden in 1929, with the intention of being an affordable racing keelboat. Its elegant sheerline, spoon bow, low freeboard and counter stern replicate the J-Class yachts of the same era. The boats were originally designed with long coachroofs and a short cockpit, creating enough room for two small berths and sitting headroom down below. The idea was to enable crews to sleep aboard overnight during regattas, although the accommodation and coachroof was removed from most boats after the war in favour of a larger open cockpit.

The first British fleets were established on the Clyde and at Hastings in 1932. By 1935, six Dragons were racing at Cowes against the Knud Reimers-designed Tumlaren double-enders. Four years later, at the outbreak of the Second World War, the Dragon had become the favoured small boat one-design at Cowes. The class gained a more prominent profile thanks to the 1948 Olympic Games, for which many new Dragons were built. Among these were DK 214 *Blue Skies* at the Clare Lallow Boatyard in Cowes and DK 192 at the Camper & Nicholsons' yard in Gosport.

Later that year, the Island Sailing Club at Cowes presented Princess Elizabeth and Prince Philip with the Camper & Nicholsons-built *Bluebottle*, the smallest official Royal yacht ever launched. From then on, the Royal couple became members of the Island Sailing Club, keeping *Bluebottle* at Cowes. Encouraging renewed interest in international yacht racing after the war, Prince Philip founded the Edinburgh Cup, a regatta set up specifically for International Dragon class yachts from any nation. The Edinburgh Cup was first held in 1949 at the end of Cowes Week and, as it is hosted by each British Dragon fleet in turn, it did not return to the Solent until 1954. On this occasion, 22 Dragons gathered at Bembridge on the Isle of Wight, with *Bluebottle* finishing second overall, achieving the best position among the Solent boats.

The modern-day International Dragon is a thoroughbred one-design racing keelboat with worldwide popularity. The Solent fleet, today consisting of about 40 Dragons, continues to be based at Cowes and has a busy annual racing and social programme.

The annual South Coast Championship takes place over the May Bank Holiday weekend and is popular both with local and visiting boats. The class has also firmly established itself at Cowes Week, when Dragons from countries throughout Europe and even sometimes as far afield as Australia take part.

Flying Fifteen

The Solent fleet, consisting of about 15 Flying Fifteens, is based at Cowes Corinthian Yacht Club (CCYC) on the Isle of Wight. Designed by the famous Cowes yacht designer, Uffa Fox, in 1947, the Flying Fifteen revolutionised small keelboat racing. With a LOA of 6m (20ft) and a LWL of 4.5m (15ft), its vee-sectioned bow and long flat run aft allow the boat to plane smoothly in winds of over 12 knots. The steel keel has been skilfully designed to enable the boat to be launched and trailed easily yet without compromising on stability.

Originally, Flying Fifteens were cold-moulded in construction, but inevitably modern materials soon took over, and in 1952 the design became one of the first production boats to be built in glassfibre. Since then, carbon fibre and composite hulls have become the norm but old wooden classics still race competitively against their more modern counterparts. The one-design rule helps ensure that all the boats are equal, regardless of age, putting the onus on the skills of the crew, rather than the size of the owner's wallet.

The Solent fleet meets every Tuesday evening from April to September and most weekends throughout the year. Since the Flying Fifteen's inauguration, 40 competitive fleets have been established within the UK, with a further 20 or so throughout the world.

South Coast One-Design

The South Coast One-Design's (SCOD) roots lie in Cowes, as it was thanks to a group of Island Sailing Club sailors that the cruiser-racer was conceived. They wanted a comfortable cruising yacht that could be raced around the Solent as a one-design class. With accommodation for four, she had to be easy to handle, and inexpensive to buy and maintain.

Charles E Nicholson was commissioned and in 1955 produced a design for a yacht that was 7.9m (25ft 11in) LOA, on a beam of 2.4m (7ft 10in). With a voluminous interior and standing headroom of 6ft (1.8m) around the galley, the SCOD proved an immediate success.

Six were launched that year – five built by Clare Lallow of Cowes – and another 21 in 1956. In total, 106 were built by various Solent boatbuilders, but it was Burnes Shipyard of Bosham that built the most.

Burnes started building SCODs when David Bowker, the yard's owner, was asked to build one because Lallows hadn't time. The SCODs were, unusually for the time, built on spec in batches of seven, with just a man and a boy working on each one.

Seaview Mermaid

Like so many of the Solent classes, the Seaview Mermaid has seen many changes in the 100 years since the design was conceived, yet it remains essentially the same as GU Laws originally intended. Designed in 1907 to supersede Seaview YC's fleet of six-year-old 4.6m (15ft) Ark class gaffers, the Seaview Mermaids were elegant in profile, with a pretty sheerline, long overhangs and reasonable-sized gaff rig. They were built by Arthur Taylor of Sandown on the Isle of Wight, but were later sold to the Medway YC and replaced with a second fleet in 1922 built by Woodnutts at St Helens. These 7.9m (26ft) bermudan-rigged, larch on ash-built Mermaids were themselves replaced in 1963 with a cold-moulded ply version, and again in 1994 by a fleet built in glassfibre. All types of construction are still competitive, and as well as a packed annual racing programme, the current fleet of 13 boats is often chartered out for corporate entertainment.

Daring class

Another Cowes-based class is the Daring. Designed by Arthur Robb in 1961, this 33-footer is one of the most prolific of the Solent classes and although not built in large numbers – 36 were built between 1961 and 1992 – nearly all remain in commission today.

With its long overhangs, clean lines and simple bermudan rig, the Daring is Robb's most enduring design and was inspired by the 5.5-Metre *Vision II*, which he designed in 1955 and which went on to win a silver medal for Great Britain at the 1956 Olympics.

Unlike the rest of the traditional one-designs mentioned here, the Daring was never built in wood, as at the time wooden boats were considered expensive to build and maintain and glassfibre construction had all but superseded it. Portsmouth-based Halmatic Ltd, who produced the first glassfibre Flying Fifteens (see p186), built the first 15 boats in the class, before construction was transferred to Island Builders of Ryde on the Isle of Wight and then John McIntosh/Souters.

Like the Solent's other traditional designs, the class is raced at Cowes Week each year and every weekend between late April and September. In recent years, it has also formed an affiliation with the Royal Navy, which has led to the Navy naming its new fleet of T45 Destroyers after the class. HMS *Diamond,* the third T45, which was named after Daring No5, is currently in build at Vosper Thorneycroft's yard in Portsmouth Harbour.

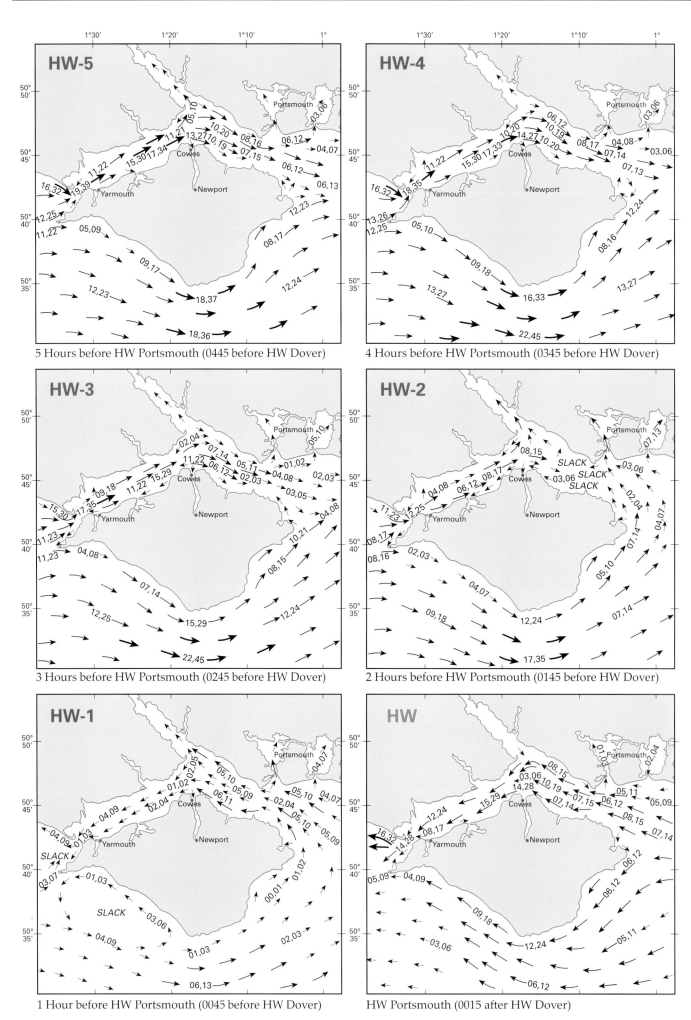

5 Hours before HW Portsmouth (0445 before HW Dover)

4 Hours before HW Portsmouth (0345 before HW Dover)

3 Hours before HW Portsmouth (0245 before HW Dover)

2 Hours before HW Portsmouth (0145 before HW Dover)

1 Hour before HW Portsmouth (0045 before HW Dover)

HW Portsmouth (0015 after HW Dover)

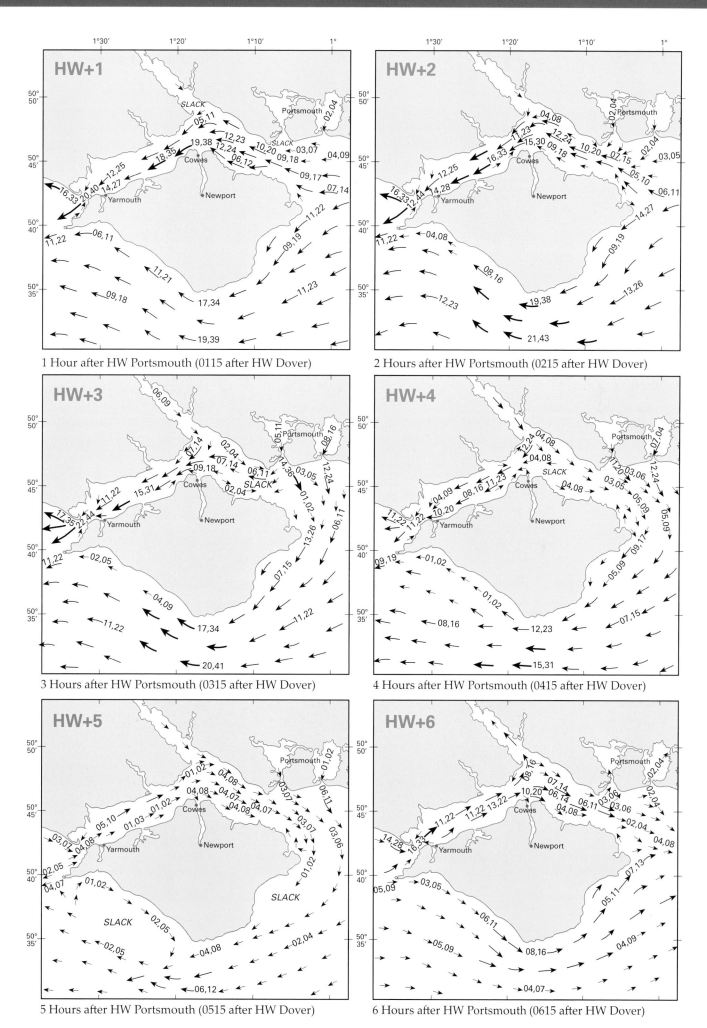

1 Hour after HW Portsmouth (0115 after HW Dover)

2 Hours after HW Portsmouth (0215 after HW Dover)

3 Hours after HW Portsmouth (0315 after HW Dover)

4 Hours after HW Portsmouth (0415 after HW Dover)

5 Hours after HW Portsmouth (0515 after HW Dover)

6 Hours after HW Portsmouth (0615 after HW Dover)

Useful waypoints

All positions are referenced to the WGS84 datum but should be assumed to be approximate

AAA Marine	50°46'.09N	01°18'.43W	Dean Tail South	50°43'.04N	00°59'.57W
After Barn	50°51'.53N	01°20'.82W	Dibden Bay	50°53'.70N	01°24'.92W
Air Canada	50°47'.34N	01°16'.84W	Dorset Yacht	50°40'.31N	01°52'.45W
Alpha (Cowes)	50°46'.24N	01°18'.11W	Dunfords ('B')	50°43'.41N	01°31'.63W
Aquaspec	50°45'.43N	01°25'.89W	Durns Pt obstn (S end)	50°45'.40N	01°27'.05W
Ashlett	50°49'.99N	01°19'.75W	East Bramble	50°47'.23N	01°13'.63W
B&G	50°48'.46N	01°15'.73W	East Hook	50°40'.58N	01°55'.22W
Bald Head	50°49'.90N	01°18'.25W	East Knoll	50°47'.96N	01°16'.83W
Barnes Ingram	50°43'.03N	01°38'.09W	East Lepe	50°45'.93N	01°21'.07W
Bay	50°46'.23N	00°58'.14W	East Looe	50°41'.09N	01°55'.82W
Bembridge Ledge	50°41'.15N	01°02'.81W	Echopilot (A)	50°42'.80N	01°32'.53W
Bembridge Tide Gauge	50°42'.46N	01°05'.02W	eDigitalResearch	50°44'.18N	01°23'.79W
Berthon (Fl Y 4s)	50°44'.20N	01°29'.22W	Elephant	50°44'.63N	01°21'.88W
Beta (Cowes)	50°46'.28N	01°17'.62W	Eling	50°54'.47N	01°27'.85W
Black Jack	50°49'.13N	01°18'.09W	Fairway (Needles)	50°38'.24N	01°38'.98W
Black Rock	50°42'.58N	01°30'.63W	Fastnet Insurance	50°47'.66N	01°13'.65W
Bob Kemp	50°45'.18N	01°09'.65W	Flying Fish	50°47'.42N	01°15'.90W
Boulder (Looe Channel)	50°41'.57N	00°49'.09W	Gales HSB	50°46'.15N	01°16'.65W
Bourne Gap	50°47'.83N	01°18'.34W	Gleeds	50°46'.12N	01°06'.42W
Bramble Bank	50°47'.41N	01°17'.15W	Greenland	50°51'.11N	01°20'.38W
Bridge	50°39'.63N	01°36'.88W	Gurnard	50°46'.22N	01°18'.84W
Britanniaevents.co.uk	50°48'.63N	01°16'.66W	Gurnard Ledge	50°45'.52N	01°20'.59W
Browndown	50°46'.57N	01°10'.96W	Gymp	50°53'.17N	01°24'.30W
Burges Salmon	50°47'.31N	01°12'.10W	Gymp Elbow	50°53'.50N	01°24'.68W
Bury	50°54'.14N	01°27'.12W	Hamble Point	50°50'.15N	01°18'.66W
Cadland	50°51'.02N	01°20'.54W	Hamstead Ledge	50°43'.87N	01°26'.18W
Calshot	50°48'.44N	01°17'.03W	Hard	50°45'.15N	01°58'.14W
Calshot Spit Lt F	50°48'.35N	01°17'.64W	Harwoods	50°42'.87N	01°28'.55W
Castle (NB)	50°46'.45N	01°05'.38W	Hill Head	50°48'.07N	01°16'.00W
Castle Point	50°48'.71N	01°17'.67W	Hook	50°49'.52N	01°18'.30W
Cathead	50°50'.61N	01°19'.24W	Horse Elbow	50°44'.26N	01°03'.88W
Champagne Mumm	50°45'.64N	01°23'.12W	Horse Sand	50°45'.53N	01°05'.27W
Charles Stanley	50°42'.68N	01°29'.70W	Horse Sand Fort Lt	50°45'.01N	01°04'.34W
Chi	50°45'.72N	00°57'.26W	Horse Tail	50°43'.23N	01°00'.23W
Chichester Bar Beacon	50°45'.92N	00°56'.46W	Hound	50°51'.68N	01°21'.52W
Citymain	50°45'.78N	01°19'.76W	HW Corporate Finance	50°49'.16N	01°15'.70W
Colten ('C')	50°43'.87N	01°30'.95W	Hythe Knock	50°52'.83N	01°23'.81W
Coronation	50°49'.55N	01°17'.62W	Jack in the Basket	50°44'.27N	01°30'.58W
Cowes Breakwater Light	50°45'.88N	01°17'.52W	Jib	50°52'.96N	01°23'.06W
Cowes No.1	50°46'.07N	01°18'.03W	KB Boat Park	50°46'.62N	01°06'.84W
Cowes No.2	50°46'.07N	01°17'.87W	Kingston & Grist	52°42'.73N	01°28'.69W
Cowes No.4	50°45'.85N	01°17'.72W	Kingston Marine Services	50°46'.10N	01°18'.87W
Cracknore	50°53'.94N	01°25'.20W	Lains Lake	50°51'.59N	01°21'.65W
Craftinsure.com	50°45'.03N	01°11'.89W	Lambeth	50°41'.53N	01°41'.69W
Crosshouse Lt Bn	50°54'.04N	01°23'.20W	Langstone Fairway	50°46'.32N	01°01'.36W
Cutter	50°49'.45N	01°16'.91W	Lepe Spit	50°46'.78N	01°20'.64W
DAKS	50°45'.53N	01°14'.39W	Lightwave	50°41'.50N	01°51'.68W
Dean Elbow	50°43'.69N	01°01'.88W	Lymington Bank	50°43'.11N	01°30'.86W
Deans Elbow	50°52'.16N	01°22'.76W	Mackley Construction	50°46'.16N	01°13'.09W
Deans Lake	50°51'.40N	01°21'.59W	Main Passage	50°45'.99N	01°04'.09W
Dean Tail	50°43'.00N	00°59'.16W	Marchwood	50°53'.98N	01°25'.57W

Mark	50°49'.56N	01°18'.94W	RYA Yachtmaster	50°48'.13N	01°14'.64W
Mid Shingles	50°41'.21N	01°34'.66W	Ryde Pier Hd (NW corner)	50°44'.34N	01°09'.72W
Milbrook	50°54'.12N	01°26'.82W	RYS flagstaff	50°45'.98N	01°18'.04W
Mixon Lt Bn	50°42'.36N	00°46'.33W	Saddle	50°45'.20N	01°04'.98W
Moore & Blatch ('E')	50°44'.61N	01°29'.52W	Sailtime	50°44'.35N	01°06'.50W
Moorhead	50°52'.55N	01°22'.90W	Salt Mead	50°44'.52N	01°23'.04W
Mother Bank	50°45'.49N	01°11'.21W	Sconce	50°42'.53N	01°31'.43W
Murrays	50°45'.62N	01°20'.14W	SE Ryde Middle	50°45'.93N	01°12'.09W
Nab 1	50°41'.26N	00°56'.52W	Shingles Elbow	50°40'.37N	01°36'.05W
Nab 2	50'41'.04N	00°56'.73W	Skandia	50°44'.83N	01°26'.09W
Nab 3	50°41'.64N	00°56'.75W	Snowden	50°46'.25N	01°17'.59W
Nab East	50°42'.85N	01°00'.80W	Solent Bank	50°44'.23N	01°27'.37W
Nab End	50°42'.63N	00°59'.49W	South Bramble	50°46'.98N	01°17'.72W
Nab Tower	50°40'.08N	00°57'.15W	South Pullar	50°38'.81N	00°49'.27W
Naomi House	50°46'.07N	01°05'.75W	South Ryde Middle	50°46'.14N	01°14'.15W
NE Gurnard	50°47'.06N	01°19'.42W	Southsea Marina	50°46'.43N	01°03'.54W
NE Ryde Middle	50°46'.21N	01°11'.89W	SP	50°45'.95N	01°19'.45W
NE Shingles	50°41'.96N	01°33'.40W	Spit Refuge	50°46'.15N	01°05'.46W
Needles Fairway	50°38'.24N	01°38'.98W	Spit Sand Fort Lt	50°46'.24N	01°05'.94W
Needles Lighthouse	50°39'.73N	01°35'.50W	Sposa	50°49'.66N	01°17'.59W
Netley	50°52'.03N	01°21'.81W	St Helens	50°43'.36N	01°02'.42W
New Grounds	50°41'.84N	00°58'.49W	Stormforce Coaching	50°49'.24N	01°17'.48W
Newtown R Buoy	50°43'.75N	01°24'.91W	Street	50°41'.69N	00°48'.89W
No Mans Land Fort Lt	50°44'.40N	01°05'.70W	Summers	50°44'.07N	01°05'.01W
Norris	50°45'.97N	01°15'.50W	Sunsail	50°46'.43N	01°15'.09W
North Head	50°42'.68N	01°35'.51W	Swinging Ground No1	50°53'.00N	01°23'.44W
North Hook	50°41'.01N	01°56'.44W	Swinging Ground No2	50°53'.82N	01°25'.12W
North Ryde Middle	50°46'.60N	01°14'.31W	SW Shingles	50°39'.35N	01°37'.38W
North Sturbridge	50°45'.33N	01°08'.23W	Tanners ('G')	50°44'.83N	01°28'.56W
North Thorn	50°47'.91N	01°17'.84W	The George Hotel (2)	50°42'.89N	01°29'.49W
NW Netley	50°52'.31N	01°22'.73W	Thorn Knoll	50°47'.50N	01°18'.44W
Outer Nab	50°41'.04N	00°56'.74W	Universal Marina	50°47'.33N	01°14'.59W
Outer Spit	50°45'.58N	01°05'.50W	Vail Williams	50°46'.83N	01°07'.34W
Paul Jackson ('H')	50°44'.33N	01°28'.25W	VT Shipbuilders	50°47'.08N	01°06'.77W
Peel Bank	50°45'.50N	01°13'.34W	W – E	50°45'.72N	00°59'.05W
Peel Wreck	50°44'.90N	01°13'.41W	Wadworth	50°43'.15N	01°27'.49W
Peters & May	50°46'.13N	01°22'.19W	Warden	50°41'.48N	01°33'.55W
Pier Head	50°53'.67N	01°24'.66W	Warner	50°43'.87N	01°03'.99W
Poole Bar Buoy No1	50°39'.31N	01°55'.16W	West Bay	50°45'.65N	01°20'.23W
Portsmouth No3 buoy	50°47'.07N	01°06'.24W	West Bramble	50°47'.20N	01°18'.65W
Portsmouth No4	50°47'.00N	01°06'.36W	West Knoll	50°47'.55N	01°17'.77W
Prince Consort	50°46'.42N	01°17'.55W	West Lepe	50°45'.23N	01°24'.09W
Quinnell	50°47'.06N	01°19'.89W	West Pole Beacon	50°45'.71N	00°56'.50W*
Rainbow Centre	50°46'.43N	01°07'.89W	West Ryde Middle	50°46'.48N	01°15'.79W
Raymarine	50°46'.58N	01°21'.46W	Weston Shelf	50°52'.71N	01°23'.26W
Reach	50°49'.05N	01°17'.65W	West Princessa	50°40'.16N	01°03'.65W
rib-it.com (G)	50°44'.80N	01°28'.47W	West Ryde Middle	50°46'.48N	01°15'.79W
Ridge	50°46'.45N	01°05'.65W	William	50°49'.03N	01°16'.49W
Roway Wk	50°46'.11N	01°02'.28W	Williams Shipping	50°47'.11N	01°18'.08W
Royal Albert	50°46'.26N	01°08'.76W	Winner	50°45'.10N	01°00'.10W
Royal Southampton	50°51'.76N	01°22'.28W	Wootton Bn	50°44'.53N	01°12'.13W
Royal Southern	50°48'.88N	01°15'.57W	Yachthaven ('D') ODM	50°44'.21N	01°30'.19W
Royal Southern ODM	50°42'.53N	01°29'.74W	Ynglinggirls.com	50°45'.11N	01°27'.34W
Royal Thames	50°47'.81N	01°19'.26W			

*These co-ordinates are due to change in early 2008 – see p141

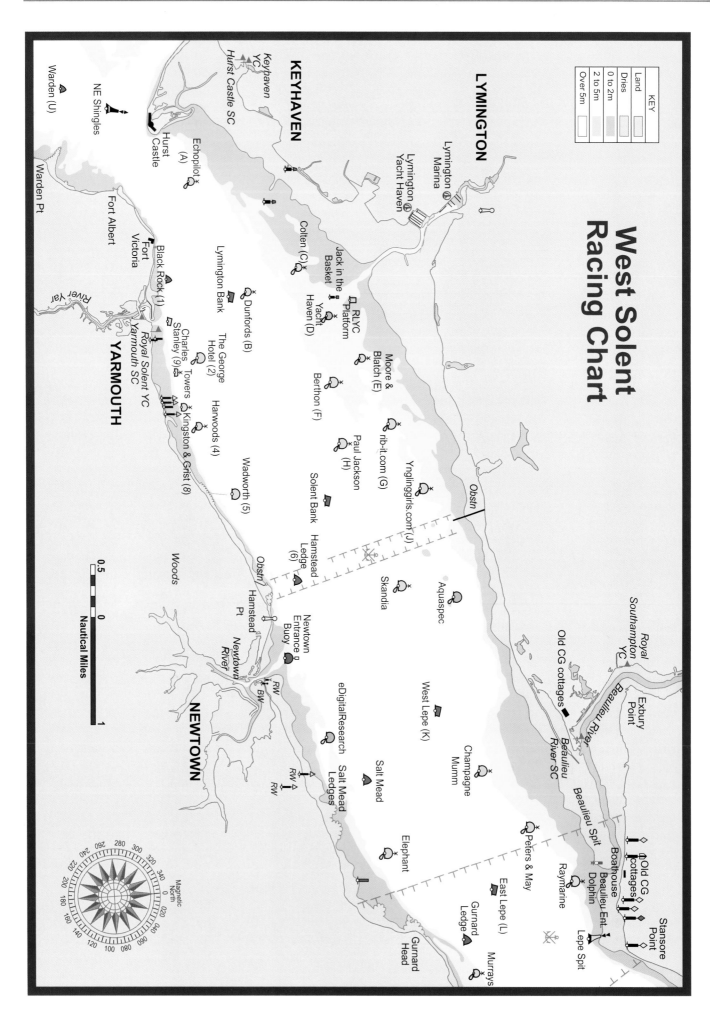

West Solent Racing Chart

LYMINGTON

KEYHAVEN

YARMOUTH

NEWTOWN

KEY
Land	
Dries	
0 to 2m	
2 to 5m	
Over 5m	

Warden (U)

NE Shingles

Warden Pt

Fort Albert

Fort Victoria

Hurst Castle

Echopilot (A)

Hurst Castle SC

Keyhaven YC

Keyhaven

Lymington Marina

Lymington Yacht Haven

Colten (C)

Jack in the Basket

Black Rock (1)

Lymington Bank

Dunfords (B)

The George Hotel (2)

Charles Stanley (9)

Royal Solent YC

Yarmouth SC

River Yar

Towers

Kingston & Grist (8)

Harwoods (4)

Wadworth (5)

RLYC Platform

Yacht Haven (D)

Moore & Blatch (E)

Berthon (F)

Paul Jackson (H)

rib-it.com (G)

Ynglinggirls.com (J)

Solent Bank

Hamstead Ledge (6)

Skandia

Aquaspec

Obstn

Hamstead Pt

Hamstead

Obstn

Newtown River

Newtown Entrance Buoy

RW

BW

Woods

eDigitalResearch

West Lepe (K)

Salt Mead Ledges

Salt Mead

RW

RW

Elephant

Gurnard Head

Gurnard Ledge

East Lepe (L)

Murrays

Peters & May

Champagne Mumm

Royal Southampton YC

Old CG cottages

Beaulieu River SC

Beaulieu River

Exbury Point

Beaulieu Point

Beaulieu Spit

Beaulieu Ent.

Dolphin

Raymarine

Boathouse

Old CG cottages

Stansore Point

Lepe Spit

Magnetic North

0.5   0   1

Nautical Miles

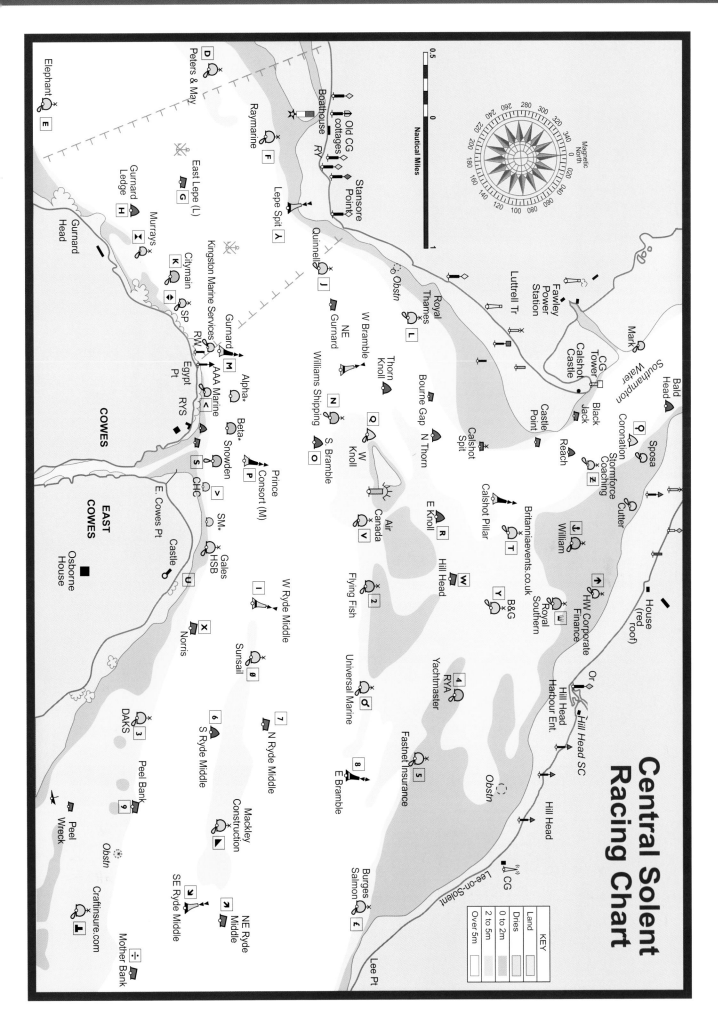

Central Solent
Racing Chart

Nautical Miles

0.5   0   1

Magnetic North

0 020 040 060 080 100 120 140 160 180 200 220 240 260 280 300 320 340

KEY

	Land
	Dries
	0 to 2m
	2 to 5m
	Over 5m

Elephant **E**

Peters & May **D**

Raymarine **F**

East Lepe (L) **G**

Gurnard Ledge **H**

Gurnard Head

Murrays

Citymain **K**

SP

Kingston Marine Services

RW

Gurnard **M**

AAA Marine

Egypt Pt

RYS

Alpha*

Beta*

Snowden **S**

Prince Consort (M) **P**

CHC **V**

SM*

Gales HSB

Castle **U**

E. Cowes Pt

Osborne House

EAST COWES

COWES

Lepe Spit **λ**

Boathouse RV

Old CG cottages

Stansore Point

Quinnell **J**

Obstn

NE Gurnard

W Bramble

Williams Shipping

S. Bramble **O**

W Knoll **Q**

Thorn Knoll

Royal Thames **L**

Bourne Gap N Thorn

Luttrell Tr

Fawley Power Station

CG Tower

Calshot Castle

Castle Point

Calshot Spit

Calshot Pillar

E Knoll **R**

Air Canada **V**

Flying Fish

Hill Head **W**

2

RYA Yachtmaster **4**

Universal Marine **Q**

Fastnet Insurance **5**

B&G **Y**

Royal Southern **W**

Britanniaevents.co.uk **T**

William **J**

HW Corporate Finance

Stormforce Coaching

Coronation Cutter

Sposa **Q**

Bald Head

Black Jack

Reach **Z**

Southampton Water

Mark

Hill Head Harbour Ent.

Hill Head SC

Hill Head

House (red roof)

Or

Lee-on-Solent

CG

Obstn

Lee Pt

Burges Salmon **3**

E Bramble **8**

Mackley Construction

NE Ryde Middle **2**

SE Ryde Middle

Craftinsure.com **L**

Obstn

Mother Bank

Peel Wreck

Peel Bank **9**

DAKS **3**

Norris **X**

Sunsail **Ø**

S Ryde Middle **6**

N Ryde Middle **7**

W Ryde Middle **I**

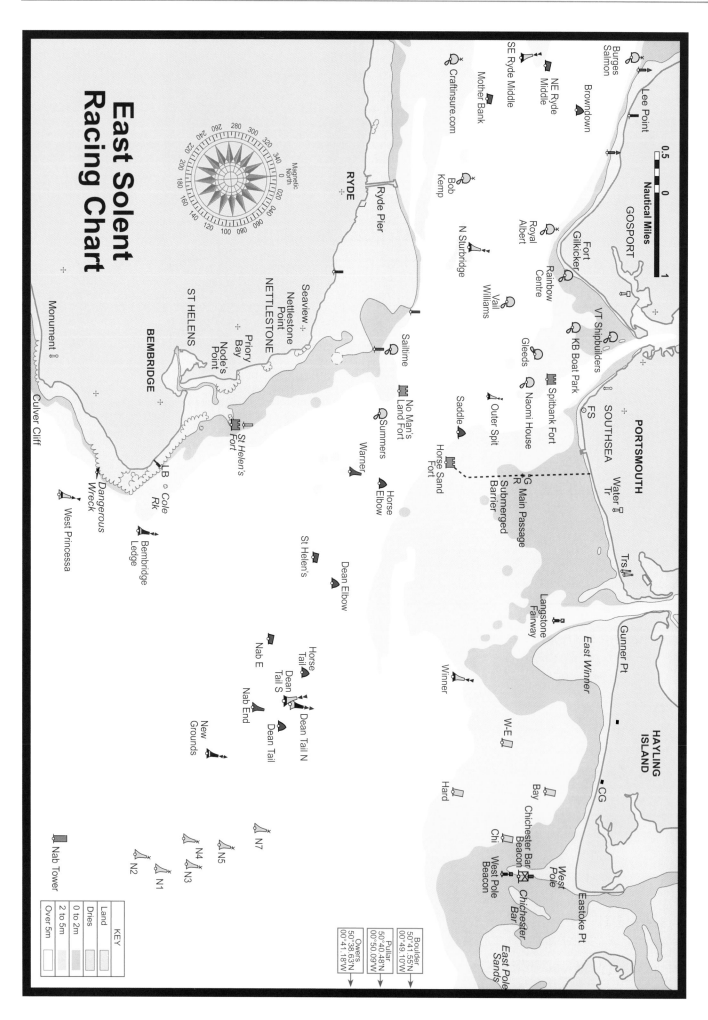

East Solent Racing Chart

Magnetic North

RYDE

Ryde Pier

Seaview
Nettlestone
Point
NETTLESTONE

BEMBRIDGE

ST HELENS

Priory
Bay

Node's
Point

St Helen's
Fort

Monument

Culver Cliff

Dangerous
Wreck

West Princessa

Bembridge
Ledge

LB
Cole
Rk

Summers

Warner

Horse
Elbow

St Helen's

Dean Elbow

Horse
Tail

Nab E

Dean
Tail S

Nab End

Dean Tail N

Dean Tail

New
Grounds

Nab Tower

N7

N5

N4

N3

N2

N1

Burges
Salmon

SE Ryde Middle

NE Ryde
Middle

Browndown

Craftinsure.com

Mother Bank

Bob
Kemp

N Sturbridge

Royal
Albert

Rainbow
Centre

Vail
Williams

Gleeds

Naomi House

Spitbank Fort

KB Boat Park

VT Shipbuilders

Fort
Gilkicker

Lee Point

GOSPORT

Sailtime

No Man's
Land Fort

Saddle

Outer Spit

Horse Sand
Fort

Submerged
Barrier

Main Passage

G
R

FS

SOUTHSEA

PORTSMOUTH

Water
Tr

Trs

Langstone
Fairway

Winner

W-E

Hard

Gunner Pt

East Winner

HAYLING
ISLAND

CG

Bay

Chichester Bar
Beacon

Chi

West Pole
Beacon

West
Pole

Eastoke Pt

Chichester
Bar

East Pole
Sands

Nautical Miles
0.5   0   1

KEY	
	Land
	Dries
	0 to 2m
	2 to 5m
	Over 5m

Boulder
50°41.55'N
00°49.10'W

Pullar
50°40.48'N
00°50.09'W

Owers
50°38.63'N
00°41.18'W

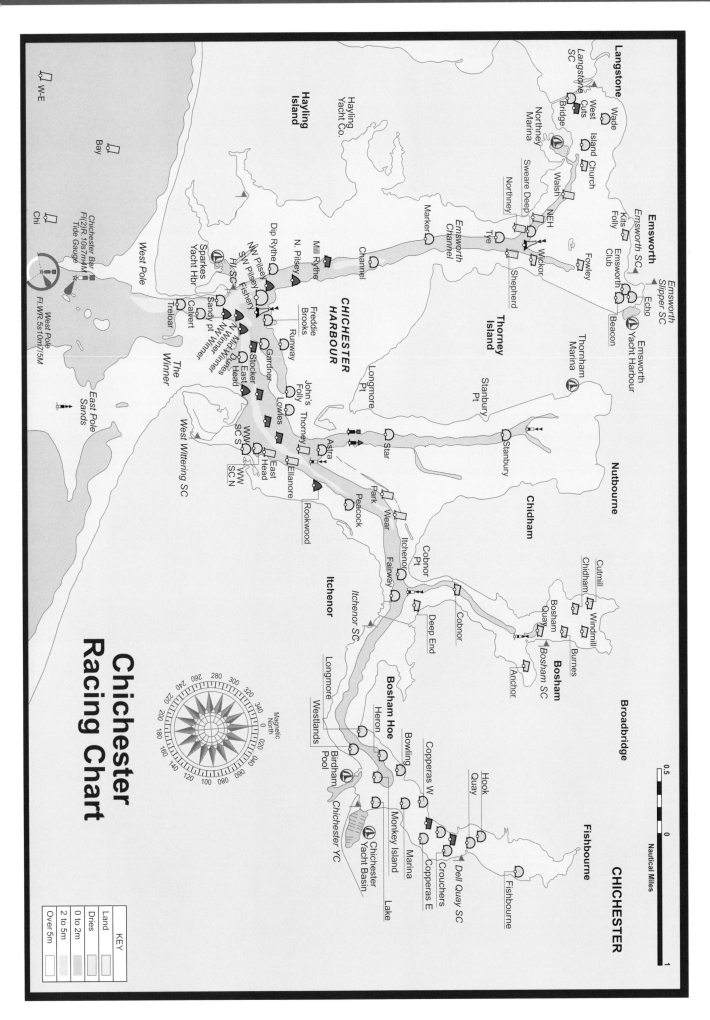

Chichester Racing Chart

CHICHESTER

Langstone

Langstone SC
Wade
West
Island Church SC
Bridge
Northney Marina
Sweare Deep
Northney

Hayling Island

Hayling Yacht Co.

Walsh

NEH
Tye
Wickor
Shepherd

Emsworth
Kits Folly
Emsworth SC
Fowley
Emsworth Club
Beacon
Echo
Emsworth Slipper SC
Emsworth Yacht Harbour

Market
Emsworth Channel
Channel

Thorney Island

Longmore Pt
Stanbury Pt
Thornham Marina

Nutbourne

Chidham

Dip Rythe
N. Pilsey
Mill Rythe
NW Pilsey
SW Pilsey
Fishery
Freddie
Brooks
Runway
Gardner

Sparkes Yacht Hbr
Calvert
Treloar
Sandy pt
N Winner
Mid Winner
Dunes
East Head
Stocker
East
Lowles
John's Thorney
Folly
Astra
Star
Stanbury

West Pole

The Winner

West Wittering SC
WW SC S
WW SC N
East Head
Ellanore
Rookwood
Peacock
Park
Wear

Cobnor
Cobnor Pt
Cobnor
Deep End
Anchor
Burnes
Bosham SC
Bosham Quay
Windmill
Chidham
Cutmill

Bosham

Broadbridge

Fishbourne

Itchenor
Itchenor SC
Fairway
Longmore
Westlands
Birdham Pool
Chichester YC
Chichester Yacht Basin

Bosham Hoe
Heron
Bowling
Copperas W
Hook Quay

Monkey Island
Marina
Lake
Crouchers
Copperas E
Dell Quay SC
Fishbourne

CHICHESTER HARBOUR

Chichester Bar Fl(2)R.10s7m4M
Tide Gauge
West Pole Fl.WR.5s10m7/5M
East Pole Sands
Bay
Chi.
W-E
West Pole

Magnetic North

KEY
Land
Dries
0 to 2m
2 to 5m
Over 5m

0.5 0 Nautical Miles 1

Solent weather

SOLENT COASTGUARD

Solent Coastguard (Tel: 023 9255 2100) broadcasts weather messages on VHF Ch86 and Ch23 after an initial announcement on Ch16 at 0130 Local Time (LT) and every three hours thereafter. Note that the forecasts at 0730 and 1930 are full maritime safety broadcasts, with all others being weather information updates only.

WILEY NAUTICAL WEATHER APPLICATIONS

Wiley Nautical has launched two new programs that let you get detailed forecasts to your mobile or laptop while you are on the move. Both the mobile and desktop program include forecasts for inshore, offshore and mainland locations throughout the UK and surrounding waters. Forecasts are updated four times daily, cover up to seven days ahead, with a detailed breakdown for each three hour period. It's good to eventually see this quality of graphical forecasts available cheaply to sailors on the go.

Get it on your mobile: Text 'WEATHER WILEY' to 60030 or visit **www.wileynautical.com/weather**. Your first three forecasts are free, future requests will be charged to you through your normal mobile bill. Latest rates and discounts are shown on the above website. Usual network operator charges for SMS text messages and downloads apply.

Get it on your computer: Visit **www.wileynautical.com/weather**. All forecasts are provided free of charge through the desktop application.

MARINAS AND HARBOURMASTERS

Forecasts and synoptic charts are put up daily at most marina and harbourmasters' offices and usually include a two or three-day outlook.

NATIONAL & LOCAL RADIO BROADCASTS

BBC general (land) forecasts: Land area forecasts may include an outlook period of up to 48 hours beyond the Shipping Forecast, as well as more details of frontal systems and weather along the coasts. The most comprehensive land area forecasts are broadcast by BBC Radio 4. See below for times and frequencies.

Local broadcasting stations: Some of the local radio stations are listed below, although it must be remembered that the information is subject to change. Broadcast times tend to be a little approximate and are in Local Time (LT).

WEATHER ON THE WEB

Most of the major marinas on the South Coast now have Wi-Fi internet connections. A range of meteorological information is available over the internet, including Met FAX marine services, two and three to five-day inshore forecasts, the Shipping Forecasts, gale warnings, coastal reports and satellite images. Visit the Meteorological Office's website at www.met-office.gov.uk.

Other useful websites that cover specific UK regions:
- www.bbc.co.uk/weather • www.onlineweather.com
- www.windfinder.com • www.chimet.co.uk (for the Chichester Harbour area) • www.sotonmet.co.uk (for the Southampton Water area) • www.bramblemet.co.uk

RADIO STATION	FREQUENCY	TYPE OF BROADCAST	TIMES
BBC RADIO 4	92.5– 94.6 MHz FM; 198kHz LW, MW	Shipping Forecast	Monday – Friday: 0048, 0520* Saturday: 0542; Sunday: 0556 LW only: 1201, 1754
ISLE OF WIGHT RADIO	102.0, 107.0 MHz	Local inshore forecast, tide times	Monday – Friday: 0630, 0730, 0830, 1630, 1730; Saturday: 0730, 0830; Sunday 0730, 0830, 0930
WAVE 105.2 FM	105.2 MHz	Inshore forecast (Solent)	Monday – Friday: 0630
BBC RADIO SOLENT	1359, 99 kHz; 96.1, 103.8 MHz	Weather, Shipping Forecast and tide times	Monday – Friday: 0533
		Shipping Forecast, local sea conditions and tide times	Monday – Friday: 0645; Saturday: 0645, 0745 Sunday: 0645, 0745
		Tide times	Monday – Friday : 0745, 1745
		Shipping Movements	Monday – Friday: 0533, 0645, 0845 Saturday: 0645; Sunday: 0645
		'Solent Sea-Dog'	Monday – Saturday: 0650
		Gunfacts	Tipnor Coastal Gunnery Range Monday – Friday: 0535, 0645, 0745 Saturday – Sunday: 0633, 0745

* The broadcasts at 0048 and 0520 also include weather reports from coastal stations. These are valid for inshore waters (up to 12M offshore) until 1800 LT and include a general synopsis, forecasts of wind direction and force, visibility and weather for inshore water areas referenced to well-known places and headlands.

FREE Mobile Weather Forecasts - in 3 easy steps

Step 1 Go to www.wileynautical.com/weather and enter your name, email address & mobile number.

Step 2 We'll send the application to your mobile. Follow the simple instructions to install the service

Step 3 We also give you 3 FREE forecasts. Just select your UK mainland, inshore or offshore location and you'll receive three 7 day forecasts for free.

After you've used up your 3 free downloads, new forecasts are charged to you through your normal mobile phone bill via your network operator. Or you can visit www.wileynautical.com/weather to get highly discounted rates and subscriptions.

Can't wait to get hold of it? Then text the words
WEATHER WILEY to 60030
right now!

WILEY NAUTICAL

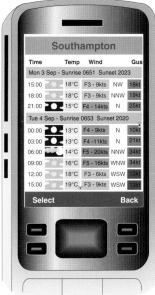

WILEY ⊛ NAUTICAL
Cruising Companions

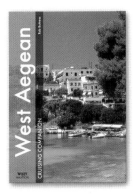

West Aegean
Robert Burtress
ISBN: 9781904358268

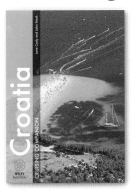

Croatia
Jane Cody & John Nash
ISBN: 9781904358282

North Brittany &
Channel Islands
Peter Cumberlidge
ISBN: 9780470988299

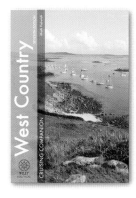

West Country
Mark Fishwick
ISBN: 9780470985694

Also available:

• **Ionian Cruising Companion**
Vanessa Bird
(ISBN: 9781904358275)

• **East Coast Cruising Companion**
Janet Harber New edition Sept 2008
(ISBN: 9780470990926)

• **The Channel Cruising Companion**
Neville Featherstone & Derek Aslett
(ISBN: 9781904358121)

• **NW Spain Cruising Companion**
Detlef Jens (ISBN: 9781904358107)

• **West France Cruising Companion**
Neville Featherstone
(ISBN: 9780333904534)

• **SW Spain & Portugal**
Detlef Jens (ISBN: 9780333907733)

Available from all good chandlers and bookshops   **www.wileynautical.com**

Index

INDEX

Old Castle Point 48
100 Guinea Cup 167
Orrery *101*, 102
Osborne Bay 45, 170
Osborne House 63, 169
Outer Spit Buoy 47
Owers SCM 8

P

Palace House 44
Palmerston, Lord 17, 93
Parsons, George 163
Pennington 15
Philante 170
Pilsey Island 142
Pilsey PHM 142
Port Hamble Marina 82–3, 84
Port Solent Marina 127–9
Port Solent YC 129
Portchester Castle 127, 128, *129*, 132
Portsdown Hill 165
Portsea 163
Portsmouth Harbour 8, 10, 47, 114–33, 160–5
Portsmouth Harbour YC 119
Portsmouth Historic Dockyard 130, 163, *162*
Portsmouth Royal Dockyard 131, 162, 163–5
Portsmouth SC 183
Pot Bank 7
Priddy's Hard 133
Prince Consort NCM 49, 64
Priory Church of St Andrew the Apostle *88*
The Prospect 55
Pylewell Lake 15

Q

Queen Elizabeth, HMS 165
Queen's HM 122

R

racing 173–79, 192–4
RAF YC 90
Rat Island 163
Red Funnel Easter Challenge 181
Robb, Arthur 187
Roman age 132, 158
Roman beacon 142
Rose, Sir Alec *128*
Round the Island Race 51, 54, 167, 178–9
Royal Albert YC 166
Royal Clarence Marina 120–1
Royal Corinthian YC 54
Royal London YC 51, 54, 166
Royal Lymington YC 30, 32, 34
Royal Marines Museum 131, 138
Royal Naval Museum 130, 163

Royal Naval Sailing Association 183
Royal Navy 120, 130, 162, 187
Royal Navy Submarine Museum 131
Royal Ocean Racing Club (RORC) 54, 170
Royal Solent YC *12*, 26, 27
Royal Southampton YC 43, 70, 77
Royal Southern YC 90, 166
Royal Victoria Country Park *76*, 88
Royal Victoria YC 92, 94, 95, 96, 97, 180
Royal Yacht Squadron 12, 51, 54, 167
Russells Lake 137
Ryde 98–102
Ryde HM 99, *100*, 102
Ryde Pier 94, 98
Ryde Sand 91, 93, 94, 98

S

St Barbe Museum 33
St Catherine's Point 112
St Edmund's Church 96–7
St Helen's fort 93, *107*
Salt Mead Buoy 37
Salt Mead Ledges 15
Sandhead 141
Sandhead PHM 142
Sandown 111
Sandy Point 143
Saxon era 132, 158–60
Saxon Wharf 72, 77
SCOD 186
Sconce NCM *9*, *14*, 16
Seaview 103–4, 107
Seaview Mermaid 187
Seaview YC *12*, 103, *104*, 187
Selsey 158
Selsey Bill 8
Shalfleet 37, 38
Shamrock IV 170
Shamrock V 71, 169, 170
Shamrock Quay 69, 71, 77
Shepards Wharf 50, 51, 52
Shingles Bank 7, 18
shipping 8, 47, 64, *67*
Shrape mud 49
Signal Station 67, 69, 73
Sinah Sands *138*
Small Boat Channel 116
Solent Bank 16
Solent Coastguard 12, 196
Solent Sky Aviation Museum 74–5
Solent Sunbeam 184
Solent Way 33
Sopwith, Sir Thomas 169
soundings 10
South Downs 139

South Folly beacon 50
SW Shingles Buoy *16*
Southampton 8, 45, 64–77, 158, 160
Southampton Boat Show 74, *75*
Southampton HM 77
Southampton Maritime Museum 74
Southampton Town Quay 67, 69, 73, 77
Southampton Water 9, 47, 64–77, *161*, 163
Southsea 92, 114, 116, 131, 137–8
Southsea Castle 132, 137–8, 161, 163
Southsea Marina 136, 138
Spanish Armada 162
Sparkes Marina 143, 144
Spinnaker Tower *116*, *122*, *124*, *132*
Spinners Garden 33
Spitbank fort 93, 116
Spithead 157, 165
Springvale 101
Stanbury Point 142
Stansore Point 45
Steephill Cove 113
Steward, Captain EH 93
Stocker Sand 141
Stokes Bay 163
Stone Point 39
submarine barrier 92, 135
Swanwick Marina 85–6, 87, 90
Swashway channel *114*, 116
Sweare Deep *141*, 142, 145
symbols 14

T

Tar Barrel beacon 29
Test, river 67, 73, 157
Thorney Channel 142, 148
Thorney Island 148
Thorney SC 148
Thorney SHM 142
Thornham Marina 142, 148
Thornycroft 165
tidal streams 188–9
tides 8–10
Titanic 74, *76*
Togidubnus 158
Totland Bay 16
Totton & Eling Heritage Centre 75
transport 13
Trap 7, 18
Trinity Landing 51
Tudor SC 138

U

UK Sailing Academy 53
Universal Marina 85, 90

V

Varvassi 7
Velsheda 168, 170
Ventnor 112–13
Ventnor Botanic Gardens 113
Ventnor HM 113
Venture Quays 51
Ventnor Winter Gardens 113
Vessel Traffic Services (VTS) 47, 64
Victoria, Queen 63, 164, 166, 167
Victory, HMS 130, 163
Victory class 183
Vosper Thornycroft 165

W

Waitegates visitors' moorings (Cowes) 51
Warden Point 16
Warrior, HMS 130
Warsash 79, 80
Warsash Maritime Centre *79*
Warsash river taxi 80
Warsash SC 80, 90
Watts, Isaac *76*
waypoints 11, 190–1
weather 10, 196
West Beach, Ryde 101
West Bramble buoy 64
West Fairway Buoy 23
West Knoll buoy 45, 49
West Pole beacon 139, 141
West Pole sands 91
West Winner 91, 134, 141
West Wittering SC 156
Western Solent 15–44, 192
Westmacott, Alfred 183, 184
Weston Shelf buoy 67
Wicormarine 125, 126
William the Conqueror *159*, 160
William III, King 163
Windeler, Cyril 178
Winner shoal 141
Wootton Bridge 96
Wootton Creek 91, 94–7
Wootton NCM 94
Wootton Rocks 91, 94

X

X One-Design 183

Y

Yar, river 27
Yarmouth *11*, 22–7, 38, 183
Yarmouth Castle 25, 27, *160*
Yarmouth HM 25, 27
Yarmouth SC 27